Rethinking modern political theory

RETHINKING
MODERN POLITICAL THEORY
Essays 1979–83

JOHN DUNN

Fellow of Kings College and
Reader in Politics, University of Cambridge

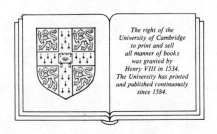

The right of the
University of Cambridge
to print and sell
all manner of books
was granted by
Henry VIII in 1534.
The University has printed
and published continuously
since 1584.

CAMBRIDGE UNIVERSITY PRESS

Cambridge
London   New York   New Rochelle
Melbourne   Sydney

Published by the Press Syndicate of the University of Cambridge
The Pitt Building, Trumpington Street, Cambridge CB2 1RP
32 East 57th Street, New York, NY 10022, USA
10 Stamford Road, Oakleigh, Melbourne 3166, Australia

First published 1985

Printed in Great Britain at
the University Press, Cambridge

Library of Congress catalogue card number: 84–21360

British Library Cataloguing in Publication Data
Dunn, John
Rethinking modern political theory: essays 1979–1983
1. Political science
I. Title
320'.01   JA71
ISBN 0 521 301300 hard covers
ISBN 0 521 316952 paperback

M.I.F.

discipulus magistro

Contents

vii

Contents

Preface

THE ESSAYS in this collection were written (or in one instance, extensively rewritten) between 1979 and 1983. I am grateful to many friends and colleagues for encouragement and assistance in connection with them. I should particularly like to thank Anouar Abdel-Malek, John Barber, Cynthia Farrar, Bianca Fontana, Paul Ginsborg, Geoffrey Hawthorn, Istvan Hont, Susan James, Jonathan Lear and Quentin Skinner.

I am grateful to the editors and publishers for permission to reprint those chapters which have been previously published or which were prepared for other occasions:

Chapter 1 was first printed in Reinhard Brandt (ed), *John Locke Symposium. Wolfenbüttel 1979*, W. de Gruyter & Co., Berlin and New York 1981.

Chapter 2 was first printed in Richard Rorty, Jerry Schneewind, and Quentin Skinner (eds), *Philosophy in History*, Cambridge University Press, Cambridge 1984.

Chapter 3 was first printed in Istvan Hont and Michael Ignatieff (eds), *Wealth and Virtue*, Cambridge University Press, Cambridge 1983.

Chapter 4 is reprinted from *Ethics*, XCII, January 1982, 229–315, by permission of the University of Chicago Press.

Chapter 5 is reprinted from *Totalitarian Democracy and After: Colloquium in Memory of Jacob Talmon*, The Israel Academy of Arts and Sciences, Jerusalem 1985.

Chapter 6 was prepared for a Colloquium at the Istituto Gramsci, Firenze on the centenary of Marx's death.

Chapter 7 is reprinted from Christopher Lloyd (ed), *Social Theory and Political Practice; Wolfson College Lectures 1981*, Oxford University Press, Oxford 1983, by permission of the President and Fellows of Wolfson College and Oxford University Press.

Chapter 8 was prepared for the United Nations University's Colloquium on Development Alternatives held in Algiers in December 1981 and is reprinted with the permission of the United Nations University.

Chapter 9 was prepared for a colloquium on the Crisis in Liberalism organized by the Guelph-McMaster Doctoral programme in Philosophy at the University of Guelph in June 1983.

Chapter 10 was prepared for the United Nations University's Colloquium on Europe and North America held at the Fondazione Feltrinelli in Milan in November 1982 and is printed with the permission of the United Nations University.

JOHN DUNN

April 1984

Introduction

POLITICAL THEORY, as both Charles Taylor and Alasdair Mac-Intyre have recently insisted,[1] is principally an attempt to understand 'what is really going on in society'. What sets the agenda for political theory, accordingly, is what actually is going on in society. Its task is the understanding of a historically given practical world, not the recycling of a more or less antique vocabulary of moral appraisal.

Modern political theory requires rethinking because it is philosophically so feeble and politically so maladroit. Both of these characteristics are readily explicable. To understand how its philosophical weakness has arisen, it is necessary to study in detail and with some sensitivity the history of western philosophy over at least the last three and a half centuries. To understand how its political insufficiency has arisen it is necessary, by contrast, to consider closely the very concrete history of political, economic and social organization over at least as lengthy a period. The degree of academic division of labour which prevails at present in western societies means that virtually no scholar is likely to make a serious attempt in the course of an intellectual lifetime to master both of these massive cognitive fields. Since no thinker, however impressive their personal abilities, is likely to prove very successful in carrying through such an endeavour, and since there are deep intellectual reasons as well as trivial institutional pressures that underlie the present academic division of labour, this is neither a surprising nor a wholly regrettable state of affairs. But it stands massively and intractably in the path of attempts to remedy a condition of cognitive confusion and discomfort which is becoming increasingly hazardous both for particular human collectivities and for the species as a whole.

The essays in this book certainly make little contribution to such a remedy. (It would perhaps barely be possible in principle for any single scholar to make *much* of a contribution.) But they do at least attempt to address the issue of why modern political theory should be so

I

unimpressive; and they explore from a variety of angles where its main weaknesses lie and how they might in principle be remedied.

The principal intellectual device which they deploy, tacitly if not often very explicitly, is the separation and reassembling of two very different forms of history and analysis. Ethical and political concepts certainly have a history. They appear in human speech and reflection (and sometimes disappear from these) within particular spans of time; and their existence, whilst they are in this way extant, is surrounded by a multiplicity of pressures, intellectual and pragmatic, which lends to them an endless variety of shading and modulation. But although, like all human artefacts, they are indeed deeply historical in each of these two senses, their history has a very different shape and rhythm from the more concrete history of human states, societies and economies; and to understand this history with any power and delicacy requires a very different approach from that which the historian of wealth, power, or in the broadest sense culture, needs to adopt. Yet, sharply distinct in both structure and rhythm though these two historical trajectories certainly are, they are not in any sense causally independent of one another; and neither, accordingly, at any particular point in time, can be understood at all precisely without a careful and accurate appraisal of the other. Political theory, of all surviving academic disciplines, is most bluntly charged with the responsibility of identifying such inter-sections between the historical planes of power and meaning and with weighing the causal pressure of each upon the other. In this way it is committed by its central tasks to a rejection of the intellectually, educationally and politically disastrous divorce between a purely historicist history of political ideas, a style of political philosophy committed to political inconsequence by the self-conscious purity of its methods, and a political science ludicrously aping the sciences of nature and uninformed by any coherent conception of political value (and thus at the mercy of the most superficial of local ideological perspectives and sentiments).

The first three essays discuss aspects of the historical shaping of liberal conceptions of political value. They emphazise the decisive break in the history of these conceptions between an understanding of individual practical reason premissed, as in Locke's case, on the cultural authority of a Christian way of life, and one which centres on the presumed causal properties of whole societies, economies or states. The first and third essays stress the degree to which Locke's own thinking was formed by the effort to avoid resting his conception of practical reason on an appropriative and calculating individual egoism and a view of the causal properties of societies or states which he regarded as essentially superstitious. The second explores the implications of this fundamental commitment for Locke's conception of the nature of politics itself and argues that it enabled him to develop a clearer-headed and less credulous understanding of politics than subsequent thinkers have contrived to fashion.

The first essay also explores the roots of this primary theoretical commitment in Locke's own experience of the society of his day, treating this as a problem in the theory of ideology and stressing the degree to which a conceptually legitimate ideological explanation of complex thought must centre on the effort to understand the processes through which a human being's social imagination comes to be shaped, rather than confine itself to assessing the pragmatic interest which a given adult person might possess in publically professing particular opinions. This first essay is the most determinedly historical in focus; but if its claims are essentially correct the intimate links between Locke's rejection of a purely terrestrial pursuit of individual advantage as a sufficient account of human practical reason and the positive content of his conception of political duty must be seen as a product of his explicitly Christian commitments. In the light of his theory, accordingly, the instability of any liberal theory of political value which is linked to practical reason only through a conception of the rationality of egoistic individual appropriation or which, worse still, lacks any determinate theoretical links to practical reason at all, becomes all too easy to understand.

The second essay discusses the category through which Locke attempts to link human practical reason to the causal field of politics: the moral relation of trust. It shows how far Locke's thinking throughout his intellectual life was addressed to the question of what human beings could, and should rationally, trust and explains the rationale of his eventual assessment of the indispensability and the necessary limits of political trust. Because he saw trust as both indispensable and ineliminably hazardous, he developed a particularly strong and evocative understanding of the nature of political responsibility, both on the part of the rulers or leaders who are the recipients of such trust and on the part of the ordinary citizens who bestow it, for the most part with little if any hesitation, but who also, in this instance and in this world, may and indeed must be prepared always to reconsider whether their bestowal has proved justified. The view of human institutions in general, and of political institutions more particularly, as a tissue of more or less well-conceived or misguided trust is not a substitute for assessments of their causal properties; and Locke himself in no way supposed it to be such. But what it emphatically is is a necessary complement to a vision of human social and political institutions simply as bearers of their causal properties. No one actively involved in the workings of modern political organizations or institutions is likely to be unaware for long of the heavily situated character of political responsibility in any modern state. But by the same token, and notoriously, anyone trapped within this field of constraint is likely over time to find it exceedingly hard to sustain and focus a clear conception of their own responsibility as an active political agent. Given the appalling history of organized political power in the modern world, Locke's steady insistence on the moral impossibility in principle of abandoning responsibility for the exercise of power to ruler or government or party has a trenchancy and a relevance which, at least in this respect, is unmatched by any other major political thinker.

The third essay, 'From applied theology to social analysis', discusses the transition between Locke's theocentric world view and the modern and more anthropocentric understandings of politics developed by his eighteenth century Scottish successors David Hume and Adam Smith. It naturally makes no attempt to defend the intellectual cogency of theocentrism itself. But it emphazises a number of respects in which the deployment of Locke's imaginative energies within a theocentric framework of thought[2] gave him a more searching and critical under-standing of the nature of his contemporary society and polity than that developed by his successors. Hume and Smith unite together two modern theoretical doctrines, a conception of individual practical reason which relativizes this in the last instance to the desires, senti-ments and evaluative opinions of individuals and a conception of social reproduction as a potentially autonomous process which can certainly be subverted by political incompetence or misfortune[3] but which does not depend to any large degree for its viability upon political inten-tions. The union of these doctrines with the epistemological conviction that existing human nature is the sole and final criterion for human value at any particular time implies that the limits of men's social duties are the limits of the socializing capacities of the societies within which they are nurtured. Locke by contrast rejects not merely the view that egoistic individual calculation within this world can and will ground an adequate schedule of human cooperative practices and obligations,[4] but also the Scottish complement to this fond hope, the judgement that social reproduction, through the socializing mechanisms which form individual belief and sentiment, will prove to be a relatively automatic process. Not only did he foresee, albeit in shadowy outline, the familiar paradoxes of modern economic theories of politics (the problems of free riding etc.); he also refused absolutely to accord instead any automatic value to the social specification of purely human power, and rejected accordingly the possibility of seeing the existing substance of social relations as a sufficient foundation for human value. This set of rejections plainly does not in itself amount to a coherent alternative viewpoint which is still genuinely accessible today. But it does present a strategically better positioned conception of the demerits of either individualist egoism or whole-hearted social holism as theoretical foundations on which to specify human political value. At least as critic of his successors, if not as a constructive theorist in his own right, Locke remains a major ally in the project of rethinking modern political theory.

The next three essays shift the focus from the history of ideas to the vicissitudes of an extremely concrete, if internally differentiated, tradition of political action. Since the middle of the nineteenth century, political exponents of socialism have sought to supplant the political vision of Hume, Smith and their successors as the basis on which to shape modern communities. The first of the three essays considers a question essentially of social and political explanation: what it is that causes major socio-political revolutions to occur. The initial Marxist understanding of the nature of socialist revolution saw this as the compulsive political working through of the internal socio-economic dynamics of a given territorial society. Socialist revolution was to be a local solution in a given locality out of local resources which was also in the long run (by composition) a universal solution everywhere since all societies potentially possessed the relevant capacities for self-transformation and since, in their economic, cultural and political interaction with other societies, all in the last instance confronted the same need for self-transformation. The most powerful recent account of the nature of social revolutions in general (and hence of socialist revolutions in particular), Theda Skocpol's *States and Social Revolutions*, qualifies this initial Marxist understanding in two important respects. Social revolutions remain local outcomes; but their occurrence does not depend solely either on the socio-economic characteristics of the society in question or indeed on its purely domestic attributes in their entirety. In contrast with Skocpol's position, 'Understanding revolutions' argues that a structural conception of the causation of revolutions must be both causally inadequate and politically misleading. It must be causally inadequate because it is committed to failing (or refusing) to recognize the causal role of belief, judgement and political will in the making of revolutions. It must prove politically misleading because it commits those who choose to adopt it to ignoring

5

(or pretending not to see) this causal role, and thus distracts them decisively from the urgent and exceedingly difficult political task of assessing frankly the prospective causal contributions of particular beliefs, judgements and efforts. Looked at under the general aegis of practical reason, as human beings have good reason to perceive it, it is impossible to see how competitive political process could be crimped in its entirety into the frame of necessity. But even if it were possible to see how to conceive competitive political process wholly under the rubric of necessity, it would remain just as impossible to ground upon any such conception an honest and self-aware approach to political action. Both the political force and the political queasiness of the Leninist tradition derive directly from these theoretical features.

The second of these essays, 'Totalitarian democracy and the legacy of modern revolutions', assesses the degree of political responsibility which should be ascribed to the Leninist tradition (and to Marxism more generally) for the sorry outcomes of twentieth-century socialist revolutions. It does so in the first instance by appraising the strengths and weaknesses of the late J. L. Talmon's celebrated analysis of the sources of 'totalitarian democracy'. On balance it endorses Talmon's judgement that the socialist political telos affirmed both by Marx himself and by his self-identified successors is fused with the analytical scheme for historical explanation that accompanies this solely by a quite unwarranted optimism. It also accepts the consequent judgement that it is this arbitrary fusion which lays a mode of social and political understanding which is in many respects sceptical and demystifying open to a quite illegitimate exploitation as a doctrine of monopolistic political authority. But it rejects the view that these defects in themselves suffice to explain much of the social and political demerits of post-revolutionary socialist states. What does explain these, rather, is the politically corrupting and barbarizing consequences of intense domestic political conflict and the bitter geopolitical clashes of interest produced by the patchy but substantial advance of socialist revolution in the twentieth century. The structure of Marx's own political theory gave quite inadequate weight to these consequences; and the politically most important twentieth century heir of his analysis, the Marxist-Leninist doctrine of state, which certainly does accord them all the weight they deserve, has decomposed morally in the course of learning to do so. But more important than these purely political disasters, two thirds of a century after the Russian revolution, has been the incapacity of post-revolutionary socialist states to recover effectively from their political degeneracy. On this point the essentially Machiavellian pragmatism[5] which serves effectively enough to explain the political character of revolutionary advance or frustration offers only the most superficial illumination. Here a fundamental theoretical misjudgement of Marxism is far more important: the gross overestimate by Marx himself and by virtually all subsequent Marxist thinkers of the ease with which an economy founded upon common ownership of the means of production can be organized to produce efficiently.[6]

The third of these essays, 'Unimagined community', considers another theoretical misjudgement which is arguably fundamental to Marxism and which, in this instance, is linked closely to one of Marxism's most powerful explanatory insights. Marxist politics are founded upon a fusion of two fundamental considerations: a rejection of all conceptions of a right to ownership in the means of production (and most particularly of the conception of entitlement on which the capitalist mode of production depends) and an acceptance of the historically given and humanly advantageous character of the world-wide framework of economic exchange created by the expansion of capitalism. The first of these lends to Marxism much of its moralizing force. The second furnishes much of its explanatory power in the face of twentieth-century history. Taken together they imply that socialism must indeed be international if it is to be established at all. But neither together nor separately do they offer any clue as to how socialism in this full and benign sense could in fact exist internationally. It is not just that they fail to suggest how international socialist cooperation could come about through political struggle and economic change (a lacuna which history might in due course be charitable enough to fill on their behalf). Far more importantly, they also fail to indicate, even in the vaguest outline, what such a social, political and economic order might consist in. Whilst a domestic socialist economy was until 1917 described rather thinly by socialists and imagined with undue optimism, the intellectual substance of an international socialist economy is virtually exhausted thus far in a string of edifying abstract nouns. The scepticism of the Marxist critique of entitlement is thus reversed in application to a world of uneven and combined economic, social and political development by a comprehensive but contentless moralization of possible modes of well-intentioned cooperation, without the provision of even the flimsiest intellectual warrant.

The last four essays turn back towards the history of western political theory and consider the implications for its present intellectual standing of the postwar development of academic philosophy in the west. The first, 'Social theory, social understanding and political action', focuses on the striking contrast between the causal importance of social theory in shaping modern political projects and its purely intellectual debility. It distinguishes between three distinct modes of social understanding: amateur social theory (the attempt to understand the social setting and significance of their lives in which every human being necessarily engages), official social theory (the cognitively overblown and morally overbearing dogmas about the nature and organization of societies today which form the basis of all modern claims to political authority and the pretext for the use of all those modern analogues of rack and thumbscrews which maim and sear human flesh somewhere on earth every hour of every day) and professional social theory (the comparatively systematic attempts to grasp the properties of societies by modern social scientists). In the modern world official social theory is in large part a heavily edited version of professional social theory, transposing the claims to cognitive authority made by the latter into grounds for disregarding the motley array of amateur social theories espoused by its unruly subjects. In a secular world full cognitive authority over the nature and organization of human society would be a conclusive title to political power. It is certainly the responsibility of any professional social theorist to seek to understand the causal properties which they elect to study as deeply and accurately as he or she can. There is no reason to doubt the sincerity of professional social theorists in pressing their conclusions as advisers to princes, ancient or Modern. But there certainly is reason to doubt their moral and practical discretion in so doing. The academic idiom which has emerged from the last two centuries of struggle to understand the nature and organization of human societies massively overstates the degree of cognitive mastery attained. The intellectual basis for such overstatement is a conception of the nature of philosophy and perhaps also of the character of the sciences of nature which can no longer be plausibly defended. One of its main political consequences is a large measure of complicity in, and of responsibility for forming, a morally improper and politically inexpedient understanding by modern rulers of their relation with those over whom they rule.

'Identity, modernity and the claim to know better' considers the implications of recent criticisms, particularly by Richard Rorty and Alasdair MacIntyre, of the self-understanding of western philosophy for the cultural conflicts between different national societies in the world today. The struggle between the wealthier and more powerful and the poorer and weaker states in the world today, as in some measure the struggle within these between particular communities and classes, takes place, as the Italian Marxist Antonio Gramsci affirmed so evocatively, just as intractably in the idiom of human belief as it does in

8

that of physical coercion. In this incessant and painful encounter the claim to know better, about many matters from the efficient organization of production to the valid understanding of non-human nature and the appropriate form in which for power to be exercised politically, is one of the principal weapons. Because the role of this claim is ideologically so prominent and so effective, the long drawn out effort of western philosophy to understand and explain human cognitive success and failure is of major political importance. As a claim it is frequently resented by those at the receiving end, particularly in the Third World, and experienced by them more as an assault on surviving social and cultural identities than as a benign civilizational contribution. This resentment is not difficult to understand; but it is not necessarily at all well-conceived. Insofar as modern western philosophers continue to accept the more successful sciences of nature as paradigms for human cognitive success, any repudiation of their cultural status will also, at least in the longer run, be a repudiation of practical instruments for the accumulation and exercise of power. And, insofar as modern western philosophers have begun to recoil from the corrosive existential impact of an epistemology which privileges the sciences of nature, both the grounds for their revulsion and such intellectual contribution as their views are potentially in a position to make would be just as culturally benign for other human communities as they could be in the West. If all human cognitive authority is intra-cultural in the last instance[7] it is hardly surprising that criteria for assessing the comparative merits of human practices should prove to be pretty elusive.

'The future of liberalism' discusses the development of liberal political thinking since the end of the Second World War, considering the main experiences which have shaped its development and asking which of the resulting intellectual styles is likely best to withstand the intellectual and practical discouragements of future political experience. In the last fifteen years the most influential of these styles has been the revival of a strongly moralizing liberal individualist political philosophy of predominantly North American provenance. As political theory this belongs firmly to the Utopian genre, albeit more inadvertently so in some instances than in others. But its metaphysical foundations are too flimsy to ground a powerful and durable mode of Utopian political theory. In its politically more robust versions, liberalism does at least attempt to put at its theoretical centre the virtue of prudence and to offer itself as a comparatively firmly located branch of human practical reason. To do this successfully, it would have to develop a far more effective conception of political causality and to reconstruct itself, with the aid of such a conception, as a theory of modern politics, predicated on the economic, social, political and military realities of the world in which we now happen to be living. A number of strands of contemporary liberalism (the critique of totalitarian rule, utilitarian ethics, political economy) have focused to some effect on particular aspects of this world. But it cannot be said that any liberal political theorist has recently made a serious effort to consider the relations between all of them. Until such an effort is made, it will be hard to judge whether liberalism just happens at present to be an array of shreds and tatters of past ideological improvisation and highly intermittent current political illumination, or whether it necessarily and in principle lacks the resources to transform itself into a more oecumenical, more realistic and more effective conception of what is of political value to the members of the human species now.

The final essay seeks to assess the future for academic political philosophy in the west. This future will, of course, depend in part simply upon the future of philosophy itself. At present both of the two principal traditions in modern ethical theory, the utilitarian and the Kantian, are continuing to exert a strong and in some respects vitalizing influence upon political philosophy. But neither of them has ever contrived to give a very coherent and philosophically satisfying account of the nature of the relations between human value, human agency and the material universe. The more sceptical and pragmatist tinge of recent western philosophical conceptions of natural science and epistemology contrives to give less strained answers to these problems largely by dint of refusing to answer them at all – by pure evasion. At least in political philosophy, such evasive tactics, however elegantly deployed, will hardly suffice. Unless and until it can be remedied, the philosophical weakness of modern conceptions of practical reason[8] will by itself preclude the construction of a political philosophy of any great power.

But it is not only the philosophical deficiencies of modern conceptions of practical reason which stand in the way of any such construction. It is also, and at least as decisively, their crude political inadequacy. The most important instance of this inadequacy, unfortunately, is to be found in the political tradition which has most determinedly cast itself as a general theory of social and political practice: Marxism. There can be no reasonable doubt by now, especially in the light of the perfunctory efforts which Marx himself initially made to specify what forms of political action could hope to prove benign, of the grave political defects of Marxism. Whilst in several respects it possesses the appropriate theoretical form for a modern political theory – that of a theory of collective prudence for the members of a species obliged to share a common habitat in permanent danger and on the basis of limited mutual concern – it severely underestimates the dangers which they face, and offers dismayingly little practical guidance on how they might reasonably hope to meet these. Moreover there is good reason to suppose that much of the guidance which it does offer is highly misleading.[9]

To build a more adequate theory of collective prudence today it is necessary to start rather closer to the historical ground on which we stand and to attempt to take in the full character of this terrain. It is necessary to consider soberly the nature of economic exchange, across the globe and within particular national societies, without presuming in advance that either capitalist or socialist conceptions of property right could in themselves suffice to render this morally unproblematic on any possible (let alone any likely) future basis. It is necessary to consider soberly the character and mutual relations of modern state powers and of the fearsome and very poorly controlled[10] destructive capabilities with which they now menace us all. It is necessary to consider realistically how human beings do in fact see and feel about each other in the settings in which they live and which they understand (and always will understand) so poorly. At the time when the leaders of the most powerful nations on earth may at any moment find themselves with at best a few minutes in which to decide whether or not to unleash thermonuclear war,[11] it is hardly open to rational dispute that human beings have a more urgent and a more baffling need to grasp what prudence really is than they have ever had before. Nor is it readily disputable that the political project of reconstructing the states and societies to which we belong to embody such prudence is apocalyptically more complex and formidable than it must have looked to a would-be Legislator in the Greece of the fourth century B.C. or in eighteenth-century Geneva. Political prudence is not a purely ideal value; it necessarily embodies a conception of how the world could, in historical reality and through real human agency, be changed to meet its requirements. A cosmopolitan and ethically alert conception of what it is for human beings, individually, collectively and as a species, to be prudent in the world which we all now inhabit would have to take the measure of very much which political philosophers today make little (if any) effort to consider. Yet it is only with such a conception at its heart that a modern political philosophy could hope to be altogether serious.

This is a very old understanding of the nature of political theory. But no one has deployed it with much authority for many decades; and the more contemporary intellectual idioms which have replaced it, an ignorant and self-righteous moralism and a bigotedly parochial instrumentalism, can offer for it only the most lethally inadequate of surrogates.

The time has more than come to try again.

Chapter 1

Individuality and clientage in the formation of Locke's social imagination

A book is the product of a different self from the one we manifest in our habits, in society, in our vices. If we mean to try to understand this self it is only in our inmost depths, by endeavouring to reconstruct it there, that the quest can be achieved.

> Marcel Proust, *Contre Sainte-Beauve*
> (translated and quoted in George D. Painter,
> *Marcel Proust, Vol 2*, Harmondsworth 1977,
> p. 120)

Nothing tends so much to corrupt and enervate and debase the mind as dependency, and nothing gives such noble and generous notions of probity as freedom and independency.

> Adam Smith, *Lectures on Jurisprudence*
> (1762–3 Report, ed. R. L. Meek, D. D. Raphael
> and P. G. Stein, Oxford 1978, p. 333)

WHAT makes a human being the person he or she is? What gives them a personal identity and endows them with a self which is truly their own? How does it come about and in virtue of what is it true that 'every one is to himself, that which he calls *self*[1]? Locke's analysis of personal identity in the second edition of the *Essay Concerning Human Understanding* was an original and courageous attempt to dissipate 'this ignorance we are in of the Nature of that thinking thing, that is in us, and which we look on as our *selves*'.[2] Arising out of his complicated quarrel with the thought of Descartes and focusing firmly on an ethical puzzle about the nature of responsibility which the metaphysical doctrines (or at least strategy) of the *Essay* had posed,[3] the theory of personal identity which Locke advanced is still the fulcrum of modern dispute about what it is to be a person. It has retained this centrality, to be sure, not by the felicity in detail of the solution which it offered to his own difficulties, but rather by raising relatively clearly for the first time a problem of evident depth and significance which subsequent thinkers have as yet proved unable convincingly to resolve.

The compatibility between an analysis essentially in terms of mental connectedness and continuity and any conception of personal *identity* is still in the sharpest dispute.[4] The inadequacy of Locke's account to resolve the particular problem which he had set himself (to show how men can justly be held responsible for their own actions and only for actions of their own: Person 'is a Forensick Term appropriating Actions and their Merit; and so belongs only to intelligent Agents capable of a Law, and Happiness and Misery')[5] was pointed out by his friend William Molyneux as early as 1693.[6] As a general account of personal identity it was criticized severely by philosophers such as Joseph Butler and Thomas Reid (who were in no position to improve on it)[7] and by a decidedly more profound critic, Leibniz, who saw it as symptomatic of Locke's 'lax' and implicitly materialist metaphysics.[8] How far an analysis of personal identity in terms of mental connectedness and continuity is compatible with the type of strongly Protestant doctrine of individual responsibility which Locke set himself to rationalize is still a very open question in ethics and the philosophy of mind.[9]

There are many ways of characterizing the fundamental coherence and incoherence of Locke's intellectual and personal ventures: the struggle to articulate a given nature as norm for human culture,[10] the attempt to vindicate (or to elude the need to vindicate) a natural theology which would guarantee the foundation in nature of Christian moral values,[11] or the attempt to display the human agent as a natural creature somehow coherently and rationally self-conceived as committed to the (as even Locke recognized)[12] in *some* measure historically contingent values of a certain version of Christianity.[13] A choice between such characterizations may be simply the selection of a mode of representation. But there is a more general and abstract way of conceiving Locke's thinking, a way which does at least attempt to do justice to the force of both the rationalist and the historicist dimensions of our contemporary consciousness: to see it crudely as an encounter between a wholly historically contingent personal will and the wholly objective constraints of conceptual possibility. Locke, like perhaps most courageous and imaginative human beings, set himself to do something which cannot in fact be done. We have been exploring ever since why precisely it is that what he set himself to do cannot be done (and what else, in the extremity of its impossibility, is to be done instead). With the privilege of hindsight, we are necessarily better placed, if we can only muster the calm and the clarity of mind to take advantage of our location, than anyone in Locke's day could have been, to see why the task which he set himself to complete could not be accomplished. The best of contemporary philosophical intelligence is not too much to bring to bear in the elaboration of such understanding. It would be a very foolish and vain historian who chose to volunteer their services for the task. What a historian may sensibly seek to do instead is to cast some light on the idiosyncratic and contingent personal will which committed Locke to his project. How did he come to acquire, and why did he retain, the highly distinctive intellectual and moral identity, the continuity of aspiration, which made his intellectual creativity possible? How and why, begging all the questions of personal identity, did he become *himself*?

The constitution of personal identity, the establishment of a relatively constant temperament or character[14] in an individual, is an intricate and conceptually elusive process and one in the face of which our present level of bafflement presents severe problems for the development of an adequate ethics or philosophy of mind or even empirical psychology of human development. As a result of the scholarship of the last few decades many aspects of Locke's intellectual trajectory have become rather well understood.[15] The identification of a broadening range of theoretical problems and a sequence of varyingly successful attempts at their resolution, executed in the interstices of an often busy and sometimes valetudinarian existence, make up an extremely full intellectual life. The internal sequential rationality of the trajectory is now rather clearly displayed. Its complexity and intellectual force together preclude any hasty external 'explanation' of the structure of thought as a whole, whether in the idiom of psychological or sociological determinism. It is natural to see it as the self-unfolding of reason, an impressive exemplification, in the terms of Martin Hollis,[16] of the autonomous rather than the plastic model of man. Certainly the *active* and inventive character of the thinking in Locke's case makes more readily apparent than it is in much of human performance, the absurdity of any attempt to *explain* what is being brought about as though what was bringing it about was not effortful intentional action.[17] Any serious account of Locke's reflections, whether in the end it be sympathetic or hostile to the broad lines of thinking which he undertook, must necessarily regard many aspects of his thinking and writing as the products of a paradigmatically free intellectual agent. What cannot, however, be intelligibly conceived as the *product* of paradigmatically free intellectual agency is the centre of more or less consistent purpose and aspiration which, to use a crass pair of metaphors, fuelled or activated this agency. To observe Locke's intellectual identity shaping itself within his historical social setting is not to derogate from the intellectual energy and creative power of his life's work. But it is to keep open the question (a question which remains of pressing significance for everyone) of how precisely the lines between choice and fate are drawn in human intellectual life. Is the concept of ideology simply a characteristic symptom of modern credulity or is it an as yet feebly specified and clumsily deployed theoretical instrument for demarcating this boundary?

Provided the concept of explanation is used in a sufficiently unexacting manner, almost any aspect of human performance can be explained after a fashion. Since ideology purports to be an explanatory concept of exceedingly general import, it is scarcely surprising that in use its reach should often (or indeed usually) exceed its grasp. In no context is this excess of promise over performance more apparent than in relation to the thought of great individual thinkers. (Predominantly psychological explanations of the genesis of Newton's *Principia* or exclusively sociological explanations of the character of Locke's political theory, even when executed with great scholarship and intellectual vigour,[18] are necessarily mildly preposterous.) But it is unclear that a consideration of the role of ideology in intellectual life need commit us to such facilely reductive and pseudo-causal interpretations. For, even if psychological determinism were true, it would still have to be the case that the reasons which cause 'my actions are *my* reasons, the wants and beliefs which actually enter into my practical reasoning, the wants and beliefs which find expression in the fiats and statements which constitute the premises from which I infer how I should act'.[19] As a hypothesis, psychological determinism offers the analyst no excuses for shirking the duty to show the workings of the subject's deliberative rationality in full. It is within the elaborated and effortful thinking of real individuals that this shadowy boundary between rational reflection and compulsive judgement on the part of the intellectual agent contemplating politics is to be found (if it is to be found anywhere at all). Ideology, as it concerns a major thinker, cannot be simply a mnemonic term for the prevalence of a multiplicity of agreeable (and false) social truisms amongst the intellectually insincere and thoughtless, but rather a recognition, more or less clear in character, of the credibility in the last instance of an entire web of belief, an acknowledgement of the genuine causal force of its credal centre of gravity. The heuristic promise of ideology as a category is better preserved and its adequacy to reality better secured by abandoning claims which are obstreporously causal and concentrating interpretive energy on seeing how far it is possible in detail to illuminate the question of why intellectual agents have one set of purposes, wants and beliefs rather than another which they readily could have had (and more particularly to illuminate the question of why they choose to adopt one set of beliefs in preference to another which they explicitly consider). It is under any circumstances a subtle question how far men can appropriately be said to decide or choose their beliefs.[20] But the language of choice and decision can scarcely be withheld completely in the face of situations which agents themselves characterize in such terms; and the concept of theory choice is of such prominence in recent epistemology as to give historians of ideas the strongest of motives for concentrating on the relatively few contexts in the intellectual lives of their subjects in which it is clear a-posteriori that fundamental theoretical options have been adopted.

How, then, was it that Locke became the sort of person who could choose the most fundamental of theoretical options as he in fact did? How did he acquire his own (and not some other historically available or accessible) intellectual identity; and how did this identity in its turn impose more or less compulsively upon him a particular distribution of intellectual *akrasia*? The intellectual identity is probably less controversial in its implications. Every human being begins to think at some time and in some place and, soon enough, within some language or other. Location is a prerequisite of human thought; and, however commandingly the thought advances, it seems inconceivable that it should ever be *quite* wrenched loose from such moorings, dislocated. Some of what explains the trajectory of its advance must simply follow from – be furnished by – this siting of its starting point and of the territory through which it seeks to make its way. Seeking to explain the akrasia is, however, a touchier matter. In the case of the tolerably foolish the explanation in detail of intellectual error is likely to prove unrewarding. Intellectual akrasia can be an exceedingly random affair, a sustained demonstration, well within the capacities of most human beings, of their inability to *think* in the full light of their own best reasons. But to identify intellectual akrasia in the thinking of Locke is to identify a response which is very markedly not random. What makes Locke such a powerful thinker is less the striking originality of his conceptual invention than it is the capacity to hold in an extremely stable relation a variety of different lines of thought and to work through with great care and attention the intricate structures which relate them. His deepest intellectual ambition was to think constructively, rather than destructively.[21] It is possible, without major distortion, to see his entire intellectual career, a career which spanned four decades, as the working through of a rather small number of problems at an extremely high level. It is a mark of his sheer intellectual distinction that so much, strategically considered, of his working through of his line of thought explains *itself* so handsomely, as the unfolding of reason ideally should. Seeing how much of what he originally took for granted he became in due course, simply under the force of his own reflection, not merely willing to doubt but unable any longer to believe, seeing, that is, his intellectual identity *shape* itself, we have good reason to consider with some attention just why exactly in the end he should have chosen to resist or shy away from conclusions towards which his thinking would appear (to us) to be dragging him. The intellectual akrasia of the immensely intelligent is not merely more fascinating to reflect upon than the akrasia of the intellectually incoherent. It is also for anyone interested in political philosophy – and in the relationship between political philosophy and ideology – potentially far more important and revealing. It can scarcely be denied that the beliefs and sentiments of most of us on matters of political value are largely (though not, of course, exclusively) an unexacting exercise in credulity. But what someone of Locke's intelligence and of Locke's – it can be unsentimentally said – *will* to understand managed to convince himself of in the teeth of his own better reasons, surely does show something of the social limits of human rationality, of the reality of ideology in the sense in which that term may indeed refer to a profound aspect of the human condition and not merely to the bleary cynicism of the educated contemporary political vision.

In what follows it is presumed firstly that the carrying through of an extended piece of reasoning can be validly represented as the performance of a somewhat complex type of action and that at least some of its characteristics cannot be validly represented in any other manner. Secondly and more hazardously it is presumed that the types of action which very able and intellectually very *serious* thinkers are apt to perform in the case of passages of very extended reasoning are to be explained both by their natural (and culturally realized) capabilities, their skills, as reasoners and by their social identities. Thirdly it is presumed that the explanation of such agency is to be sought in the first instance not in neurophysiology (where Locke is presumably now safe from our attentions) but in terms of the dispositions, commitments, values etc. of the agent and of the orientation which these render it rational for him or her to adopt towards the context to which their thought is addressed. The principle of rationalization[22] can be applied over very different time horizons, to split seconds or to whole lifetimes. Intellectual akrasia over split seconds would be unlikely to be instructive even in the case of Locke. But intellectual akrasia lasting over most of a lifetime in a great philosopher eminently deserves explanation. (In relation to fundamental questions of social and political value, even the akrasia of the somewhat bemused would be sociologically illuminating, if described with any fidelity and analysed at all perspicuously. All societies face persisting difficulties in ingratiating themselves at all plausibly with their members; and these impediments are often correctly seen not simply as affective obstacles but as intellectual anomalies.) How far is it still possible to identify just what did set the limits of what a political philosopher of Locke's stature found that he could or could not believe, found plausible or unthinkable, found himself able to doubt and even rationally to abandon or unable even to *conceive* of doubting?

Two genuinely deep philosophical issues arise in the attempt to specify these relations more clearly: the question of the criteria for the rationality of beliefs and the question of how to conceive the process by which men make their selves. Adopting, very broadly, a conception of beliefs as an intricate web upon which experience at any point in time bears only at the periphery,[23] the key question is how radically it is appropriate to relativize the rationality of belief change to the existing web of beliefs. Very drastic relativizations might be attempted, relativizations which in effect preclude identifying a fundamental choice of the kind which Locke is here presented as making as an instance of akrasia at all. Such radical historicism (in effect the making of dissent a criterion of the failure to understand: 'Do I seem to you to contradict myself? Very well then, that shows that you have not contrived to understand me') probably cannot be stated coherently and is certainly counter-intuitive to most human beings. (The category of ideology, for example, could scarcely retain a use if it were accepted; and it is extremely dubious whether most of our more fundamental concepts could survive its acceptance. But it does represent the logical terminus ad quem of a line of reflection on which very many contemporary thinkers are firmly embarked and a line on which there appear to be few, if any, natural stopping points.) The character of Locke's central credal choice will be (dogmatically) presented here as an instance of intellectual akrasia. By the same token, the possibility (perhaps resting on some version of a coherence theory of truth) that the incapacity of many today to adopt the same credal choice for the (to us, very feeble) reasons which he was able to give for adopting it merely demonstrates that he is not us will be ignored.[24] A subsidiary difficulty within this general puzzle is the question of what sort of conceptual model of the nature of such a choice it is appropriate to adopt. The choice is presented here as the decision of an embodied (and very much *socially* extended) intellectual will,[25] as an intellectual *action*. The model chosen is a model of agency. It is however, at least implicitly a somewhat more determinist *type* of model than can readily be defended in the case of individual human actions. In relation to individual action the insistence that wants are not circumstances,[26] that the locus of wanting is precisely the gap between circumstances and action, the gap left by the unpredictability of action from circumstance,[27] is well placed. In relation to a credal commitment which lasts over many decades, the attempt to explain the persistence of a credal disposition represents a more crudely causal type of inquiry. Conceptions such as those of a consistent sadist or a compulsive believer in the truth of Christianity may not be legitimate; but, if they *are* legitimate, it seems strained to deny that they are (at least in intellectual intention) causal in character. (Conduct which one has perfect reason to expect an agent to perform has become a causal property of the agent.) In relation to each particular choice which a man makes it may well be true that the best explanation which can be given is the reason which led him to choose as he did. But in relation to a strong pattern of choices extending over a whole adult lifetime it is not plausible that the only valid explanation which can in principle be given of this pattern is the set of reasons which led him to make each particular choice of which the pattern is compounded precisely as he did.[28] To possess a character, perhaps even to be a self, is, amongst other considerations, precisely for there to *be* pattern in a person's choices.

How then is it appropriate to conceive the emergence (or creation?) of such a self? Harry Frankfurt offers an illuminating suggestion, in the course of discussing the case of a choice between the satisfaction of two desires which are both incompatible and inconsistent.[29] He presents such a choice as a process in which the agent renders one desire external to himself and identifies himself with the other, stressing that it is by making a particular kind of decision that the relation of a person to his passions is established and suggesting that it may be a decision of this kind which lies behind every instance of the establishment of the internality and externality of the passions. Modelling this process from the outside is rendered practically manageable by the fact that most human beings do not remain in a state of flighty existential nebulousness, resisting self-definition for the sheer charm of the gratuitous. If the range of individual plasticity characteristically increased throughout the human lifetime, instead of decreasing, a biographical approach to the constitution of the self would be merely perverse. But since in most (if not in all) cases, it very definitely does not do so and since it is in many ways illuminating to see the self, at a particular time, as a web of feelings as well as a web of beliefs,[30] and to see these as displaying over time rather similar balances of causality and rationality, there is (men being taken as they are) real merit in seeing the earlier stages in the constitution of social identity as setting relatively firm constraints on the range of credal and affective potentiality for an individual. It is not (it must be emphasized) a matter of doubting whether there is emotional or intellectual life after fifty (or indeed after twenty-five). The movement from relatively credally and psychically inchoate to relatively credally and psychically determinate is not a form of loss. Clearly defined intellectual (or existential) puzzles and deeply felt dilemmas are scarcely the prerogative of youth. Equally, the movement is not one in any sense *beyond* the range of experience but rather one towards a condition in which experience has relatively determinate implications.

What is attempted in the remainder of this paper is a very brief (and unoriginal) sketch of the central intellectual choice of Locke's life and an equally sketchy, though lengthier consideration of the social and personal context within which Locke formed the self which could be guaranteed to take this choice in the direction in which he in the event did take it. ('Guaranteed' should be read as a rhetorical flourish and not as a theoretical claim. It is extremely doubtful whether we ever know enough about any human being – ourselves included – to warrant using such a term in relation to choice. But some of our expectations become extremely stable and, of these, *some* are never disappointed.) In considering this process of the formation of a self particular attention must be paid to the terms in which Locke himself described the social world which he was entering and described his own experience of it.

Because Locke's thinking was so elaborate and because it touched on so many different topics, it is clear that different aspects of his developing social identity must stand in an explanatory relationship to different facets of his thinking. Even in relation to his political thought, the variety of contexts to which he addressed himself and the diversity of his personal interests on different occasions must necessarily be invoked in any attempt to explain its development in detail.[31] But the central aspect of his political thinking which requires explanation is quite simple. As a whole this thinking can be legitimately represented as the attempt to think through the political implications of a rather chastened Puritan Christianity within the political frame of an inherited constitutionalist state[32] and in the light of an epistemology which gave great epistemic weight to sensory experience.[33] The resulting theory, as it can be elicited from the published works as a whole (though not necessarily as it strikes a casual modern reader of the *Two Treatises of Government*), represents a precarious balance between a strongly felt religious individualism and a potentially incompatible and heavily sceptical theory of knowledge (with a peculiarly corrosive impact upon the Puritan conception of the Church as an authoritative community).[34] This tension can in principle be resolved decisively in one or other direction – in the direction of a resolute fideism (as in the case of Pascal, or, on some readings,[35] Pierre Bayle) or in the direction of a comprehensive secularism (as in the case, at least consequentially, of Thomas Hobbes or, still more overtly, David Hume). An essentially fideist position could incorporate, as it did in the case of both Pascal and Bayle, a considerable body of taut and sceptical epistemological and psychological reflection. But, as the term itself implies, it rested its intellectual conclusions on foundations which were set firmly beyond the reach of rational argument. Why Locke should not have embraced this theoretical option – why indeed he should have in some measure abandoned it after initially espousing it[36] – is obscure. All we know in effect is that he was ill at ease with and disinclined to remain content with such explicit irrationalism, once the latter was clearly conceived as such. It is this disinclination which provides the dynamic of his intellectual life, driving him forward from one intellectual resting place to another, until he arrived at the relatively intellectually passive pietism of his last years. After the early *Tracts on the Civil Magistrate* we have no evidence that Locke ever contemplated simply opting for such an irrationalist solution. Even the devotional writings of the last decade of his life represent less a theoretical adoption of a fideist position – a denial, implicit or explicit, of the epistemic doctrines of his maturity as set out in the *Essay concerning Human Understanding* – than a tense and exhausted attempt to change the subject of reflection to a more emotionally reassuring theme. The fact that Locke should have spurned the comforts of a fideist solution is, then, something which we are perhaps in a position to applaud but scarcely to explain.

Is it possible, by contrast, to offer any explanation of why he should not have chosen to resolve the tension in a decisively secular direction? The most noteworthy recent attempt to *explain* the individualist character of Locke's political theory, Professor Macpherson's racy and trenchant *The Political Theory of Possessive Individualism*, sees this in broadly functionalist sociological mood as simply ideologically propitious for the capitalist society of late seventeenth-century England, fashioned because it was capable of doing some ideological service. This perspective might in principle illuminate the potential implications of Locke's political writings for the ideological viability of British society in the eighteenth century (though the historical record of their reception does little to confirm this expectation[37] and it is worth noting the penetrating and deeply concerned judgement of David Hume, both in youth and in maturity, that they presented on the contrary an appreciable threat to this ideological viability).[38] In the absence, however, of any theoretically clearer and better-grounded teleology than is supplied by a generalized functionalist theory of ideology, the fact (if it is a fact) that Locke's writings might have had this consequence is in itself quite insufficient to explain his actions in settling down to write them. With this problem, the challenging issue of just how ideology comes to be *made*, it is necessary to attempt a bolder intellectual tactic.

The nub of this problem can be stated quite briefly. Why did Locke not in practice elect to follow what subsequent intellectual history has hinted obtrusively enough to be the natural development of his recognition, as early as the *Essays on the Law of Nature*, of the primacy of sensory experience in the derivation of true knowledge (as opposed to potentially all-too-misguided belief) and simply abandon the intellectual practice of deriving substantive conclusions from explicitly theological categories? Not only did Locke not *abandon* this intellectual practice, either explicitly or tacitly; he in fact committed himself to it in a singularly whole-hearted and self-conscious fashion, affirming ringingly, as late as his writing of the *Conduct of the Understanding* that the science of theology was incomparably above all other sciences and that 'containing the knowledge of God and his creatures, our duty to him and our fellow-creatures, and a view of our present and future state', it amounted to 'the comprehension of all other knowledge directed to its true end; i.e., the honour and veneration of the Creator, and the happiness of mankind'. It was a study in which every man had the duty to engage and which 'every one that can be called a rational creature is capable of'.[39] The persisting effort to unite a theological rationalism and a sensorily-based conception of man's place in nature presented major intellectual difficulties; and, at least from July 1676 onwards,[40] his adoption of an explicitly hedonist psychology imposed severe theoretical strains upon the natural theology framework which he retained. Because of the astonishing intellectual career of Thomas Hobbes we can be certain that the option of abandoning the practice of drawing substantive ethical conclusions from theological categories was not merely theoretically open to Locke (as it is reasonable for *us* to regard it as being theoretically open to any thinking person at any time) but also genuinely *historically* open to him in the exceedingly strong sense that it was directly presented to him in an intellectually forceful and distinguished fashion.

His continued adherence to such a profoundly theological framework of thought thus cannot be explained by invoking structuralist dogmas to the effect that no alternative was at the time genuinely conceivable nor even to the less strained hypothesis that he simply never encountered any such intellectual possibility. On the contrary, we not merely know that he could well have conceived of such a consistent naturalism as a genuinely possible intellectual option but also that its intellectual charms were put very actively and stylishly in front of him. If he did not succumb to its charms, if indeed he rejected them with a certain tortured asperity, it is legitimate to infer that he did so, over more than twenty-five years of very active thinking, because he found their seductions on balance very plainly outweighed by their menace.[41] Whether or not Hobbes himself did believe in God (and whatever sort of God he can be intelligibly said to have left himself intellectual licence to believe in), it is plain enough that he did *not* believe in permitting theological categories to *deflect* human terrestrial judgement. The option which Locke rejected – and rejected by profound intellectual commitment, whether or not he rejected it by a process of protracted and consciously reasoned reflective choice – is precisely the option of preventing theological categories from deflecting human terrestrial judgement. The grounds for supposing that in making this intellectual commitment Locke knew very well what he was doing (however little insight he may have had into just why, causally speaking, he was so acting, and however long or short a time of deliberation he may have consciously devoted to the issue) can be seen clearly in a brief passage from one of his abortive mature sketches for a demonstrative ethics: 'The original and foundation of all Law is dependency. A dependent intelligent being is under the power and direction and dominion of him on whom he depends and must for the ends appointed him by that superior being. If man were independent, he could have no law but his own will, no end but himself. He would be a god to himself and the satisfaction of his own will the sole measure and end of all his actions.'[42] This is no hastily and fecklessly seen shape of a possible world view, rejected from unthinking prejudice or imaginative indolence. It is the considered verdict of a man who has seen clearly a vision from which he recoils in horror. The thought which he rejects is in no sense a thought intrinsically unthinkable in itself. Rather it is a thought which Locke, the embodied thinker, could not endure thinking, could not bring himself to believe true.

Why should Locke have recoiled in horror from this conception? On this point at least Macpherson's explanatory stance offers little assistance. Since he at no point seriously considers the place occupied by the deity in Locke's reflections on any matter, it is scarcely surprising that he should be in no position to illuminate Locke's continued intellectual adherence to a theological framework of thought after the stage at which intellectually powerful temptations to abandon this had become obtrusively apparent within the latter's own thinking. But if the question at issue is the question of how ideology is made and remade, such perfunctory treatment can hardly suffice. If the category of ideology is taken seriously (as at least reaching for – and at most *capturing* – an understanding of just precisely how the bounds between the thinkable and the unthinkable do come to be set within an individual and within a society), then such a clear-sighted encounter between intellectual will and intellectually powerful temptations is an ideal point at which to attempt to apply it. By contrast, to seek to explain the development of a structure of beliefs, while ignoring what in the view of the thinker in question was its major theoretical term and while neglecting to consider the context in which this central term was explicitly put in theoretical jeopardy, is a necessarily ill-conceived venture.

Locke's distinctive balance between a demanding and highly repressed religious individualism and a theory of knowledge and individual psychology which could have subsisted perfectly well (as indeed in later thinkers they frequently *did* subsist) quite independently of any such religious repression, certainly cannot be explained by any broad sociological characterization of the (partially) completed transition from feudalism to capitalism. But it can perhaps be illuminated by taking somewhat more precise account, on the one hand, of the familial religious culture in which Locke was reared and in which, like most other human beings he learnt more or less successfully to repress himself[43] and, on the other hand, of the distinctively dependent cliental social position which he occupied within the English society of his day, a position, in terms of the etiquette of social relations, at least as deeply marked by 'feudal residues' as it was by capitalist novelties. The blend of internal repression and external dependence was exceedingly punishing. The discomfited precariousness of the resulting life rendered any theory of human existence in which it was seen as exhaustively rational to pursue one's pleasures without inhibition or external responsibility, within the limits of instrumental prudence, too ironical to endure. Locke had no difficulty in understanding such thoughts. What was beyond him was to attempt to live his life on the basis of believing them. Such allegations are inherently vague and inferentially loose. It is certainly too despondent to presume that we have no means in principle of bringing any evidence at all to bear upon them. But it would be idle to deny that we possess at present no uncontentious intellectual routines for deciding on their merits in a particular case. Such confidence as we are likely to succeed in mustering in our capacity rationally to make up our minds about them is apt to be predicated upon very elaborate evidential access (access which is certainly seldom – and arguably never – adequately available in the case of the distant past). In the case of Locke, the exceptional bulk of his private note-books and working materials gives us better access than we possess for all but a handful of seventeenth-century figures. By now these materials have been explored with thoroughness and imagination by a large number of scholars. It is now possible to supplement them with a systematic chronological study of Locke's correspondence, conveniently assembled for the first time as a whole and in chronological order by Dr E. S. de Beer.[44] What this last source offers is a picture of Locke's developing characterization, in detail and over a lengthy period of time, of the social world in which he lived and of the social relations within which he found himself situated. It enables us to see, on occasion, to be sure, a trifle fitfully, but on occasion also with striking clarity, Locke's own sense of the historical and personal milieu to which he was obliged to orientate himself, not ideologically abridged into some compressed and carefully aimed thrust of argument but casually disclosed in the course of everyday life. In it Locke can be seen describing this social world to himself and to others and, in effect, negotiating with interlocutors with their own distinct social identities on just how it was becoming to see and to feel about this world. To watch someone in this fashion learning to describe his world is potentially to see very deeply into the central axis of a man's developing thought. Faced with the arbitrary palimpsest of the historical record, such an inquiry can hardly be systematic – a matter of taking carefully spaced readings of man's developing descriptive tastes and powers throughout infancy and childhood, youth and maturity. Brief passages of intense light cannot wholly compensate for the lengthy tracts of profound shadow. But within this corpus of materials, patient and careful inquiry may reasonably hope to get at, to capture imaginatively, a real thinking and feeling person, relatively off their guard, unposed, unmade-up (or, if on their guard, posed and made-up in relation to quite distinct types of audience from that for which the elaborated works were staged). Here we may encounter Locke's consciousness not in the painstakingly moulded and impacted guise of presented doctrine but in the disaggregated and relatively relaxed ambiance of ordinary life. In doing so we may hope to discern an intellectual agent endowed with his own independent attributes to set over against the works themselves and to aid in the explanation of at least some of their characteristics which do not contrive – and perhaps *could* not contrive – to explain themselves.

Three types of relation which appear in the *Correspondence* may help to define more precisely the intellectual and emotional persona that stood behind the public works and caused them to be penned broadly as they were and not otherwise. The first of these is a set of relations of client and patron, deeply revealing as to the etiquette of social relations and, of course, of key importance in determining the material character of most of Locke's life. The second is a set of broadly familial relations, also highly illuminating but casting light in this case not upon Locke's place within a system of social stratification but upon the texture of dutiful valuing, concern and no doubt moral pretence, the complicities of a relatively concrete way of life into which he was inducted in his childhood and from which he does not seem ever emotionally to have made his escape. Third, and perhaps equally revealing, is the more egalitarian and less externally responsible idiom of discussion with his friends in Oxford and elsewhere as to the practical strategies for personal social mobility and the appropriate moral mood in which to contemplate them, somewhere between a loftily pious disinterest and an eye frenziedly alert to the main chance.

The central tension disclosed by these three relations lies in the apparently antithetical intimations of the first two. Insofar as it is resolved theoretically in Locke's thought and feeling at all, it is so in the precarious synthesis offered by the third relation. It can be seen relatively clearly by juxtaposing to a pair of programmatic statements of Locke's confidently universalist religious theory a comparatively casual acknowledgement, taken from the *Two Treatises of Government*, of the inherent particularism of at least some human relations of dependence in which even the most intelligent of dependent beings may find themselves placed. The existential urgencies of the social realities which lay behind this acknowledgement for Locke himself can be sensed in the form in which he expressed his own recognition of what he owed to the contingencies of his dependence.

The first of these statements is the classic proclamation of creaturely dependence on the Creator on which Locke bases the central argument of the *Second Treatise*.[45] 'For Men being all the Workmanship of one Omnipotent, and infinitely wise Maker; All the Servants of one Sovereign Master, sent into the World by his order and about his business, they are his Property, whose Workmanship they are, made to last during his, not one anothers Pleasure.' The second occurs in the course of his discussion, in a letter to Edward Clarke of 22 August 1685, of the attitudes towards all sentient creatures in which human

27

children ought to be reared and of the ready transition from cruelty or insensibility to the plight of animals to the same sentiments in relation to human beings:[46] 'Children, then, should be taught from the beginning not to destroy any living creature unless it be for the preservation and advantage of some other that is nobler. And, indeed, if the preservation of all mankind as much as in him lies, were the persuasion of every man, as it is indeed the true principle of religion, politics and morality, the world would be much quieter and better natured than it is ... And, indeed, I think people should be accustomed from their cradles to be tender to all sensible creatures, and to spoil or waste nothing at all.' Against these should be set the revealing assertion, also from the *Second Treatise*, of the scope and limitation of human jural equality:[47] 'Though I have said ... *That all Men by Nature are equal*, I cannot be supposed to understand all sorts of *Equality: Age or Virtue* may give Men a just Precedency: *Excellency of Parts and Merit* may place others above the Common Level: *Birth* may subject some, and *Alliance* or *Benefits* others, to pay an Observance to those to whom Nature, Gratitude or other Respects may have made it due; and yet all this consists with the *Equality*, which all Men are in, in respect of Jurisdiction or Dominion one over another, ... being that *equal Right* that every Man hath, *to his Natural Freedom*, without being subjected to the Will or Authority of any other Man.'

To be subject to such observances might well mean to be expansively open to the duty of obsequiousness. The importunities of patronage in which Locke's career began and the forms in which he felt it appropriate to display his gratitude for receiving it make this painfully clear. Excellency of parts and merit were in due course to make open to him an intricate but in the end very grand career. But the career could be kept open to his talents only at the price of the sustained capacity to display appropriate gratitude. The consciousness of the need to pay this price is seldom long absent from the correspondence. In May 1652 he writes ('tuus obedientissimus filius') to his father from Westminster School on the prospects for securing a scholarship in the election at Christ Church, making very plain his awareness that, without the aid of patronal wire-pulling, the best of talents in Latin or Hebrew, whether or not they were necessary conditions for success, might well prove insufficient to ensure it; 'for we heare that there will be very few chosen'.[48] Two further letters may be set against this, one of which, from 1660, was certainly addressed to his patron Alexander Popham and the other, probably dating from 1652, may well have been. Both are concerned with the moral obligations of the client's role and discharge their responsibilities with graceful literary embellish-

ment. Popham was an important man, a member of the Council of
State in both 1652 and 1660, a Member of Parliament for a variety of
seats in the West Country, a political luminary in the Somerset political
circles of Locke's comparatively humble father, and certainly the cause
of Locke's getting his foot on the first rung of the career ladder and
being at Westminster School at all. In the earlier letter, written in Latin,
Locke adapts a passage from one of Cicero's letters to press his case:[49]
'Others perhaps will think it presumptuous in me, most excellent
patron, to be still importuning with fresh prayers one from I have
already received so many kindnesses. But I consider it rather to be the
mark of a candid and not ungrateful mind to wish to owe yet more to
one to whom one owes so much.' He ends with a brief verse exercise on
the bringing of thankofferings to the gods by grateful suppliants:[50]
'This is how gods are made [*Numina et hinc fiunt*]. May you pardon me
for asking you so many things, for I show by the frequency of my
requests that you are my god [*deum*].' Alliance or benefits can exact
pretty fulsome observances.

In 1660, at another high point of Popham's fortunes, Locke recapi-
tulates his sense of obligation with equal pains, offering his services in
the education of Popham's son, then opportunely at Christ Church:[51]
'The greatest advantage I demand of my studys is an ability to serve you
with them, and I shall thinke those years I have spent in Oxford not lost
when I perceive they have rendered me any way usefull to him that first
placd me there . . . I would not willingly give you a reason to thinke that
your care of Learning is a fruitlesse thing and such as from whence you
must expect noe return. This makes me diligently eye all occasions that
may beccon me to your service, which should I oversee or be lesse
carefull to observe it might justly be thought that in a place where all
others improve their knowledg and become quicksighted I alone grew
blinde and stupid . . . if then I have made any acquisitions in learning tis
fitt I dedicate them to you as their first author . . . It will equally
unbecome me either to promise any thing for my self more then a zele
to this undertakeing or to prescribe to you what way you shall make
use of me. I shall only take leave to minde you that I am an utinsill
wherein you have a propriety . . .' 'An utinsill wherein you have a
propriety' is hardly a becoming phrase for someone who supposed men
to be 'his Property, whose Workmanship they are' to find himself
employing. It is scarcely surprising that an intelligent but undeniably
dependent being should have found it hard to reconcile the demands of
human social power with those of God's natural Power.

The strains can be seen again from other angles in three further
letters written probably between 1658 and 1660. The first, addressed

to Locke's father, discusses the latter's political prospects and the threats to their success.[52] In it Locke proclaims bitterly that, if his father's plans miscarry, 'it will teache me this caution, to withdraw my dependences from such windy props, to forbid my hopes and fears a commerce with their frowns, or promises, and to use them as they use us, only as long as serviceable. I cannot overvalue those accidentall differences that chance doth place on men, and are noe reall ones, but as they are usd. Pardon me Sir if I have dwelt to long on this and perhaps to hotly. But I cannot see your services soe rewarded, repeated promises so slighted and jugling in a great man without being movd.' In contrast to these sentiments over 'those accidentall differences that chance doth place on men' may be set a particularly feeling and attractive letter of some two years later, again addressed to his father, 'more than all other relations', which urges the latter to treat his own needs as an overriding claim upon the family's resources since Locke himself could always, if necessary, rely on his own 'head, and hands and Industry'. 'I cannot', he proclaimed,[53] 'distrust that providence which hath conducted me thus far'. Accidental differences between men are the arbitrary product of an unmoralized *Fortuna*; but Locke's sense of his own life was the sense of an axiomatically moralized dispensation of Providence.

The third letter is already justly famous. Addressed in 1659, probably in Dr de Beer's judgement, to a Christ Church friend Thomas Westrowe, it reflects upon the question of how a human being ought to live in the light of the dominance of fantasy in human experience:[54] ''tis Phansye that rules us all under title of reason, this is the great guide both of the wise and the fooleish, only the former have the good lucke to light upon opinions that are most plausible or most advantageous. Where is that Great Diana of the world Reason, every one thinkes he alone imbraces this Juno, whilst others graspe noething but clouds ... Tis our passions that bruiteish part that dispose of our thoughts and actions, we are all Centaurs and tis beast that carrys us, and every ones Recta ratio is but the traverses of his owne steps ... Truths gaine admittance to our thoughts as the philosopher did to the Tyrant by their handsome dresse and pleaseing aspect, they enter us by composition, and are entertained as they suite with our affections, and as they demeane themselves towards our imperious passions, when an opinion hath wrought its self into our approbation and is gott under the protection of our likeing tis not all the assaults of argument, and the battery of dispute shall dislodge it? Men live upon trust and their knowledg is noething but opinion moulded up betweene custome and Interest, the two great Luminarys of the world, the only lights they walke by. Since therefor we are left to the uncertainty of two such fickle guids, lett the examples of the bravest men direct our opinions and actions; if custome must guide us let us tread in those steps that lead to virtue and honour. Let us make it our Interest to honour our maker and be usefull to our fellows, and content with our selves. This, if it will not secure us from error, will keepe us from loseing our selves, if we walke not directly straite we shall not be alltogeather in a maze ...' The providence which Locke *could* not distrust was the providence which had conducted him thus far, the sense of moral aid and meaning in a blatantly socially and ideologically arbitrary world which left him at ease with his own good intentions[55] and his own sense of effort, within a continuing frame of moral significance. Within that frame, but only within that frame, he knew very early, he ran no risk of losing his self and within that frame he could not distrust providence, whereas outside that frame, however high the accidentall differences that chance doth place on men were to carry him (and in later life they carried him very high indeed), he could never muster the assurance to rethink the whole of the human condition simply in their terms. In this sense *Recta ratio* for Locke himself in his intellectual maturity was very much the traverses of his own steps. Seeing him in these early years groping for a self which he might hope to retain, it is easy to see that for *him* at least it was simply not a real option to conceive his entire human environment with unflinching instrumental poise as a flat unmoralized field for the exercise of whatever appropriative ingenuity he could muster.

In these (somewhat arbitrary) epistolary juxtapositions an image can be discerned of a self in formation. Within at most a decade and a half of the first of these letters a very fully formed self is to be found determining the direction of Locke's intellectual exploration.[56] To see the intellectual itinerary of his maturity as simply the traverses of his own steps is, at first sight, to adopt a crudely relativist perspective. But if the direction of interest is altered slightly and stress is laid instead on the extraordinary length of this itinerary and on the numbers of those amongst his contemporaries and successors whom Locke in due course compelled to accompany him imaginatively along it, some of the crudity can perhaps be avoided. If we choose to reflect, in addition, on the process through which these steps *became* fully Locke's own, it becomes still less clear in what precise sense this is a relativist perspective at all. The formation of a self is a process of choice within constraints, the more or less successful creation of an order within which life can be lived, intellectually and emotionally, the more or less successful transcendence of the possibility of an experiential chaos within which life can barely be lived at all. It is possible to identify the constraints to some degree from the outside; but the process of creation itself is as yet (and may always remain) inscrutable to us. To study human thinking as ideology is to study some of the constraints on our capacity to create rational order, not to seek to deny this capacity to whatever degree men succeed in displaying it.

The self which Locke formed in the midst of a confusing welter of kinship and friendship and cliental relations,[57] by espousing some purposes and attitudes within himself and rejecting others, was not a comfortable creation. Throughout the period of his life which lies within our view he distrusted most of those on whom he in any way depended (whether kin, friends or patrons) and fiercely resented their frequent disappointment of his expectations. But it was a self which both sustained him in his highly dependent pursuit of social mobility and exacted from him the most strenuous intellectual and moral effort. The effort was the price for accepting dependence and its disciplines – in particular the sustained display of gratitude and respect as a prudential investment, whilst retaining a personal sense of moral purpose. In contrast to David Hume's often expressed aversion to 'all connexions with the Great', his 'Disdain of all Dependence',[58] Locke's feelings were inescapably ambivalent. The central importance of relations of dependence in social experience, the dominant intellectual obsession of the Scottish Enlightenment,[59] was the theme above all others that Locke had set his intellectual imagination to pass by on the other side. His individualism was predicated on the individual incidence of social and spiritual fate, not on a concern with the sociological preconditions for the realization of men's 'natural liberty'. For him individuality was always primarily a human achievement and never simply a social provision. Had Locke been less ambitious or had he been socially more advantaged, his intellectual itinerary might well have been very different. But, at least by the early 1660s, he had formed an identity which was truly his own; and from this point, if not earlier, it is appropriate to think of this identity as a determinant of the itinerary which he followed and as what *made* the steps which he traversed truly his own.

The broad limits of what is thinkable, at least in political theory and in ethics, are set far more rigidly and narrowly for those who think superbly than they are for the vast majority of the rest of us, whose minds move inconsequentially through the fogs of intellectual bemusement and confusion, as selective inattention and infirmity of conceptual grasp permit them, restrained at best feebly and intermittently even by the laws of logic. For Locke, though, it was not at all like that; and less so over the most fundamental of his concerns than over the surface detail of the arguments. In the broad (and still fundamental) choice in political theory between linking the rationality of individual action and the reality of a public world either by trusting in a morality of individual intention or in the moral substance of a set of concrete social relations or in a practice of purely egoistic utility maximization, what Locke trusted in was intention and not a moralized social order or individual appropriativeness. Individual intention is an apt focus for the faith of an anxious Christian, just as individual appropriativeness seems to most today a more natural vehicle for the trust of the comfortably pagan.[60] But the rejection of the social frame of seventeenth century English society, either in its capitalist or in its pre-capitalist dimensions, either as market or as skein of cliental dependence, as a self-subsistent focus of value and the rejection of instrumental egoism, the appropriate moral mood for an operating capitalist society, left Locke with nothing to trust in but his own good intentions and the theological framework which defined the merits of these intentions to himself. The fundamental terms of Locke's theory of the human condition, politically, socially, morally, religiously, were set not by Professor Macpherson's market society nor by its accompanying psychology of possessive individualism. Nor were they set by the obtrusive ideological residues of the lordly way of life – 'a style of living and a scale of values which had flourished from the days of Beowulf to those of Sir Philip Sidney'[61] – residues in the midst of which Locke had, very practically, to make his eminently dependent life. What did set them rather was the simple frame of Puritan religious values which Locke inherited from his father and within which he rethought the meaning of human existence throughout more than four decades of very active intellectual life. This is how ideology *is* made, in the formation of men's social imagination, a tense and eventful process in every human being and in a human being with the emotional force and intellectual depth of John Locke, one of very high drama. The formation of social imagination cannot be a peripheral concern for political theorists. For the limits of social imagination are what determine what men in the last instance can place their trust in. Men, as Locke said, *live* upon trust. And there is simply no conceptual truth in political theory more fundamental than the truth that men trust in what they *can*.

Chapter 2

'Trust' in the politics of John Locke

BECAUSE in politics the most fundamental question is always that of what particular human beings have good reason to *do*, and because what they do have good reason to do depends directly and profoundly on how far they can and should trust and rely upon one another, I take the central issue in political philosophy (properly so called) to be that of how to conceive the rationality of trust in relation to the causal field of politics.

In this essay I discuss the thinking of Locke, firstly because I consider that he made a more systematic and determined effort to think about this question than any other and more recent political philosopher, and secondly (and, of course, connectedly) because the attempt to think comprehensively about this conception has essentially disappeared from modern political philosophy, both in its Marxist and in its liberal or conservative variants. (There are, to be sure, important analytical idioms in modern thought – such as game theory – and key moments in the construction of particular political theories – such as John Rawls's original position – in which the issue is treated with great assurance.) The explanation of this disappearance is a complicated and somewhat obscure matter, and not one suitable for treatment in this context. But that it is so would be difficult to deny.

To discuss Locke in this fashion is not to argue that we should today espouse all – or any – of Locke's own detailed conceptions, but it is implicitly to suggest that we do have good reason to treat his conception of political philosophy as examplary – as a model which there is still every ground for our trying to emulate.

To most modern philosophers, the question 'What is the bond of human society? What in the last instance holds it together?' will seem a pretty odd one. There is, to be sure one entire tradition in modern social theory which is still more or less united in the last instance in the view that what does hold human society together is the indispensability of cooperating in the production of material goods. But this is certainly not intended as a psychological allegation about human dispositions or attitudes. And it remains one of the most pressing difficulties of Marxist theory that its conviction of what *does* secure the reproduction of human social arrangements is not accompanied by any very clear or cogent explanation of just how and why human agents can be confidently expected to be either disposed to, or able to, execute the task which the theory assigns to them.[1] When John Locke in his *Essays on the Law of Nature* described *fides* as the *vinculum societatis*[2] (the bond of society) there is no reason to believe that he drew a clear distinction between what he took to be the central virtues or ethical requirements of a good social life and what he took to be the causal explanation of the existence of such a life. At the time, indeed, he had no particular reason to think especially hard about the latter question. Modern thinkers, by contrast, are inclined to separate out these two questions with some completeness, often electing to confine themselves solely to considering either the internal relations of a set of ethical concepts or the political sociology of the conditions for reproducing a particular regime or mode of production. Those who are interested predominantly in explaining the reproduction of particular social and political patterns would not, on the whole, be inclined to look for answers at the psychological level. (A partial exception would be Barrington Moore's explanation of the historical record of human passivity in the face of *Injustice*[3] in terms of imaginative habituation, eked out by rational pessimism.) Even if they were prepared to essay a psychological account of the cement of human society, most modern social thinkers would probably offer a fairly variegated list of contributory factors: greed, fear, lust, conviviality, habit, hope, despair, indolence, an extremely high degree of selective inattention – and so on.

The most famous single criticism of Locke's political philosophy (and in some measure of the entire contractarian tradition) is David Hume's attack in the *Treatise of Human Nature* and more particularly in his essay 'Of the Original Contract' on the absurdity of any attempt to resolve the obligation of allegiance into the obligation of fidelity, to explain political obligation by invoking the duty to keep promises.[4] There is, in my view, abundant doubt as to how far Locke himself did intend to *explain* political obligation through the duty to keep promises and, more particularly, as to how far he regarded personal consent as a precondition for valid political obligation.[5] But what is true is that his moral and political thinking as a whole (and indeed the central burden of his philosophical thinking in its entirety) was directed towards an understanding of the rationality and moral propriety of human trust. The purpose of this essay is to try to show how and why this preoccupation dominated his thinking, to show that it was (and is) a coherent preoccupation and to suggest that modern political philosophy has not gained but lost from its fastidious and scrupulous avoidance of such gross and promiscuously constituted issues. I take it that, to the extent that my purpose is successfully realized, what could reasonably be drawn from the line of argument is, in the first place, a fairly robust understanding of the integrity and force of a past piece of philosophical thinking of very high quality and secondly, and much more tentatively, a not necessarily altogether flattering perspective on the tacit framing of much political philosophy in our own day.

The rationality of trust within particular structures of social and political relations is a pressing issue in political understanding in any society of the modern world. It features prominently (and pertinently enough) in the characteristic analyses of the politics of communist states constructed by western scholars, just as it does in those of capitalist states developed by Marxist scholars. It is a salient preoccupation of such ambitious essays in the theoretical assessment of modern society and its travails as that of Jürgen Habermas. But, as far as I know, only one major social theorist has recently chosen to consider it directly. The German functionalist sociologist Niklas Luhmann published ten years ago a lengthy synthetic essay on the problem of trust in modern society. Some of the main lines of thought set out in this work offer an instructive contrast to Locke's approach. Like Locke, Luhmann sees trust as central to sustaining a society in operation. Like Locke again, he sees trust as making possible a massive extension of men's capacity to cooperate, not by means of cognitively rational calculation but through the provision of a measure of buffering between indispensable hopes and expectations which are necessarily partially disappointed. Trust, fundamentally, is a technique for coping with the freedom of other human beings,[6] for extending the availability of time and thus rendering possible the choice of delayed gratification,[7] for increasing men's tolerance of uncertainty,[8] for the contrafactual stabilization of expectations.[9] Without trust, confidence in their own expectations of others, men or women could scarcely nerve themselves to get up in the morning.[10] The working of all complex political or economic institutions, government bureaucracies or monetary systems,[11] depends directly upon trust and, at least in part, on trust generated in the more intimate and cognitively accessible contexts of each human being's everyday life.[12]

Luhmann's book does not present a particularly bold and clear line of thought. But it does extend this range of judgements, any or all of which Locke might well have shared, in one distinctive direction, a direction dictated by Luhmann's emphatic commitment to a functional conception of society. Modern societies, Luhmann believes, depend less on normative experience and more on purely cognitive assumptions than did their historical predecessors.[13] 'The contrafactual stabilization of experience is the function of normative experience.'[14] This function is less central to modern societies because of the degree to which these require for their working not emotional trust in known and familiar persons but system-trust predicated on the ways in which institutions, practices and the incumbents of distinct roles present themselves to us.[15] Individual trust is seldom reflexive in its base, founded upon trust in the viability of trust itself;[16] but confidence in economic institutions such as a particular currency is characteristically grounded in this way. Because of this sharp change in the balance between emotional and presentational, between direct and systemic, trust in the operations of earlier societies and in those of today, issues of the rationality of trust today depend for their assessment predominantly on the causal analysis of society and thus cannot be handled by an ethical theory of the appropriate criteria for the allocation of individual trust.[17] This view of the part played by the cognitive apprehension of, and the instrumentally rational response to, social causality in cementing social cooperation is sociologically more plausible in relation to the Federal Republic of Germany of the late 1960s than, for example, to the Great Britain of the early 1980s. But however questionable its sociological judgements, it does indicate one strong contrast between modern social thought and the perspective of Locke: the very limited extent to which the latter's conceptions of rational and moral conduct for individuals or groups in particular contexts depended upon explicit judgements of the causal properties of societies or of particular social institutions. One of the judgements defended here is that, despite the indispensability of causal analysis of society,[18] there is considerably more than we normally recognize today to be said for the pre-modern, Lockean, perspective on this question.

Its most important merit is the directness with which it addresses the question of just what particular human beings (ourselves included) have good reason to *do*. A great deal of modern political philosophy, whether utilitarian or Kantian in its moral inspiration,[19] gives very arbitrary or uncertain accounts of how in a particular historical situation any particular agent has good reason to act. There are, of course, many other types of question which require an answer in political philosophy. But because of the historically given character of political conflict and political power, and the consequent need for the conclusions of political philosophy to intrude themselves into existing fields of force and meaning,[20] no adequate political philosophy can simply take the form of a theory of what is intrinsically desirable. (It cannot, in the last instance, because the question 'Desirable for whom?' is the prototypically political question.) At the very least any such theory must also offer an account of what sort of claims in the face of what sorts of costs the intrinsically desirable can rationally levy upon individual historical agents or groups of such agents. If these claims constitute at all a heavy burden, it must add at least a sketch of the reasons why such agents would themselves be epistemically well-advised to regard the claims as valid.

Two powerful imaginative tendencies have made it particularly hard to generate such reasons today. One, plainly, is the rather steady pressure of moral scepticism, motivated essentially by the contrast between the presumed epistemic solidity of human understanding of non-human nature and the cognitively relatively whimsical status of judgements of human value. The second is the increasingly alienated vision of the nature of human societies and polities which has developed over the last two and a half centuries. If the entire field of political and social relations surrounding an individual agent is taken as given, and his or her potential contribution to politics is then assessed in purely instrumental terms, virtually all political action will appear as necessarily futile; and the balance between comparatively certain cost and highly uncertain gain will become prohibitively discouraging to political agency.[21]

This is not the place to try to take the measure of either of these imaginative pressures. But I mention them briefly at this point because they do press so hard on all of us and because, in the realm of politics at least, their conjunction is so obviously culturally malign. John Locke wrestled for forty years with the problems presented by the first: the epistemic status of moral judgements. But, for reasons which I shall try to make clear, he was never compelled to face the menace of the second. The failure of his attempts to rebut moral scepticism[22] mean that we can hardly today employ his philosophy to order, discipline and sustain our own fondest political intuitions. But the boldness with which he conceived human societies as historical creations for which their members can and should always try to assume an active responsibility can perhaps still be of some real aid. Certainly in my view it holds a better and wiser balance between agent responsibility and external social and political causality than any political philosopher or political scientist of the last half century has managed to achieve.

I turn now to the development of Locke's thinking about the place of trust in human life and consider firstly the justly famous letter, written in his late twenties to an unnamed friend, probably Thomas West-rowe.[23] It is the most striking expression of moral scepticism that Locke ever penned. Passion and fancy, not reason, rule human life. Human beings select their beliefs to suit their desires and rational argument has little, if any, power to alter them.

'Men live upon trust and their knowledg is noething but opinion moulded up between custome and Interest, the two great Luminarys of the world, the only lights they walke by.'

The diagnosis of this predicament is lengthier, more eloquent and considerably more definite than the remedies which are suggested to meet it. Custome and interest are uncertain and fickle guides and the conclusions which they suggest are surprisingly conventional:

'Let the examples of the bravest men direct our opinions and actions; if custome must guide us let us tread in those steps that lead to virtue and honour. Let us make it our Interest to honour our maker, and be usefull to our fellows, and content with our selves. This, if it will not secure us from error, will keepe us from loseing our selves, if we walk not directly straite we shall not be alltogeather in a maze.'

Apart from the somewhat erratic pragmatism of the proposed attitude towards the deity, the stalwart conventionality of the recommended response stands in marked contrast with the existential urgency of the predicament itself. As agents, human beings make their own selves; but they do so in circumstances and out of materials emphatically not of their own choosing. Because they have such good reason to distrust the materials with which they must work and the beliefs on the basis of which they must act, and because so much of their lives necessarily depends upon custom and habitual expectation, only the clearest conceptions of virtue, held imaginatively at some distance from the immediate importunities of their own lives, can exercise a benign directive pressure upon these. To continue to act at all, men must be able to trust, to believe with confidence. But they can hope to form beliefs which epistemically deserve their trust only by a subtle and unrelenting suspicion of their own motives and a steady contemplation of ethical models which are wholly independent of their own immediate desires.

In Locke's first extended writings on politics, the *Two Tracts* of the early 1660s dealing with the extent of a magistrate's legitimate authority over indifferent things (actions neither directly commanded nor directly forbidden by God's law), the issue of trust does not explicitly arise. The magistrate's authority derives immediately from the will of God: 'God wished there to be order, society and government among men. And this we call the commonwealth. In every commonwealth there must be some supreme power without which it cannot truly be called a commonwealth; and that supreme power is exactly the same in all governments, namely, legislative.'[24] It is not clear that any such power over human life could in principle derive its authority simply from the consent of men.[25] Not only is political power indispensable for human security. It is also compelled by this very indispensability to determine its own scope in practice, since the partiality of individual human judgement and the geographical and cultural variety of men's evaluations precludes their being left to determine its scope in the light of their own individual beliefs. 'Our deformity is others' beauty, our rudeness others' civility, and there is nothing so uncouth and unhandsome to us which doth not somewhere or other find applause and approbation.'[26]

None of these considerations simply disappeared from Locke's later thinking; but the practical conclusions which he drew from them notoriously altered sharply. They did so in one sense, as is well known, as a consequence of his involvement in the busy political intrigues of the Shaftesbury entourage. But they did so, perhaps more profoundly, because of the theoretical instability of the position which Locke adopted in his English *Tract*. In this, the magistrate, in the exercise of the authority 'settled on him by God and the people'[27] is uniquely entitled to 'follow the dictates of his own understanding', while all other men, in the matter of indifferent things, must submit their conduct in its entirety to this authority, whether or not they personally believe it to be religiously permissible to do so. In this respect Locke's mature philosophical position, centering on the precept of the *Essay* that 'Men must think and know for themselves',[28] reverts to the perspective set out in his youthful letter to Thomas Westrowe and constitutes a systematic attempt to confront the problems which this raises.

When Locke attempted, not long after writing the *Two Tracts*, to develop a coherent account of the status and binding force of the law of nature, it was the twin threats of the partiality of individual judgement and the cultural heterogeneity of evaluative standards which he took as his major challenges. Each plainly militated against the view that natural law was in any helpful sense innate or that its standing could be established firmly in the general consent of mankind. The former had particularly lethal implications for any attempt to ground men's knowledge of the law of nature upon tradition: 'since traditions vary so much the world over and men's opinions are so obviously opposed to one another and mutually destructive, and that, not only among different nations but in one and the same state – for each single opinion which we learn from others becomes a tradition – and finally since everybody contends so fiercely for his own opinion and demands that he be believed, it would plainly be impossible – supposing tradition alone lays down the ground of our duty – to find out what tradition is, or to pick out truth from among such a variety.'[29] Cultural heterogeneity militates especially severely against any attempt to ground the law of nature in the general consent of mankind: 'there is almost no vice, no infringement of natural law, no moral wrong, which anyone who consults the history of the world and observes the affairs of men will not readily perceive to have been not only privately committed somewhere on earth, but also approved by public authority and custom. Nor has there been anything so shameful in its nature that it has not been either sanctified somewhere by religion, or put in the place of virtue and abundantly rewarded with praise.'[30] Individual partiality and cultural heterogeneity do not merely pose practical obstacles to the observance of the law of nature. They also constitute epistemic obstacles to its reliable identification in the first place.

In practice, in large measure, human beings do learn how to act, what is virtuous, what is obligatory, what is prohibited or disapproved, from the responses of other human beings and especially from their speech: 'ab aliis fando'.[31] Tradition, therefore, offers a perfectly appropriate and plausible causal explanation of most of human sentiment and belief.[32] But insofar as this explanation is exhaustive and valid, what it implies is that the authority behind human moral sentiments and beliefs is merely the dictates of *men* and not those of reason.[33] If the law of nature were to be learnt from tradition, it would be an example of faith rather than knowledge, since it would depend upon the authority of a speaker rather than on the evidence of things themselves.[34] Faith (*fides*) stands in epistemic contrast to knowledge (*cognitio*). But it also stands in practical contrast to the vice of untrustworthiness. The virtue of keeping one's promises is the virtue of *fides*.[35] If the law of nature were founded solely in individual worldly advantage and utility the duties of human life would be at odds with one another. What reason could there be, on this presumption, for fulfilling a promise when to do so would be to one's own personal disadvantage?[36] On the assumption that individual worldly advantage is the basis of the law of nature no coherent account of the content and binding force of human duties can be constructed. Any real conception of a society is subverted, and with it *fides* (trustworthiness) the bond (*vinculum*) of society.[37]

That Locke happens in the *Essays on the Law of Nature* to employ the same term to mark the epistemic contrast between faith (or belief) and knowledge and between interpersonal trustworthiness and undependability in itself tells us only a fact about his Latin vocabulary. But it also serves handily to draw our attention to three very profound assumptions behind his thinking: firstly, that any acceptable human society depends upon the recognition of moral duties which cannot be validly derived from the rational assessment of individual worldly advantage; secondly, that the most important and encompassing of these duties is the duty to act towards fellow human beings in a way which deserves their trust; and thirdly that the most important theoretical question about human duties is the question of how far and in what sense we can *know* the content of these duties and how far and under what conditions we must rest our assessment of them in the last instance simply on faith. In his letter of 1659 Locke had underlined the compulsiveness and the radical undependability of human moral judgement; but he had also emphasized the extent to which human beings retain the capacity to take responsibility for, to modify and even to dispose of their own beliefs. The *Essays on the Law of Nature* explore the sceptical threat posed by this judgement, without doing much to clarify or to reinforce the optimistic injunction which accompanies it. But they also extend its implications from the existential problems of the individual into the life of civil society at large. Trustworthiness, the capacity to commit oneself to fulfilling the legitimate expectations of others is both the constitutive virtue of, and the key causal precondition for, the existence of, any society. It is what makes human society possible. For Locke (unlike for David Hume) there is a real and potentially systematic antithesis between individual terrestrial interest and individual moral duty; and there is no reason at all to trust in the moral validity of any individual's or even any society's moral socialization. The duty to be trustworthy simply *is* more fundamental than the moral conventions or positive laws of any society, because none of the latter is necessarily morally valid and because, without the former, human society would not be possible at all. It is an individual duty, not a naturally given attribute of human nature – and without its display human society simply cannot exist.

The most dramatic proclamation of this judgement in Locke's works comes in the famous explanation in the *Letter on Toleration* of why it is that, although anyone whose religious beliefs and sentiments do not directly imply the political subversion of a legitimate political authority has a *right* to the toleration of the civil powers, no atheist can possess any such right. His reasons for taking this view go back to a brief section added to the final draft of his 1667 *Essay on Toleration* in which he had insisted that 'the belief of a Deity is not to be reckoned amongst purely speculative opinions', for it represents 'the foundation of all morality, and that which influences the whole life and actions of men, without which a man is to be counted no other than one of the most dangerous sorts of wild beasts, and so incapable of all society'.[38] One reason given in the *Letter of Toleration* for denying a right of toleration to atheists applies only to those perverse enough to claim such a right in the name of religion. Since Locke's defence of the right to toleration defends this *as* a religious right, he is quite consistent in denying it on these grounds to an atheist. But the first and more striking reason which he gives echoes the judgement of 1667. No one who denies that there is a God is entitled to toleration.[39] For 'neither faith [*fides*], nor agreement nor oaths, the bonds [*vincula*] of human society can be stable and sacred for an atheist: so that, if God is once taken away, even simply in opinion, all these collapse with him.' (Or, as William Popple's 1689 translation puts it, 'the taking away of God, even only in thought, dissolves all'.)[40] Locke's judgement here notoriously clashes directly with that of his Protestant contemporary Pierre Bayle who denied that there was any reason at all why a society of atheists should not prove perfectly viable in practice.[41] From the perspective of modern scholars, Bayle's judgement appears self-evidently correct, while Locke's is at best an embarrassingly superstitious anomaly in one of the great advocates of the liberal value of freedom of thought and expression.

In Locke's own thinking, however, there was nothing vaguely anomalous about the judgement. Indeed it lay at the very foundation of his theory of the content and binding force of moral duty. The reason why atheists posed such a threat was not a causal hypothesis about the degree to which on any given occasion they would in practice prove emotionally susceptible to the authority of the law of opinion or reputation (the moral traditions of the community to which they belonged).[42] Rather, it was a logical presumption about the necessary absence for them of any good reason, in the last instance, for curbing their own selfish and socially destructive desires. It was the rational implications of atheism for human practice, not its external and contingent causal pressure upon human moral dispositions, which expelled it from the protected arena of free intellectual exploration. Almost any set of religious, or moral, or speculative opinions *might* in Locke's view contingently affect men's moral demeanour for the worse. But this consideration alone could not possibly justify the repression of any particular set. What was unique about atheism was that if its premiss was once accepted, then it rationally *should* affect men's moral demeanour as a whole dramatically for the worse.

If trustworthiness, fidelity, the keeping of agreements and promises, and respect for oaths were in this way the bonds of human society, what in Locke's eyes *makes* it possible at all, it is obviously important to understand how he conceived the extent of human trustworthiness in practice and what he considered to determine its incidence. It is essential here to separate firmly what Locke believed to be the necessary obligations of all men under the divine law of nature from what he judged to be the reasons for action which any particular human being contingently happens to possess on a particular occasion. He had no doubt that under the divine law of nature all human agents had a clear obligation to keep their promises. Faith and the keeping of faith belong to men as men and not as members of society.[43] Promises and oaths 'tye the infinite Deity' himself.[44] 'The Obligations of that Eternal Law ... are so great, and so strong, in the case of *Promises*, that Omnipotency it self can be tyed by them. *Grants*, *Promises* and *Oaths* are Bonds that *hold the* Almighty.'[45] This can be so, in Locke's view, because it is legitimate to say that 'God himself cannot choose what is not good; the Freedom of the Almighty hinders not his being determined by what is best.'[46] Divine freedom, in this respect, is analogous to human freedom. It is not a curb upon, or diminution of, our freedom but a perfection of this that we are determined 'to desire, will, and act according to the last result of a fair *Examination*'.[47] In addition to the full divine law of nature with its panoply of infinitely punitive and rewarding sanctions in another life, Locke also attempts in the undated manuscript 'Morality' to develop an account of the obligatory force of promises which is purely terrestrial and naturalistic in structure.[48] Men have not made themselves nor any other man; and they find themselves at birth in a world which they have not fashioned. Hence they have, on the basis of their own attributes, no original and exclusive right to anything in the world. In this condition, they will inevitably be subject to want, rapine and force and will fail to attain the happiness which only plenty and security can make possible. In order to avoid this predicament, they have no choice but to determine each other's rights by compact. Once they have done so, they have established the duty of justice as the first and general rule of their happiness, since the making of compacts would be incoherent and pointless without the commitment to observe them. 'These compacts are to be kept or broken. If to be broken their making signifies noe thing if to be kept then Justice is established.' This naturalistic would-be demonstration is clearly at odds with the theory of property right set out in the

Second Treatise – a point of some interest since there is good reason to suppose it to have been written well after that work was completed. But in the present context what is more important is that the structure which it suggests for the obligation to keep promises is so weakly related to Locke's theory of the reasons for individual action. The claim that promise-breaking is irrational because it is literally self-contradictory was defended notoriously some three decades later by William Wollaston in his *Religion of Nature Delineated*[49] (and later still mocked unmercifully by David Hume).[50] But the moral objection to breaking a promise is that it deceives others, not that it involves the assertion and denial of an identical proposition; and, of course, to deceive others it is necessary for a promise to cause them to attribute a particular meaning to it and to shape their expectations accordingly. To make a promise would signify nothing at all unless it signified a commitment in due course to keep it in practice. But to choose to keep a promise in due course is still to decide to act in a particular manner; and, given Locke's hedonic theory of the grounds or determinants of an agent's choice, it is entirely possible for any agent in practice to find that they possess more pressing motives or more immediately cogent reasons for breaking a past promise than they do for choosing to keep it.[51] The signification which a promise necessarily possesses is the signification which enables it to play an important role in the deception of others. It is not a signification which necessarily in practice, on this account, gives the maker of the promise a *sufficient* reason or a *determining* motive to observe it.

How far then, in Locke's view can men be trusted? This question has been a focus of considerable, and rather poorly articulated, controversy in the interpretation of his political theory. Commentators such as Leo Strauss and Richard Cox[52] have seen the core of Locke's politics as the conviction that humans are as radically untrustworthy as Hobbes depicted them as being, and have insisted accordingly that Locke's conception of the state of nature is distinguishable from that of Hobbes only by the degree of evasion with which Locke elects initially to describe it. The state of nature is a state not of peace, but of war. But this interpretation simply mistakes an account of the structure of rights between men (in which the state of nature and the state of war are in fact by definition incompatible with one another)[53] for a description of the practical character of social relations in the absence of legitimate governmental authority. The latter, Locke fully recognizes, are likely to be both hazardous and disagreeable, particularly after the attainment of any great measure of economic advance and consequent social and economic inequality. To the question 'How far can man be trusted?', Locke has no simpler and more readily applicable general answer to offer than does Niklas Luhmann. It depends on many different sorts of considerations: on the contingencies of individual disposition, of the prevailing culture of a particular community and of the practical structures of material interests which are at issue. If Locke had been obliged to construct a theory solely on the basis of judgements of practical prudence, he would therefore have been hard put to it to proffer any firmer and more concrete direction[54] on the pragmatics of allocating individual trust than Luhmann (or indeed we ourselves) can readily muster.

But if human trustworthiness, like any other instance of weakly structured probability, can in practice only be assessed with a large margin of error, Locke does of course possess a conception of the nature of its determinants. It is not perhaps an entirely coherent conception, particularly in its understanding of the fundamental character of human agency, where he has been plausibly accused of vacillating between a robustly hedonist mechanical theory of motivation and a distinctly less determinate theory of reasons for action expressed in a misleadingly hedonic language.[55] (On this point, there seems little doubt that the most lasting impulse of his thought, reflected in the major amendments to his account of free agency, and in the treatment of personal identity, added in later editions of the *Essay* was to secure at virtually any cost men's responsibility for their own actions.[56] But whether expressed in the terminology of pleasure, desire or uneasiness, or in that of reason, the main determinants of human trustworthiness can be identified with some confidence.

There are four positive components. The first of these is the rational understanding, or the revelation, of God's requirements for his creatures, weakly enforced by prudential sanctions within this life but backed by overwhelming sanctions in the next.[57] The moral content of this determinant is ex hypothesi perfect – the divine law of nature – but its immediate motivational incidence on particular human beings is regrettably fitful. The second component is the emotional impact of moral socialization within a particular family and community,[58] the law of reputation, enforced by men's desire for each other's approval and their aversion to each other's blame. (As an epistemic criterion for the true law of nature, the moral traditions of particular communities are irretrievably unreliable. But in practice their content does overlap to a considerable degree with the divine law of nature[59] and their motivational impact is reassuringly vigorous. Such trustworthiness as most human beings contrive to display in their interpersonal relations is in fact the product, in this manner, of their moral socialization.)[60]

The third component is the public law of particular political communities, backed by the coercive sanctions at the disposal of their rulers. (On all matters which are morally indifferent in communities where these rulers possess legitimate political authority, such laws constitute authoritative extensions of the divine law of nature. But the mere fact that something is the public law of a particular political society offers no guarantee that its subject matter falls within the class of indifferent things or that the rulers of this society possess legitimate political authority.[61] In civilized and economically developed countries, much human trustworthiness does in fact depend upon the existence of effective governmental power. But wealth is no guarantee of political legitimacy; and no constitutional form can ensure that the subject matter of public law is confined to the class of morally or religiously indifferent things. Even illegitimate political authorities may well make a real contribution to sustaining human trustworthiness in some domains of activity (and their subjects may even owe them duties of obedience because of their provision of these services).[62] But they themselves have no right to be obeyed; and their commands, as such, carry no necessary moral authority. Even the commands of a legitimate sovereign lose their authority when what they order is in breach of the divine law of nature.) The fourth and final positive component of human trustworthiness is not an external pressure upon men's wills, but an aspect of their motivation: what is sometimes referred to as their 'natural sociality'. Locke presents this both in the *Two Treatises* and in the *Essay* as a motive for men's entry into continuing social relations at all: 'God having made Man such a Creature, that, in his own Judgment, it was not good for him to be alone, put him under strong Obligations of Necessity, Convenience, and Inclination to drive him into *Society*, as well as fitted him with Understanding and Language to continue and enjoy it.'[63] The God who gave men all things richly to enjoy[64] gave them also a judicious combination of practical compulsions and capacities to enter and sustain society and psychic inclinations to seek out and to enjoy it. What makes a relatively unforced human trustworthiness readily attainable under some conditions is the fact that human beings can and do take pleasure in each other's company. It is men's natural sociality which enables the law of reputation to have such a vivid impact upon their sentiments and causes them to care so keenly what other men feel about them.

To balance these positive components, the motivational pressures, external and internal, which promote human trustworthiness, there are also, of course, negative components, motivational pressures which militate more or less decisively against it. Some of these are also external, most importantly the simple and unstartling recognition, expressed as early as the *Essays on the Law of Nature*,[65] that human material interests do conflict regularly and directly with each other. In conditions of limitless abundance, as Locke clearly acknowledges in the *Two Treatises*[66] and Hume later insists so effectively in the *Treatise of Human Nature*,[67] the concepts of property rights in material objects and of justice would be otiose. But material scarcity implies the permanent possibility of acute conflicts of material interest.

It is quite clear from his discussion of the character which the state of nature would in practice be likely to assume in conditions of moderate economic progress and complexity, that Locke recognized the causal significance of this external and negative motivational pressure upon human trustworthiness. But in itself, as Hume's subsequent analysis brings out, scarcity serves merely to explain[68] men's invention of the institutional forms (ownership, promise-making and keeping, and the rules of justice) best calculated to minimize the threat which it poses. It has no determinate implications for how to conceive men's motivation in relation to these institutional forms; and it offers no basis for assessing the prospective punctiliousness with which they can be expected to observe these norms in practice.

The basis for such assessment in Locke's thinking is provided by his theory of human motivation and his conception of men's reasons for action. These two were not very successfully distinguished by Locke himself; and it cannot be said that their implications harmonize very successfully. The mechanical hedonist account of motivation, as initially elaborated even in the *Essay* itself, makes it very unclear how men can be genuinely responsible for their actions and has correspondingly pessimistic implications for the assessment of human trustworthiness. The revised account of the nature of the will and of human freedom, with its stress on the agent's capacity for rational suspension of practical choice to enable him or her to reconsider more soberly what is at stake,[69] is certainly less destructive of agent responsibility and offers more insight into how a human agent can in principle be worthy of trust (and not simply dispositionally unalarming). But the revised account, for this very reason, is less well fitted to serve as a basis for the practical assessment of trustworthiness. Its implications are less pessimistic precisely because they are less clear and less determinate.

Because, on Locke's analysis, human beings are free agents, responsible for their own actions, they are in principle capable of taking responsibility for many aspects of their own beliefs. This consideration is central to the understanding of human trustworthiness because only human beings who do fully understand what is at stake in their choices can be *depended* upon to have sufficient reason to be consistently worthy of trust. As natural creatures, all men are 'liable to Errour, and most Men are in many points by Passion or Interest under Temptation to it'.[71] Unless they anticipate a future life (as in Locke's view they have good reason to do), they are perfectly rational in pursuing whatever terrestrial pleasures happen to appeal to them.[72] Some of the terrestrial pleasures which do happen to appeal to them can readily have highly deleterious consequences. 'Principles of Actions indeed there are lodged in Men's Appetites, but these are so far from being innate Moral Principles, that if they were left to their full swing, they would carry Men to the over-turning of all Morality.'[73] Locke's image for the cognitively appropriate mechanism for inhibiting *these* principles of action is quaintly archaic: 'a Pleasure tempting, and the Hand of the Almighty visibly held up, and prepared to take Vengeance'.[74] But its archaism cannot simply be brushed aside. To be rationally and consistently trustworthy, for Locke, a human being must fear the wrath of God. It seems clear that his *Essay* was centrally motivated by the desire to show how human beings can take full responsibility for the content of their own beliefs and discharge this responsibility in an edifying manner.[75] Given the key role of the Hand of the Almighty in securing an acceptable content for the outcome of men's rationally assessed motives, it is not surprising that the *Essay*'s implications for the epistemology of morals should have fallen so far short of Locke's hopes. Nor would it be surprising if, as I shall suggest is in fact the case, the political conclusions of the *Two Treatises* seem appreciably bleaker to those of us who cannot discern the Hand of the Almighty than they did to Locke himself.

The central premiss of the *Two Treatises* is that men belong to their divine Creator and that their rights and duties in this earthly life derive from his ownership of them and from the purposes for which he fashioned them. The law of nature articulates these purposes as rationally intelligible authoritative commands. Its interpretation and enforcement within the natural world is left to human reason and human force. Every man or woman must judge rationally for themselves what its precepts are and how these bear upon their conduct; and every human being possesses the executive power of the law of nature, the right and duty to enforce these precepts when they have been flouted. This structure of rights, duties and powers is given by the character of the natural order, seen as a divinely created order which expresses in its entirety the purposes of its Creator. This is the proper understanding of what the state of nature is.[75] But in itself it offers (and seeks to offer) no explanation whatever of why human beings for the most part within the real history of their societies find themselves subject to the additional coercive power of political authorities. To this question, 'Why does political power exist at all?', Locke gives two very different but in no sense incompatible answers. The first answer specifies what benign purposes such power can serve and is worked out with some tenacity in the *Second Treatise* as a whole. The second answer simply indicates the extremely prominent role in the history of political power of purposes which are in no sense benign. Even illegitimate political power can and will serve, intermittently, some of the benign purposes which political power is capable of serving; and even the most legitimate political power can always be diverted to wholly deplorable ends. But, ex hypothesi, the grounds for viewing legitimate political power with some measure of trust are far more substantial than those for viewing illegitimate political power in this light. In the latter case indeed, although some measure of trust is likely to be accorded if the power is used at all benignly in practice, *trust* as such is scarcely an appropriate attitude. Human beings are, and have to be, very trusting creatures. But illegitimate political power even where in detail it deserves acceptance cannot deserve trust. It cannot deserve trust because it is in no way reciprocal in character.

The more important analytical question for Locke, given the moral and legal coherence of the order of nature as such, is why political power can serve benign purposes, why human history contains instances of legitimate political power and why such power, while it sustains its own legitimacy, does deserve the trust of those over whom it is exercised. The answer to this question is simple enough. Human beings are not merely liable to error (cognitively fallible) in the interpretation of their rights and duties under the law of nature, they are also often 'by Passion or Interest under Temptation to it'.[76] It is the inherent partiality of human practical judgement in the face of temptation which ensures that human beings will in practice often misinterpret the law of nature and abuse their own power to enforce this. The benign end which wholly legitimate political power is plainly able to serve is the institutionalized provision of clearer epistemic standards (known standing laws)[77] and of less partial enforcement agencies for the structure of rights and duties specified in the law of nature. The need for such institutionalized provision becomes more pressing as human society develops in complexity and social scale and as the potential conflicts of immediate interest within it sharpen, as they plainly must with the genesis of massive disparities in economic entitlements. All men, rulers as much as ruled, legitimate rulers as well as illegitimate ones, are partial in their own case and liable to error in their judgements. But in practice they vary very widely indeed in the degree to which they succeed in controlling their impulse to partiality and in judging as reason prescribes that they should. The two opposite extremes which define this range of variation are reason and duty, God's way for man, and force, arbitrary power and personal pleasure, the way of beasts,[78] who cannot suspend the execution of their desires[79] and must accordingly respond without internal check to the full swing of the principles of action lodged in their appetites.

When men confer power upon other men and establish a legitimate political society by doing so, they seek to provide against the inconveniences of the state of nature, the practical hazards posed by the general partiality of mankind. But they also expose themselves more acutely to the potential partiality of the particular human beings who always in practice constitute the holders of governmental power.[80] Political power is presented 'to the Governours, whom the Society hath set over it self, with this express or tacit Trust, That it shall be imployed for their good, and the preservation of their Property'.[81] The metaphor of a legal trust which Locke employs at a number of points in the *Two Treatises* to express the nature of the relation between subject and sovereign in a legitimate polity was not original to him;[82] and it carries little or no distinctive weight in his argument. (To conceive of a legal trust as tacit represents at least a decisive an etiolation of the concept as with the more notorious instance of tacit consent.) But the more elaborated metaphor does serve to express more sharply the implications of his pervasive insistence on the centrality of the psychological and moral relation of trust to the benign working of political authority. For political power to serve the purposes for which men need it, it *has* to be subject to drastic and potentially destructive abuse. The legal concept of trust captures nicely three features on which Locke is anxious to insist: the clarity of a ruler's responsibility to serve the public good, the existence of a structure of rights external to the practical relation of ruling on which a sovereign's claim to authority must depend, and the inescapable asymmetry of power between ruler and ruled which precludes the latter from exercising direct and continuing control over the former.

In the chapter on Prerogative in the *Second Treatise*[83] Locke insists on the degree of this asymmetry. The power of a legitimate sovereign rests on the law. But in the English constitution at least, where the ruler holds not merely the executive and federative powers but also a share in the legislative power, it extends beyond into areas where the law is silent; and it can rightfully be exercised, where the public good requires it and the people acquiesce in its use, even against the direct letter of the law. Prerogative is *'the Power of doing publick good without a Rule'*.[84]

Discretion is intrinsic to its use. Indeed, whatever the laws prescribe, discretion must always be intrinsic to the use of that concentrated coercive power which all rulers derive from the accumulated executive powers of the law of nature which their subjects have surrendered to them. The prerogatives of the English monarch give legal status to the practical opportunities which no ruler can in practice be denied. But the status depends upon the use of this power to serve the public good. Should its possessor elect to follow his or her own whims, and to make force, the way of beasts, to be his rule of right, his subjects have no duty tamely to submit. Human beings must and do trust their rulers. They trust them on the whole far beyond the latters' deserts, and to the damage of their own interests. But in the last instance they retain (and indeed have no power to abandon) the right and duty to judge for themselves how far their trust has been deserved and where and when it has been betrayed. And if they do judge it to have been betrayed, they have every right to act in concert and seek to re-establish for themselves a form of sovereign power in which they can, once again, rationally place their trust. For Locke, political participation is a burden, not a pleasure or a privilege: something to be abandoned gratefully when one's community is fortunate enough to be ruled well.[85] But it is also, where the public safety is genuinely in danger (as, alas, it often is) both a duty and a right. Political virtue does not necessarily require an activist disposition. But it does require, in the last instance, a genuine commitment to the public good and a preparedness to make sacrifices on its behalf.

In the *Two Treatises* Locke expounds the political duty of trustworthiness for both rulers and ruled, and sets out clear limits on the duty of the ruled to act trustingly in the face of bitter experience. In doing so he vindicates the rights of all men to take political action in defence of their own interests. But he also stresses repeatedly their corresponding duty to judge for themselves, soberly and scrupulously, when and where and how to exercise this right. Prior to the question of what is to be done, there is the question of what is to be believed. This too, as John Passmore has insisted, is essentially an ethical question for Locke.[86] Before men can discern how they should act, they must ascertain what they *should* believe. To learn how to act responsibly, it is first necessary to learn how to take full moral responsibility for the content of one's own beliefs. This is a puzzling and barely coherent conception in the eyes of many modern philosophers. The ethics of belief may play a minor interstitial role in modern epistemology – in parts of the philosophy of natural science, for example. But most of any person's beliefs at a particular time must surely be a matter of fate rather than choice. Yet, odd though Locke's conception may look to us, there is little doubt that it was this queasy project of *taking* responsibility for the content of one's beliefs to which the *Essay concerning Human Understanding* was principally directed. Credally, human judgement on the occasion of its occurrence is, in Locke's eyes, just as compulsive as human knowledge. But, unlike his more confidently offered candidates for knowledge, judgement is plainly an activity under a substantial measure of voluntary control and one which offers ample opportunity for the suspension of our more pressing desires, to permit a wider and less hasty consideration of just what is at stake in our actions.[87]

The *Essay* does in fact offer an elaborate analysis of the factors which enable men to assume a large measure of responsibility for the content of their own beliefs and judgements, and which therefore justify their being held responsible for these. But, especially in the case of specifically ethical beliefs, it is discouragingly undirective on the topic of what men have reason to do. One conclusion which it does draw, however, is the impossibility of supplanting, over most of the field of human belief, the discretionary condition of active judgement by the compulsive condition of knowledge. It is a decisive implication of Locke's epistemology that over much of the field of human belief there is no possibility in principle of escaping the need to rest one's beliefs on epistemically insufficient grounds. Credally, just as much as politically, therefore, men's existence requires them to put their trust in what may well in practice prove to betray them. All human life is an encounter with hazard; and the best that men can do in the face of these hazards is to meet them with, as Locke put it in 1659, 'virtue and honour'.[88]

In his last major work *The Reasonableness of Christianity*, Locke sets out a clear and simple account of how for an English Christian in 1695 trust may be more confidently and securely disposed. There is no doubt that his answer to this question – the faith that Jesus was the Messiah and the promises attendant on this faith – lay behind and sustained his thinking throughout his intellectual life. What above all, it sustained and rendered rational was the systematic scheme of good intentions which made an ethics of belief a plausible approach to epistemology and which enabled him to undertake his extraordinary intellectual odyssey.

It was this scheme of good intentions which made it possible for Locke to see human political society as a whole as the historical contrivance of a creature, man, whose empirical characteristics ensured that he could never become particularly trustworthy; and yet for him to retain his own intellectual and moral nerve in the face of this vision.

In its political implications his view stands at the opposite extreme to modern functionalist social holism. So far from every array of productive forces, for example, being guaranteed in due course the capacity to engender a social apparatus capable of ensuring their continued expansion, for Locke nothing about human history or human society was or is guaranteed, except perhaps its starting point and its eventual destination. All the rest is made by the actions of individual human beings, every one of which is prospectively consequential, and the relations between which are wholly contingent in their impact. Men, not languages, or cultures or societies or productive forces, make human history. It is always human individuals, one by one, who are responsible for the sustaining and shaping of human societies. In contrast with the alienated modern conception of the context of political agency[89] and the predominantly instrumental view of its character which dominate modern political thinking, Locke combines a radically individualist conception of both the human significance and the rationality of political agency with a wholly unalienated conception of its social context. Because his conception of political agency depends for its structure and stability on a personal relation between the individual human agent and the deity it can scarcely be adopted as a basis for grounding modern political identities. But when held up against the more prominent candidates for such adoption in the political world in which we live our lives, it does bring out dramatically the devastating imaginative poverty and evasion which are characteristic of these.[90] If the synthesis of trust (the creation and sustaining of trust) remains, and will always remain, an indispensable human contrivance for coping with the freedom of other men, it is scarcely conducive either to virtue or to honour to have to make do with such deformed and superficial conceptions of how to trust one another or to be trustworthy, individually or politically. And now that the human race has acquired the power to destroy itself for ever, this is a theme which must surely be at the very heart of any philosophy which aspires to take *politics* at all seriously.

Chapter 3

From applied theology to social analysis: the break between John Locke and the Scottish Enlightenment

THE DUTY OF MANKIND, as God's creatures, to obey their divine creator was the central axiom of John Locke's thought. The entire framework of his thinking was 'theocentric'[1] and the key commitment of his intellectual life as a whole was the epistemological vindication of this framework.[2] It is still a controversial question precisely what the religious opinions of David Hume and Adam Smith in fact were. But it would certainly be a profoundly implausible claim to make in relation to either that the *framework* of their thinking was in any sense 'theocentric'. Whether or not either was in any theoretical sense an atheist, it is fair to describe each as being, as David Gauthier terms Hobbes,[3] 'a practical atheist': someone for whom, if God does exist, at least his existence makes no practical difference to the sane conduct of human life. It is scarcely surprising that the acquaintance of a practical atheist like Hume should have troubled the neurotic and credulous James Boswell, whose conduct even when Hume was virtually on his deathbed fully merited the latter's lapidary rebuke on an earlier occasion that 'it required great goodness of disposition to withstand the baleful effects of Christianity'.[4] But it is historically more striking and more illuminating to notice that their (on the whole very discreet) practical atheism would certainly in Locke's eyes have put Hume and perhaps even a wholly honest Smith,[5] at least in later life, beyond the pale of toleration: 'Promises, covenants, and oaths, which are the bond of human society, can have no hold upon or sanctity for an atheist; for the taking away of God, even only in thought, dissolves all.'[6] Hume certainly had little hesitation in subtracting God in thought; and there is some evidence that Smith became increasingly ready to do so (or perhaps merely increasingly ready to acknowledge having done so) towards the end of his life. But each of them set himself with considerable determination to establish that the bonds of human society, human moral sentiments, neither depended nor needed to depend for either their prevalence or their rationally binding force upon an authority external to human society or to the human race as a whole.

In their earliest major works both Hume and Smith explain, painstakingly and determinedly, that so far from its being true that everything (and in particular all human obligation) is dissolved by considering such obligation independently of the purposes of a concerned creator, all that human society requires in order to be causally viable is the dependable genesis of the sense of such obligation in individuals, as these become socially adult. In lieu of theological reassurance, their readers were offered what we today would see as *sociological* reassurance, sophisticated, modern and disenchanted, an offer still readily applauded as 'scientific'. By contrast, Locke's views on the untrustworthiness and the objectively intolerable attributes of atheists are normally passed over with some discomfort by modern commentators[7] who, even if they are not all now theoretically atheists to a man, are certainly apt all to be practical atheists (and in so far, for example, as they elect to keep their promises, would be most unlikely to mention their beliefs about God in listing their reasons for doing so). Few would now be prepared to regard Locke's views on this topic as an index of much sociological acumen. But it should at least be easy enough to perceive historically that this sociological obtuseness was not a matter of mere intellectual oversight, indeed that Locke had the deepest and most closely considered reasons for refusing to regard descriptive sociology as an appropriate standard for human practical reason. For Hume and Smith, all there normatively is to individual human existence and to the reproduction of human society is the fact that human beings individually (and thus collectively) hold certain beliefs, the internal reasons with which history has furnished individuals, constrained in their individual distribution by the mechanisms of social reproduction.[8] Property, justice, allegiance, loyalty, duty, fidelity, all human rights and all human duties, are in the last instance functions of opinion.

In considering the development of political economy in eighteenth-century Scotland – a special and theoretically powerful aspect of the systematic causal analysis of society to which Hume and Smith committed themselves – it may thus be illuminating to see their adoption of this analytical project very directly in contrast with the thinking of Locke. For to do so does not merely have the merit of historical relevance (in that both Hume's and Smith's moral thinking was initially much preoccupied with remedying what they saw as the defects of Locke's thought and the politically deplorable consequences of its vulgarization). It also offers an imaginative backcloth against which it should be easier to see clearly the relations between the intellectual dynamic of Hume's and Smith's thinking and the historical limits of their comprehension. It is hard for us even today to grasp the profundity of this caesura in the history of liberalism. But if we commence our efforts to grasp it from the fact that Locke had, in a sense, consciously set himself to *establish* it, we may contrive to draw some assistance in grasping it from the forceful and highly explicit reasons which led him to do so.

Both Hume and Smith, in different ways, vindicate an extremely strong theory of human practical reason: the theory, that is, that the rational grounds for human action are, within the laws of physical nature, reasons internal to individuals,[9] restrained from chaos or arbitrariness solely by the causal processes of society. All *good* reasons for human action and human effort are founded on this single blunt (if complicated) fact that human beings hold certain beliefs. And any reasons for human action and human effort which are not founded on this fact cannot be good reasons.[10] This is certainly a very modern view; and there is some reason to suppose that both Hume and Smith were sharply aware of its modernity. But what they cannot have been aware of was the degree to which Locke's thought by contrast was devoted precisely to its rejection. The break in social thought between Locke and the great Scottish thinkers was not in essence (as the effortless Whig perspective on history inclines us to see it) a break strenuously established by the latter. Rather, it was a break established prophylactically by Locke himself, a refusal of the future as it was to come to be. To speak anachronistically, both Hume and Smith in effect subordinate human practical reason to the contingencies of sociology, seeing history as real causal process, and value for human beings as engendered within this process, and setting themselves to identify the logic of this process. History, they supposed, very much in the modern view, must be taken as it comes. Locke, by contrast, chose (and chose very early in his life) to devote his intellectual energies to shoring up human practical reason against the contingencies of sociology. Indeed at a purely personal level it is biographically correct to say (though it is, of course, not something which he would have said for himself) that his purpose in setting himself to vindicate epistemologically the theocentric framework of his thought was precisely to uphold human practical reason against the contingencies of sociology.

It is important to be clear about the implications of this endeavour. It was not that Locke was in any sense less interested than Hume or Smith were in the social causation of human beliefs, any more than it is true, for example, that he was uninterested in the causal properties of the

British monetary system.[11] He did not hesitate to apply moral categories not merely to human rights,[12] but also explicitly to market exchange as such.[13] There is, indeed, no single theme in Locke's intellectual life as a whole about which he thought as hard and long and into which he inquired as systematically as the social processes which sustain moral and religious beliefs.[14] But what was crucial in determining the significance of his inquiries was not the degree of his preoccupation or the extent of the inquiries to which this preoccupation led him but, rather, the single-mindedness with which he rejected any conception of the causal processes of human belief as a self-subsistent locus of value.[15] His fiercely reductive view of socially realized human belief as intrinsically ideological in character set the problem which, in varying forms, all his major works from the *Two Tracts of Government* to the *Reasonableness of Christianity* sought to resolve epistemologically. Naturally all men everywhere are born cognitively free. But in real social history all men everywhere are reared in credal chains. Natural freedom (the candle of the Lord which presumptively shines bright enough for all ethically legitimate human purposes) and social servitude are reconciled theoretically throughout his thinking by a highly unstable balance of social explanation and individual moral blame.[16] Within his social theory, social explanation came close in effect to entailing moral blame. True beliefs reflected the use of the cognitive capacities with which God had endowed all human beings, undeflected by the abuse of the moral freedom with which he had also elected to endow them.[17] False beliefs reflected the abuse of these cognitive capacities, an abuse which in the field of morality he explained by the socially institutionalized or the individually devised distortion of experience, in both cases under the pressure of discreditable desires. The field in which Locke's necessarily rather intricate[18] 'ethics of belief'[19] was worked out most elaborately was the assessment of religious belief systems; and the clearest insight into his conception of the potential for human individuals to transcend the disorder of human credal history comes in his extensive correspondence with those few friends whom he profoundly trusted and who shared his commitment to the intellectual and practical battle to extend religious toleration.[20]

In a deservedly famous letter of 1659, earlier than any of his formal writings,[21] Locke set out with great force this sense of the epistemically treacherous relation between human desire and human belief. He also made it plain that he conceived this relation not simply as a theoretical puzzle in academic philosophy but as an urgent problem of practical reason and a pressing threat to the constitution and sustaining of a viable sense of identity.

At least on occasion, in his later life, Locke expressed remarkable optimism over the extent to which human beings could hope to secure themselves from error. The truth needs no assistance from the holders of power and authority amongst mankind and can be confidently expected to prevail through its own force.[22] There are few purely theoretical issues on which the honest and impartial will disagree if only they take the trouble to make themselves clearly intelligible to one another.[23] But for the most part his expectations of men's actual cognitive and moral performance remained considerably more despondent throughout his life.

It was this despondent view of how on most occasions most of his fellow men would probably behave which made it easy for his contemporaries to assimilate his views to those of Thomas Hobbes. (More recently it has led others to make the same error.)[24] In the eyes of Locke's contemporaries, the thought of Hobbes himself — and still more its vulgarized ideological outcome, 'Hobbism' — amounted in essence to a union of two theoretical components: an extremely pessimistic descriptive social psychology (which emphasized mutual untrustworthiness as being fundamental to human nature) and a decisive abandonment of the theocentric framework of thought. The relation between these two components, none too clear in Hobbes's own thought,[25] was not conspicuously clarified either by Locke's contemporaries or by his successors of the early eighteenth century.[26] In the case of Hobbes himself this residual opacity may have been simply a consequence of the author's own prudence. But in the case of later thinkers it was plainly almost entirely a product of intellectual confusion. On this issue at least, however, Locke himself was certainly far from confused. Not merely did he succeed with some ease in distinguishing the two components of vulgar Hobbism from one another, he in fact premissed his entire intellectual project on the need to keep the distinction absolute. It was not simply that, in large measure, he shared Hobbes's views of the empirical properties of human beings as such but happened nevertheless to dissent from Hobbes's views of the place of the deity in specifying what is of value for man. Rather, he set himself to vindicate a conception of what is rationally of value for man which centred on the will of a benevolent and omnipotent creator because, in the face of human beings as he experienced them, he could see no other way in which to guarantee a sense of meaning in his own life or of assurance in the stability of his own identity.[27]

His sense of the inherent untrustworthiness of human performance was not focused, as with Hobbes, on men's individual psychological properties (their ineluctable concern with the imperatives of their own

59

preservation and, in many instances, their fundamental mutual malignity) but on the arbitrariness of their *social* relations, however these were institutionalized. Hobbes saw the attaining of social order for a creature so disorderly in its individual properties as unambiguously a good. But for Locke, whatever social order was attained through institutional design and the causal mechanisms of human belief and human passion, although it might and did vary considerably in moral acceptability, afforded under all circumstances too shaky a basis on which to found a sound sense of moral identity. A viable moral identity depended upon stable and unambivalent goods – goods which could not be derived from the properties of (and which will at best be very imperfectly realized within) human social institutions. He expressed this fundamental refusal to accord value to the social specification of purely human power (a refusal which formed the core of his later rejection of the political theory of Filmer) very early in his life, in bitter response to the political misfortunes of his father and to the strains and indignities of his personal situation of social dependence:

it will teach me this caution to withdraw my dependences from such windy props, to forbid my hopes and fears a commerce with their frowns, or promises, and to use them as they use us, only as long as serviceable. I cannot overvalue those accidentall differences that chance doth place on men, and are noe reall ones, but as they are usd.[28]

The determination to use the nexus of patronage and cliental dependence in a purely instrumental spirit was not, of course, in any sense a choice to eschew whatever facilities for enhancing his personal social mobility (within the limits set by his own moral susceptibilities) which that nexus could be induced to offer: as his Somerset friend John Strachey put it, 'a man of parts, lett him study but complyance, hee need want noe preferment'.[29] Nor, once such investments had been made, did it preclude the human relations which embodied these from coming to carry a heavy load of moral responsibility.[30] But what was moralized was in each instance a relation of reciprocity between individual agents and never the social matrix itself within which this relation was set. It is clear both theoretically and biographically that in this rejection of the substance of social relations as a foundation for human value, Locke was in part simply affirming the intimations of his familial religious background, however decisively his subsequent thinking was to transform the implications of this heritage in a consequentially more secular direction.[31] (No human being can pluck a moral identity out of thin air.) It is also clear that both affirmation and rejection are actively present in the deep significance which, in his later life, Locke attached to the practice of friendship.[32] Friendship is the only psychically worthwhile form of terrestrial riches because it is the only relationship between human beings in which moral solidarity may be depended upon. Seen in this light, his persistent determination to construe churches as voluntary associations appears not as a further instance of his sociological ineptitude or as a mere ideological convenience in the battle to make the social world safer for his personal religious beliefs, but rather as a forlorn attempt to stretch human moral solidarity to its limit. If the irrelevances of force and power could be extruded from religious institutions and the latter could be confined to their true end, what would a church be but a tissue of somewhat overextended friendship?

From an existential point of view it would be hard to exaggerate the precariousness of this synthesis. But if it was inherently evanescent as a historical possibility, its theoretical consequences are nonetheless clear. For Locke, to put this theocentric framework in jeopardy was to imperil the rationality of human existence in its entirety.

A dependent intelligent being is under the power and direction and dominion of him on whom he depends and must be for the ends appointed him by that superior being. If man were independent he could have no law but his own will, no end but himself. He would be a god to himself and the satisfaction of his own will the sole measure and end of all his actions.[33]

By the same token, to specify value for human beings was in the last instance to construe the implications of the theocentric framework. Even in 1790 Adam Smith appears to have been little, if any, more enthusiastic than Locke at the prospect of dispensing with belief in a benevolent deity:

... the very suspicion of a fatherless world, must be the most melancholy of all reflections; from the thought that all the unknown regions of infinite and incomprehensible space may be filled with nothing but endless misery and wretchedness. All the splendour of the highest prosperity can never enlighten the gloom with which so dreadful an idea must necessarily over-shadow the imagination.[34]

Nor was he any more attracted than Locke was to a discrete 'internal reasons' conception of the character of value for man:

A wise man ... does not look upon himself as a whole, separated and detached from every other part of nature, to be taken care of by itself and for itself. He regards himself in the light in which he imagines the great genius of human nature, and of the world, regards him. He enters, if I may say so, into the sentiments of that divine Being, and considers himself as an atom, a particle, of an immense and infinite system, which must and ought to be disposed of, according to the conveniency of the whole. Assured of the wisdom which directs all the events of human life, whatever lot befalls him, he accepts it with joy, satisfied that, if he had known all the connections and dependencies of the different parts of the universe, it is the very lot which he himself would have wished for. If it is life, he is contented to live; and if it is death, as nature must have no further occasion for his presence here, he willingly goes where he is appointed.[35]

What was theoretically crucial, however, was that Smith's rejection of the moral and epistemic sufficiency of individual internal reasons did not depend, as Locke's did, on 'entering into the sentiments of the divine Being', but derived more directly from his treatment throughout his analysis, both in the *Theory of Moral Sentiments* and in the *Wealth of Nations*, of sociology and psychology as theoretically coordinate terms. Because his approach never centred upon, and was never theoretically extrapolated from, God's purposes, but instead was concerned throughout with the systematic causal analysis of social relations and social systems, it failed to shift at all drastically (let alone to narrow, as Locke's would have done, to a nihilistic individualism), when Smith in later life experienced greater difficulty in entering into the deity's sentiments. This fundamental choice gave to Locke on the one side and to Hume and Smith on the other two drastically different fields for the deployment of their imaginative energies. At the centre of the one field lay the vindication of the intelligibility and validity of the purposes of a divine creator and the interpretation of the implications which these purposes bore for the life of man. At the centre of the other lay the identification and explanation of the causal properties of human societies and economies and the systematic analysis of the services and hazards to a life which was genuinely good for human beings which these economies and societies presented.

This division of imaginative attention comes out very clearly in the differing attitudes of Locke on the one side and Hume and Smith on the other towards the rational basis of political obligation. For Locke the duties of most human beings towards terrestrial political authority are in the first instance altruistically prudential specifications of their duties, as common creatures of God, towards their fellow men.[36] The celebrated central argument of the *Two Treatises of Government* is not merely an ideological defence of the legitimacy of resistance to political authority, where the latter is abused. It is also a decisive theoretical defence of the categorical limits of the rights of political authorities and a demonstration of the consequent asymmetry between the scope of these rights and the markedly more extensive scope of the politically relevant duties of subjects. It was *not* Locke's theory that all human political duties were necessarily exclusively derived from consent; and it indisputably was his theory that all valid human political duties were rationally to be interpreted as specifications of God's purposes for man. Political duty was a theoretical derivative of natural theology. Both Hume and Smith criticize Locke's *Two Treatises* severely, taking it as symptomatic of the provincial superstitions of vulgar Whiggism[37] and developing at some length an alternative analysis of the nature of allegiance which they presume to be both less superstitious and more cosmopolitan. Neither was at all a careful critic of Locke's text and neither appears to have grasped even the essentials of its argument,[38] though each certainly mounts an intellectually and polemically effective enough critique of vulgar Whig shibboleths. Neither in particular appears to have grasped the theoretical dependence of Locke's entire analysis upon natural theology, though it is plain enough that both of them would, if anything, have regarded such a theoretical dependence as an aggravation rather than a mitigation of the intrinsic intellectual weakness of his position.[39]

Hume's critique is developed particularly in Book III of the *Treatise of Human Nature*, the *Enquiry concerning the Principles of Morals*, and in the famous essay 'Of the Original Contract'. He takes the Lockean account as claiming that men are only politically obliged as a result of promises and that their existence within the borders of a state constitutes such a promise. He has no difficulty in demonstrating that this view bears little resemblance to most men's understanding of political obligation and that it does little justice to the facts of their political situation: 'it being certain that there is a moral obligation to submit to government, because every one thinks so; it must be as certain that this obligation arises not from a promise; since no one, whose judgment has not been led astray by too strict adherence to a system of philosophy, has ever yet dreamt of ascribing it to that origin'.[40] The theoretical basis of his criticism was the analysis of justice as an artificial virtue, an analysis which rendered absurd any attempt by contractarian theorists to 'mount higher'[41] and resolve the obligation of allegiance into the obligation of fidelity. Thinking both causes men's acceptance of moral obligations and furnishes the rational grounds for their accepting these in practice. Obligation, property and right in human society all depend upon the stability of possessions.[42] All of them are natural in the sense that they are made necessary by the intrinsic characteristics of human beings. But all of them are also artificial in the sense that they do not arise directly out of human emotions, do not intuitively accord fully with these, but are effectively inculcated by determined social indoctrination. Property right is presented as the outcome of an essentially arbitrary process of allocation, rationalized only in the most perfunctory manner. What is important about property right is simply that it be clear and well-defined in practice. The social function of government, above all the protection of property, is the institutionalized protection of men's individual and collective long-term self-interest against their individual short-term self-interest, an instrument for securing the command of their calm over their violent passions. Government is the greatest of all civilizing agencies.[43] The duty of allegiance is securely grounded in prevailing human sentiment, a sound criterion of its moral validity[44] and a causally effective guarantee of its furnishing any government of any practical merit with the political support which it both deserves and requires. In the *Treatise* itself Hume expounds his own view, revelling in its originality and its intellectual radicalism.[45] It was not until he turned to a more explicitly political attack on 'vulgar Whiggism' that he took the trouble to develop his position as an explicit criticism of Locke.[46] But in the essay 'Of the Original Contract' of 1748 he made clear his assimilation of the positions criticized in the *Treatise* to those which he now assailed in Locke's work.[47]

Smith's moral theory, like that of Hume, was an essentially naturalistic theory of the character and causation of human moral sentiments. Both the duty to obey a government and the right to resist one must rest upon the realized psychic conditions of human beings. Once any form of effective rule has been established in a particular society, most men in most countries at most times simply do in fact recognize a duty of allegiance towards it.[48] In so doing they accept, compulsively but also rationally,[49] the 'principle of authority'.[50] The rational component of their acceptance is in part[51] simply a matter of immediate egocentric prudence, but it is also in part a matter of the reflective and socially responsible judgement of the long-term advantages and disadvantages of resistance to governmental authority.[52] The principle of authority is solidly rooted in the pre-reflective zones of human psychology 'in the naturall modesty of mankind'.[53] But it is balanced by the more detached and rationally critical criterion of utility,[54] a criterion which in some instances firmly vindicates the legitimacy of popular resistance: 'No one but must enter into the designs of the people, go along with them in all their plots and conspiracys to turn them out, is rejoiced at their success, and grieves when they fail.'[55] The balance between these two criteria varies in accordance with the social and political realities of a society, since different structures of power within a society engender different distributions of popular sentiment, and different distributions of popular sentiment within a society in their turn[56] causally modify its structure of power. Different forms of regime have different causal properties, different social psychologies and correspondingly different ranges of objective moral entitlement to the allegiance of their subjects. How far this is a coherent and theoretically determinate position is a very open question in modern political philosophy.[57] But it is easy to see how firmly it distances Smith's political vision from that of Locke. For Smith, 'Every morall duty must arise from some thing which mankind are conscious of.'[58] A contractarian theory of political obligation, however firmly endorsed by 'the generallity of writers on this subject (as Locke and Sidney, etc)',[59] cannot meet this test. Belief in such a theory 'is confined to Britain, and had never been heard of in any other country'.[60] Even 'here it can have influence with a very small part of the people, such as have read Locke, etc. The far greater part have no notion of it, and nevertheless they have the same notion of the obedience due to the sovereign power.'[61] Even within its own terms the version of the contractarian theory associated with Locke and the Whigs fails, as Hume had pointed out, to resolve a number of the difficulties with which it was devised to deal.[62] For Smith, political obligation rests psychically on non-rational deference, the principle of authority, and it rests rationally on utility. But its main weight in practice plainly falls causally on the principle of authority. For him political duties, as men actually experience them, are preponderantly vertical obligations to sovereigns, not, as they are with Locke, horizontal obligations to our fellows.[63]

It is a queasy type of intellectual project to seek the roots of these differences of attitude in the social and personal experience of the three men, even if it can hardly be the case that these roots simply lie elsewhere. One very simple contrast can, however, be drawn with some confidence. Locke's social thinking, we know, began from his experience of the moral arbitrariness of vertical obligations, obligations which pervaded the social texture of the world in which he lived and on which his own individual prospects of social mobility abjectly depended.[64] Both Hume and Smith were fortunate enough to avoid any such sense of dependence, Hume in particular expressing for it a disdain which Locke himself amply shared but which, unlike Hume, he was never able to afford to express in practice. In comparison with Locke, it is plain, both Hume and Smith were very much at ease in their society and well able to take both it and their own membership within it very much for granted. Approaching it with an imaginative calm which Locke could never emulate, they found themselves free to press the causal understanding of its properties very far indeed. Each of them also, at least at some points in their lives, perhaps displayed, as an accompaniment to the imaginative calm which made their intellectual achievements possible, a certain moral complacency over the social and economic realities of the society in which they were so much at home.[65] But in Smith at least this complacency had been left far behind by the end of his intellectual life. It is historically correct to think of him as the inventor of ideological materials of extraordinary power, materials whose ideological force was a direct function of their intellectual depth. But it is historically preposterous to think of him as the ideological spokesman of his society. Indeed, the same deepening of causal understanding which enabled him to invent such ideologically powerful conceptions served to dissolve much, if not most, of the moral plausibility of his own society in his eyes. As his studies deepened,[66] and as he moved in consequence from the slightly fussy moral didacticism perhaps incumbent on a young Scots Professor of Moral Philosophy into the imaginatively chillier ambiance of a cosmopolitan theorist of the historical process, his serenity in the face of prevailing social deference shifted to a mood of pronounced moral distaste.[67]

In conclusion we may note a discomfiting historical possibility. Locke presumed that there were strict theoretical implications between the abandonment of theocentrism, the acceptance of a purely internal conception of human rational agency and the resting of all human rights and duties upon the contingencies of human opinion. He presumed this, in essence, because he put no faith in the autonomous causal process of social reproduction. Both Hume and Smith in contrast, despite their impressive insight into the dynamics of the capitalist economy, distinctly overestimated the long-term prospects of combining the dynamics of capitalist development with the deferential socializing capacities of pre-capitalist society. In their vision, we as human beings are society's creatures at any time only in so far as society has contrived to make us such. The limits of our social duties are the limits of its socializing capabilities. Hume's views of the socializing powers which can be imputed to all societies were absurdly eupeptic – at least outside the domain of religious belief. Smith certainly thought much more deeply about, and saw much more clearly, than either Locke or Hume the ways in which the individual distribution of beliefs in eighteenth-century Britain was constrained by the mechanisms of social reproduction. But even he misjudged the implications of this observation, identifying an evanescent contingency of social history with a quasi-biological property of the human species, 'the naturall modesty of mankind'.[68] Today even admirers of Hume and Smith can no longer take the causal processes of social reproduction trustingly for granted.[69] The development of a purely internal conception of rational agency has left human individuals impressively disenchanted and undeceived. But it has also left them increasingly on their own and devoid of rational direction in social or political action, prisoners in games of self-destruction to which, on these terms, there may well be no rational solutions.[70] It is easier, perhaps, now to see the connections between these menaces. If there is indeed nothing rationally to human existence, individually and socially, but opinion,[71] it will certainly be bad news if opinion ever falters. Locke's serried forty-year defence of theocentrism is a very distant battle. But its purpose, to preserve the rationality for humans of an irrational and heartless world, is disturbingly close. The real anguish which lay behind it is an anguish which we still have coming to us and which will be truly ours when we at last learn to feel what now we know. In their imaginations Hume and Smith certainly inhabited a world which was far closer to ours than Locke's world was. It is clear that, on the whole, they were well content to do so. But it is not clear that they understood its deeper structures very well.[72] Locke, on the other hand, though he devoted his intellectual life to its rejection, seems to have understood these deeper structures all too well. It has taken us nearly three centuries to begin to catch up with him.

Chapter 4

Understanding revolutions*

ANY REGULAR READER of a good newspaper knows that it is possible to explain in some fashion why quite a lot of what happens in societies happens broadly as it does. The practice of social explanation is too important and too prominent in real life for scepticism as to its possibility to be taken very seriously. (Like Monsieur Jourdain's speaking prose, we do it all our lives.) But when it comes to specifying what exactly (apart from human credulity) makes it possible, confidence is much harder to muster. On closer reflection, it can become extraordinarily hard to see how it can be possible at all. Soberly considered, the theory of social explanation is in poor shape. It is so not, as a generalized Yeatsian scepticism might presume, because the best theorists lack all conviction while the worst are full of passionate intensity, but rather because even those with the most coherent convictions have perforce and obviously grounded these on a personal choice.[1] Given the diversity of personal preferences and the variety of ways, legitimate and illegitimate,[2] in which these enter into the formation of explanatory theories, the scope of disagreement in social explanation is unsurprising. Within theoretical disputation the degree of mutual goodwill is often limited; and, even if it were unlimited, mutual understanding between the bearers of sharply distinct viewpoints would be extremely hard to achieve.

The attempts of historians, sociologists, and political scientists over the last two decades to explain the incidence and character of revolutions naturally exhibit these difficulties in a fairly blatant manner.[3] Anyone with an irritably nominalist disposition who took the trouble to plough through the now rather extensive literature which has resulted from these efforts would probably conclude that there was something irretrievably silly to the explanatory project as such. But a

---

* This chapter was written as a review of Theda Skocpol, *States and Social Revolutions* (Cambridge University Press, Cambridge 1979) and Barrington Moore, *Injustice: The Social Bases of Obedience and Revolt* (M. E. Sharpe, White Plains, N.Y. 1978).

more balanced judgement of the parlousness but indispensability of social understanding could by now draw mild encouragement from precisely the same experience. Like professional revolutionaries, social scientists seldom clearly understand quite what they are doing. But, again like professional revolutionaries, they do sometimes attain a relatively clear grasp of the implications of what they have already done; and, sometimes at least, this constitutes a marked improvement on the achievements of their immediate predecessors. With Barrington Moore's latest book and Theda Skocpol's first book it seems safe to conclude that this is now true in the case of the study of revolutions. The two works are sharply different and in some ways theoretically very much at odds with one another. But the illumination which they bring is helpfully complementary.

The initial difficulty in the explanation of revolutions is the heterogeneity of historical episodes that have been entitled 'revolutions' and the diversity of criteria on the basis of which the title has been applied. To attempt to develop an explanation of a class of phenomena without a clear conception of the necessary and sufficient conditions for including an instance within the class is optimistic. In the case of revolutions, where the nebulousness of prevailing criteria for applying the category is readily apparent, it is simply feckless. To make any explanatory progress at all with such a category there are only two plausible procedures. One is to start off arbitrarily from a set of historical instances and attempt to grasp, in the interstitial manner in which historians do, the causal dynamics of each instance, in the hope that this will facilitate the construction of more reflectively grounded typologies and the development of at least some elements of explanatory hypothesis.[4] The other is to select by determined and explicit theoretical stipulation a set of instances of a fairly complex and carefully specified explicandum[5] and seek as best one can to explain the explicandum as such. Despite the abundance of recent writings on the explanation of revolution, Skocpol's book is essentially the first to make this second attempt. That in itself is an index of her sociological acumen.

States and Social Revolutions studies three major revolutions: the French, the Russian, and the Chinese. Skocpol selects these in the first instance because, in common judgement, they do incontestably meet the criteria for what makes a historical episode a revolution. In each instance long-established state forms and social configurations are changed drastically and in some respects rapidly as a result of violent popular action and in due course are replaced by new state forms and social configurations of proven durability. The collapse of an existing state, the role of popular violence in promoting this collapse, massive consequent change in class relations, and the subsequent establishment of a renovated state form are all made definitive of what a true social revolution is. Having specified her explicandum in this way Skocpol attempts to explain in general how it is that such holistic social transformations can occur at all and to explain in particular how it was that her three selected instances took broadly the form which they did. To sharpen her analysis here she considers also in relation to these instances a number of other historical episodes which she sees as in many ways analogous to one or other of the central cases and in which revolution might well have been (and sometimes was) anticipated, but in which in practice it did not occur. Taken as a whole these particular historical explanations are intellectually the best controlled and the most impressive part of the book. But the detail of them need not concern us here.

What is important in this context is the general explanation which she offers of why social revolutions are possible at all. This explanation focuses on the role of state power in the reproduction of society, an exceedingly sensitive topic for political sociologists of either liberal or Marxist persuasion. Having specified her three *anciens régimes* as particular configurations of class relations reproduced through a distinctive state form, the agrarian bureaucracy, she explains the revolution to which these regimes succumb predominantly in terms of the vulnerability of the old state form and the potential viability of the new. What makes states vulnerable is not merely endogenous socioeconomic process, the imaginatively and practically taxing task of managing internal class relations and making whatever adjustments to these prove to be necessary. It is also external social, economic, political, and military process, the powerful external forces which have always in some measure acted upon any state power and which over the last two centuries have come to act upon both state and society virtually everywhere with increasing intricacy, insidiousness, and violence. At the heart of revolution, as Skocpol sees this, are the intricate dialectics of the frailty and robustness of the power of the modern state and the extreme consequent obscurity in contemporary political judgement as to just exactly what it is that does shape our social lives. There could hardly be a grander theme for a political sociologist.

Skocpol treats revolutions, accordingly, in the first instance as crises of states, resolved by mutations in the character of these states, partly engendered by mass political action and eventuating in substantial changes in class relations. Her grounds for doing so are strongly related to the historical grounds for conceiving revolution as a distinct form of political episode: the intitial metaphorical perception in the face of the French revolution of revolutionary process as a natural process impervious to human will, though constituted by a myriad of human performances, a conception memorably expounded by Joseph de Maistre and largely accepted by the liberal historiographers of the revolution in the succeeding century and, in a transposed form, by Karl Marx.[6] Revolution in this sense posits an ancien regime with some historical stability, a condition arguably satisfied in Skocpol's three positive cases (France, Russia, and China) and perhaps in her three negative comparisons of seventeenth-century England, pre-1848 Germany, and Tokugawa Japan, but scarcely, for example, in the case of President Batista's ageing but irretrievably parvenu regime in Cuba. Rather few societies in the world today (the United States and Great Britain perhaps most conspicuously) have the historical stolidity to be still eligible for social revolution on this criterion. Of those that are still eligible by this criterion it is arguable that none could accurately be described as an agrarian bureaucracy, as Skocpol identifies her three central examples. This is a matter of substantive importance and not merely one of theoretical etiquette since it may preclude Skocpol's admittedly loosely constructed theoretical apparatus from being in any sense *tested* either on the future or on historical episodes additional to those which she has already considered. As a piece of comparative historical explanation it has great force; and as a broad explanatory orientation towards the vicissitudes of modern state power it offers real promise. But what it promises should not be mistaken for an incipiently transhistorical explanatory theory. It is worth considering seriously the possibility that this polarity between intelligently summarized historical experience and improved prospective political judgement may well be not a regrettable debacle but simply the appropriate outcome of practising social explanation in relation to revolution.

Skocpol's approach can be best outlined as a set of rejections, with an accompanying explanatory rubric. She rejects structural-functional analysis in the manner of Chalmers Johnson[7] and aggregate psychological theories of revolutionary or rebellious action such as those of Ted Gurr,[8] reiterating the now familiar charges of vacuousness or circularity,[9] and attributing their adoption in the explanation of revolution to the supposed liberal presumption that belief and not force is the main element in social reproduction. More interestingly, she also rejects either economist versions of Marxism or more recent Marxist stresses on what are hoped to be 'the more politically manipulable subjective conditions for realizing a potential revolution when the objective conditions are present' (p. 16). Equally interestingly, though somewhat less lucidly, she also rejects (at least as a sufficient account) the approach of Charles Tilly, which presents revolutions as the outcome of organized political competition between contenders whose opportunities (and in the insurgent case whose very political existence) are dependent on structural social change.[10] What she holds against Tilly is partly the slightly two-dimensional sociological account that he offers of the social genesis of the insurgents and the comparative poverty of his analysis of the predicament of the incumbent state which they face. But, more importantly, it is Tilly's emphasis on what she calls the 'purposive-movement' character of collective revolutionary action that she rejects. What Skocpol herself is attempting is to shrink to the limits the role of agency, human understanding and will, the cognitive and affective states of human beings, within revolutionary process. In their place, she seeks to emphasize the overwhelming causal constraints imposed by objective conditions (pp. 14, 16–17, 170–71, 291, 296). She herself has an extremely strong sociological will, a determination to wrest the largest measure of social explicability out of historical phenomena: 'powerfully shaped by' is a favourite phrase in her writing. There are important advantages to this, not least the consideration that only someone who was determined to do so is in much danger of extracting the largest measure of social explicability from historical phenomena. In this endeavour she attempts to see the revolutionary process as a whole firmly from the outside and the role of human agency within this as much from the outside as possible, adopting, as she puts it, 'a non-voluntarist structural perspective' on both processes and outcomes. On the basis of this approach she constructs what are, loosely, causal models of the decomposition of pre-revolutionary states, referring as little as she can to human intention or human judgement in explicating the workings of these models. The results are extremely interesting. They lead her to stress the profound structural crises of the old-regime states, the structurally determined opportunities for and the restraints on the class action of the main agents of the states' destruction, the peasants, and the opportunities for and restraints on the reconstruction of state powers in the vacuum created by the destruction of the initial state forms.

Objective conditions within three analytically distinct but causally interrelated dimensions suffice to explain the broad outlines of these revolutions as they occurred. (Or possibly they suffice to explain them insofar as they are genuinely explicable. The inexplicable residue might be charitably consigned to the history of human action.) The three dimensions are, very broadly described, class relations arising from the relations of production; the internal extractive and repressive capacities of the state power; and the external economic, military, and perhaps even ideological pressures upon the state power. The last of these is a particularly elusive and important dimension.[11] As critics have hastened to point out, the causal interrelatedness of these three dimensions makes it exceedingly difficult for even the strongest sociological will to keep them analytically distinct. But their separability need not, perhaps, be taken too literally, while the attempt to distinguish firmly among them serves the key purpose of stressing the causal centrality within revolution of both internal state power and its external ecology. Skocpol rejects the conception of revolution as originating from endogenously generated crises of production, a conception now discarded by many Marxist scholars and perhaps never a very sensitive summary of serious Marxist understanding of the question.[12] Particularly since 1917, no serious Marxist thinker would wish to depreciate the crucial causal contributions made by the workings of the world economy or of the international state system to the occurrence or nonoccurrence of revolution.

The most drastic difference between Skocpol and the great majority of explicitly Marxist sociologists or political scientists (though not of Marxist historians) lies in the centrality and frankness of her account of state power. Here she encounters one of the most deeply ambivalent aspects of Marxist theory, the tension, as it might be formulated in relation to the politics of Kautsky or Plekhanov or the Menshevik party in general, between the wish to retain a powerfully explanatory theory of history and the wish to elude political fatalism. The intrinsic significance of state power could be denied from either point of view and must be denied by anyone who acceded to the second (the fatalism) as the price of acceding to the first (the explanation). But the easiest option at present for avoiding the second without admitting to have abandoned the first is to adopt what Skocpol calls a 'class-struggle reductionist' theory of the state (p. 28). In practice such a theory constitutes an extremely abstract and evasive redescription of states in an idiom which cannot register (and which indeed often disdains even to mention) most of their causal properties. It is in emphatic contrast to this that Skocpol insists on her own 'organizational and realist' concept of the state (pp. 31–2, 161–2), on the need to reject 'the enduring sociological proclivity to absorb the state into society' (p. 28), and on the fundamental importance of repressive force within the revolutionary process. (Here, she is very much at one with Barrington Moore.) Theoretically speaking, her conception, which owes much to Otto Hintze and which reflects a key insistence of Tocqueville, Weber, and Moore himself, is not as yet very fully elaborated. Indeed it would be more accurate to say that it is scarcely as yet a *theoretical* conception at all. But what it does enable her to offer is a splendidly direct and quite self-evidently causally relevant analysis of the role of state structures within the revolutions which she considers. Taken with her strong sense of internal class constraints and opportunities and the balance of internal extraction and external menace to which all states are heir, it makes socially perceptible (concretely intelligible) for the first time how great revolutions are a *sort* of event which can in principle happen. In this sense it is a very handsome increment to social understanding in itself; and the political sensibility that it fosters could aid in understanding a great deal more than revolutions (in themselves both an infrequent and, as argued below, a conceptually fugitive type of episode). By ostensive example, if not perhaps decisively by theoretical specification, Skocpol offers an explanatory approach which escapes being reductively historical and which certainly provides more than a list of 'pointers towards various factors that case analysts might want to take into account, with no valid way to favor certain explanations over others' (p. 34).

It is worth attempting to separate two rather different reasons for selecting the explanatory strategy of conceiving revolution in this way as a product of the causal intersection of three structural dimensions. The first of these, much emphasized and well understood by Skocpol herself, relates in several respects to her view of the intrinsically nonpurposive character of revolution. Firstly, the outcomes of revolutions are not those intended by any agent: what revolutionaries suppose themselves to be doing and what they are doing overlap rather little. Secondly, the collapse of anciens régimes is not a product of the actions of revolutionaries. Thirdly, the dynamic impact of foreign military and economic pressure, which is what in her view does explain the collapse of her three anciens régimes,[13] affects in the first instance the options of state rulers rather than those of revolutionaries (p. 24). Objective revolutionary situations, a necessary condition for revolutions, are never the causal product of the acts of revolutionaries. Three points should be made about this set of insistences. Firstly, while to reject the validity of many aspects of the belief systems of revolutionaries may well be correct[14] it in no sense follows that these invalid aspects are causally inconsequential in revolutionary process. Skocpol herself acknowledges that the availability of conceptions of possible political and economic projects from the experience of other societies, an aspect of the 'world-historical context', modifies the possibilities open to a set of revolutionaries (pp. 23, 266, 275, 286, 329–30). But she prefers to emphasize distinct material possibilities for social and

74

economic reconstruction, rather than comprehensive conceptions of the goals of such reconstruction. This preference is of some importance since, in however plastic a form, such conceptions are arguably a necessary condition for most modern revolutionaries electing to define themselves as such.[15] Secondly, even in the cases which Skocpol considers, the fact that the creation of revolutionary opportunities in the first instance depends upon social actors other than revolutionaries scarcely implies that this creation is independent of the acts of *any* social actors (and in particular of those of state rulers). Thirdly, the decisive separability of the objective revolutionary situations, in the French, Russian, and Chinese cases, from the actions of revolutionaries is not necessarily a feature of more recent revolutions (for instance, that of Cuba) and still more certainly is not guaranteed to be a feature of future revolutions. It may simply be the case that revolutionary process has been becoming (perhaps temporarily?) more voluntarist, not in the sense that the desires and intentions of revolutionaries are now having predominantly their intended effect on the historical process, but in the sense that the viability of incumbent states can now at times be threatened by the concerted actions of revolutionaries, that the latter can now play a causal role in *creating* objective revolutionary situations.

Taken together these three points raise sharply the key issue of how to conceive the nature of historical causality and the role of will and understanding within this. On the one hand they blur totally the distinction between objective external conditions and revolutionary practice. On the other they also call sharply into question more a priori grounds for adopting such a decisively anti-intentionalist conception of the revolutionary conjuncture. Social situations that are the intended outcomes of free and conscious actions may not appear either to require or to permit social explanation in the same fashion as wholly unintended social outcomes do so. (Like rational actions, in Martin Hollis's construal,[16] they may be thought in some sense to explain themselves.) It seems likely that Skocpol's choice of explicandum may well be linked in this way not merely to a conception of the nature of revolutions (pp. 4–6, 14–18, 33–4) but to a conception of the nature (or perhaps even of the purpose) of sociology or social explanation, that there can only coherently (or profitably) be a sociology of fate and not a sociology of choice. It is not merely because of its role within the history of Marxism and because of Marxism's urgent, if ambivalent, concern with it that revolutions pose this issue with peculiar poignancy. Skocpol begins from the classic conception of revolution as a process intrinsically out of human control, engendered by profound structural

strains within society and polity, thereby rejecting the modern analogues of Marx's 'alchemists of the revolution', with their 'policy-spy'
conceptions of the nature of revolutions.[17] She pins her explanatory
hopes and ambitions directly to this conception. But she also recognizes very fully that, amongst other aspects, every revolution becomes
at some point a process of violent political competition. It is possible to
model the collapse of anciens régimes very firmly and distantly from
the outside. But there is an element of absurdity in modelling the
process of revolutionary and counterrevolutionary political competition from an excessive distance. To do so is, as Hobsbawm puts it, to
exaggerate *structure* and devalue *situation*: 'Structure and situation
interact, and determine the limits of decision and action; but what
determines the possibilities of action is primarily situation.'[18] Following the archaic metaphors, the collapse of states may appear a simple
physical process with its own integral causality, essentially beyond the
reach of human will or judgement. But to see the construction of new
state powers in the midst of the violent political struggles of revolutions
as a process external to human will or judgement seems merely
perverse. No doubt most components of such a process – its variegated
cast list, its painful encounters with impossibility, even, in detail, the
judgements and hopes of its agents – can be explained severally. But
there is no reason whatever why such discrete explanatory offerings
should be expected to be theoretically additive, let alone why they
should combine to explain the whole of it from the outside in a way
which could rationally be expected to explain any other historical
sequence from the outside. On Hobsbawm's view, it is of the political
essence of revolution to be a very intricate and weakly structured
competitive game. If the structures are intricate and weak enough,
there could not in principle be an explanation of the individual
outcomes of such a game other than a historical one, while the
theoretical analysis of the range of possible outcomes and their probabilities at different points within a particular sequence would not
necessarily be strikingly more illuminating (had we the least idea how
to conduct it) than the regular reading of a good newspaper.

The unsatisfactory prospects for explanation of these aspects of
revolutionary process relate directly to the causal role of human
understanding and choice within them.[19] Skocpol never confronts this
difficulty directly. Her terminology throughout is one of possibilities,
obstacles, and options, as well as imperatives and impossibilities
(p. 171; 'specific concatenations of possibilities and impossibilities';
pp. 206, 235, 280, 286, etc.). Impossibilities are explanatory within
anyone's theory. Imperatives (when their recipients are discerning

enough to recognize them) could perhaps be regarded as in some sense necessitating. But possibilities and options, for example, have a decided flavour of choice to them. Looked at under the general aegis of practical reasons, as human beings have good reason to look at it, it is quite impossible to see how competitive political process could be crimped in its entirety into the frame of necessity. Humans may seldom know very well what they are doing and they certainly make their history under conditions unchosen by themselves. But except as seen through the eyes of God (or a comprehensive determinist theory linking human neuro-physiology to global social and political process),[20] there is no escaping the large measure of discretion which they enjoy in making their history. It is essential in social theory to distinguish why individual or collective acts are possible from why such acts are performed, to distinguish what acts *are* causally possible (environmentally permitted, etc.) from what acts are conceivable (cognitively and affectively accessible),[21] to distinguish what states can do (what their causal powers are) from what they *must* do (what, on rare occasions, is simply their *fate*).

Causal beliefs are one of the most important elements in shaping the rationality of human action. Causal beliefs about political possibility arise from historical experience and change with it. What are presumed to be identified causal properties of institutions, and prospects for political strategies predicated on these beliefs, alter what it is rational for both rulers and revolutionaries to do. Within political competition, the strategies of one set of competitors are necessarily predicated in some measure on their beliefs about the strategies of others. Revolutionaries may often strive to repeat revolutions on some particular model and their opponents to prevent their repetition.[22] But in making these very attempts revolutionaries alter sharply what would otherwise have been the outcomes of the episodes in which they take part. Revolutions accordingly do *not* repeat themselves but rather, as they sequentially occur, metamorphose constantly.[23] As a sociological explicandum, consequently, revolutions necessarily vary through time; and one of the mechanisms through which they vary in this way is the reflexive contri-bution which human beliefs make within them. The limits of social explicability are considerably more plural than the history which actu-ally occurs. And the limits of social explicability at a particular time are determined by the history which has occurred up to that time: the judgements made, the choices taken, the wills exerted, and the possi-bilities actualized up to that time. Social explanation is contextually specific and theory dependent. It cannot represent the application in a particular instance of a causally adequate theory of history in its entirety.

Skocpol herself fully acknowledges this and there is nothing superstitious in her explanatory persistence. But she is perhaps a little
insensitive to the costs of this persistence both in the nature of the
explanatory account of revolutionary process which she offers and in
the bearing of this account on how human beings have good reason to
perceive politics and to take political action. Apart from a single
gallant but weakly supported invocation in her conclusion of the
indispensability of the democratic proletarian socialism for which
Marx hoped (p. 292), *States and Social Revolutions* is written doggedly under the rubric of history as fate. Whether or not it is appropriate to see fate and explanation as coterminous for human situations,
there is certainly plenty of fate within the human experience of history,
and revolutions in many respects have little difficulty in living down to
this billing. But it is a practically consequential matter how far human
beings do see their own history as fate and a theoretically and morally
urgent question how far they are correct in doing so. In a sense
Skocpol abstracts her imagination from this question in order the
better to press the project of sociological explanation. By contrast, the
will to turn his imagination unremittingly towards it is the impetus
behind the new work of her most valued teacher, Barrington Moore[24]
(Moore 1978). Moore's earlier major work, *Social Origins of
Dictatorship and Democracy*,[25] was an extremely determined and a
highly influential exploration of the possibilities for a more structural,
materialist, and explanatory theory of social change.[26] Skocpol's first
major article was a review of *Social Origins* which sketched out with
force and economy the explanatory approach which she has put to
work in *States and Social Revolution*.[27] The extent of her debt to
Moore is as generously acknowledged as it is palpably obvious.
Accordingly the shift in Moore's perspective and the resulting clash
between it and some of Skocpol's methodological procedures is
extremely interesting. There remain important judgements common
to the two books: a common commitment against the view that the
self-understanding of modern revolutionaries furnishes valid explanations of either the incidence or the character of revolutionary
outcomes, a shared insistence on the causal role of repressive violence
in sustaining or failing to sustain state power and on the role of
structural constraints in facilitating or obstructing popular action, a
parallel stress on the class action of the peasantry as the direct
destroyer of Skocpol's *anciens régimes*. Along with the Moore of *Social
Origins*, Skocpol sees relations between landlords and peasants, the
dynamics of rural class relations, as key factors in the making of the
modern world, a judgement shared by much recent scholarship.[28] Like

Moore too, and no doubt in due course in the face of similar protests,[29] she minimizes the causal contribution of the conscious class action of the proletariat to the October revolution and its subsequent defence and consolidation. In sociological intuition the books remain in many ways extremely close; but in explanatory prescription at some points they could hardly diverge more sharply.

At least in subject matter *States and Social Revolutions* is an easy book to characterize. What it is primarily about is simply the causation of three great revolutions. The focus of *Injustice* is decidedly more elusive. What it is attempting to understand can quite reasonably be conceived as a single theme and it is as such that it is considered below. But Moore's strategy in approaching this theme is in some ways surprising; and it may therefore be helpful to give a bald outline of the markedly diverse topics treated before considering his handling of the main theme itself. What Moore wishes to grasp is why it is that men and women submit without explicit moral protest to persistent social maltreatment. He certainly accepts, in accordance with his earlier work,[30] that the main answer to this question is simply that they are compelled to do so by force majeure. But in the present work he is more concerned with the residue of the answer, with the formation and reproduction of cultures of compliance, with the internalization of force majeure and most pressingly of all with the moralization of submission. Even within a single community this is an extremely difficult topic to analyse at all clearly.[31] In the first part of the book Moore considers first of all three dramatic instances of compliance: the psychic accommodation of Untouchables to their place within the Hindu caste system, the adaptation of their inmates to the nightmare of the Nazi concentration camps, and the docile infliction of supposed pain by participants in the notorious experimental studies of Stanley Milgram. The implications of these three examples are analyzed in terms of a more general consideration of the relations between identity and social experience. Most of the remainder of the books is taken up with an examination of the same theme within the history of the German urban poor and industrial workers over the three quarters of a century between 1848 and 1920, culminating in an interpretation of the contrasts between the revolutionary experiences of Germany in 1918–19 and Russia in 1917. The concluding chapters of the book consider the relation between this historical theme and the recruitment and motivation of the Nazi party (moral resentment gone sour) and then recapitulate Moore's views on his central preoccupation. Rich, fascinating and deeply felt though it is, the book as a whole cannot be said to be particularly orderly in presentation.

79

Injustice is not any less concerned to *explain* than is *States and Social Revolutions*. But it is distinctly more metaphysical in its overt preoccupations, and what it wishes to explain is very different. Not merely tacitly but relatively explicitly, it is a book about the human condition, about the relations between the reproduction of class power in society and the fundamental properties of human nature. Like the Enlightenment liberalism of Hume or Adam Smith, though in a spiritually more troubled vein than either, it seeks to fuse together social and historical explanation with a coherent conception of what sort of creatures human beings naturally are. Its subtitle, *The Social Bases of Obedience and Revolt* is a simple extension of the perspective of *Social Origins* and aligns readily enough with Skocpol's work. But in this case the main title, *Injustice*, is considerably more revealing. What Moore wants to understand is the scope of human submission to social oppression – in apposition to the work of Ted Gurr, he is concerned with *Why Men Don't Rebel* – and the animus behind his wish to understand it is a horror at the prevalence of such oppression. Despite its sober analytic procedures and markedly unhysterical tone, in human motive *Injustice* is a modern sociological addendum to the *Book of Job*. In purely sociological terms Moore's answers to the question of why men don't rebel are as sensible as they are unsurprising: that for the most part, collectively if not individually, they find social life most of the time little worse than they expect, that they can seldom see very clearly precisely how to revolt at all effectively, and that they (on the whole all too correctly) lack optimism as to the prospective outcome of doing so. But these broad sociological intuitions leave a residue of conduct which is not simply attributable to direct experience and rational pessimism and which, in Moore's sensibility as he confronts it, remains regrettable and yet does not, at least initially, appear to be inevitable. It is on this residue that Moore's reflections on human nature are brought to bear. To consider human nature as such has been a deeply unfashionable perspective in recent decades amongst serious and historically sensitive analysts of society. When linked as it is by Moore to a stubbornly pursued but elusively presented version of ethical naturalism it could hardly in principle be offered with much authority from a standing start. Only Moore's quite exceptional honesty and unconcern with academic impression-management favour its securing a fair hearing. But, hazardous though it may be as an intellectual strategy, it does furnish Moore with an impressively direct basis from which to consider his central question and to mount a searching attack on its own home territory, on the credentials of the main modern self-understanding of revolutionary practice. If Moore is right, Skocpol's hopes for democratic proletarian socialist revolution in the advanced societies can scarcely be more than a pious wish.

The main body of *Injustice* considers at some length why it is that the industrialization of Germany did not produce a substantial revolutionary proletariat or result in a successful 'proletarian' revolution. It impresses an amateur reader as an industrious and in some respects original piece of historical inquiry. But its quality as historical research can only seriously be judged by historians of modern Germany. What are important here, rather, are the main questions which Moore addresses in this section and the main conclusions which he draws from it, these conclusions in their turn being consonant with the expectations which he had previously derived from the blunter assessment of human nature as such. When he comes to interpret the failure of the German revolution of 1918, Moore broadens his treatment to take in, at least at the level of political assessment, the coercive apparatus of the state and the range of social forces in active or potential relations with this. But for most of his account he concentrates fairly narrowly on the changing composition of the nonagricultural manual labour force, its organization and social milieu and above all on its consciousness. The movement which the book as a whole seeks to grasp (p. xiii, etc.) is the movement from endorsing or resignedly enduring oppressive social relations to actively repudiating their authority and more or less self-confidently challenging them in practice. In its fullest form this movement can legitimately be seen as the formation of revolutionary consciousness. What Moore wishes to ascertain is how far such consciousness was engendered by the life-situations of German artisans or workers at different points in their history, how far revolutionary consciousness was a natural (or even an accessible) cultural outcome of the social and economic experience of the German proletariat in the course of its historical formation. Accordingly his emphasis throughout is on the relations between the organization of work and the culture of workers, a line of inquiry which is irreproachably 'materialist' but in which what is being inquired into, the formation and persistence of culture, is prospectively discomfiting both for Marxists (for whom proletarian consciousness ought properly at least to aspire to the revolutionary) or for academic sociologists (for whom social theory should at least aspire to be strongly explanatory). Throughout Moore seeks, as best he can, to capture the experience, beliefs, sentiments, and judgements, of his historical subjects (pp. xv, 140, 174, 193, 322, 328, 332, and 457), presuming correctly that it is inordinately difficult to grasp human consciousness with sufficient delicacy to understand its internal mechanisms and fully recognizing, on the basis of his inquiries, that mustering the autonomy and imagination to reject the authority of a social universe in its entirety, on behalf of a novel and presumptively superior social order, is not a compulsive social product but rather an immense imaginative and moral feat for most human beings. (Here the confrontation with the mythic role of proletarian consciousness in Marxist politics is direct and unblinking.) Simply as a critique of political myth its honesty and simplicity make it very powerful indeed. There is nothing forensic or meretricious about it – only a worried, decent, and slightly ungainly pressing of the question as to why it is that the Marxist prophecy has failed.

But it is intended, of course, as something more than simply a critique of political myth. In the first instance it attempts to capture the key dynamics of adaptation and rejection in human culture in the face of an oppressive social reality. The dominant message, plainly, is a message of despondency: that there are almost no persisting conditions of social experience (no conditions to which in practice they *have* to adapt) to which human beings cannot and will not learn to adjust their expectations. The shadow of the concentration camps, in this analysis, lies faintly but grimly across the great bulk of human historical social experience, the experience of a creature adapting to impotence and oppression by turning at least part of its anger against itself and against its fellow victims. Expectations and their violation, accordingly, are central to the dynamics of adaptation and rejection. Even the concentration camp has its own horrid moral economy. But it is, of course, the rejection as well as the adaptation with which Moore is centrally concerned. Just as the cultural acceptance of social oppression is socially explicable, so too is its cultural rejection, the attribution of responsibility for it to malign human agents, the will to resist these agents and even the conception of (and the struggle to actualize) a comprehensively novel structure of social relations. (This last Moore on the whole presumes to be in no sense the *product* of proletarian social experience.[32]) The autonomy, the nerve, and the imaginative freedom to reject the legitimacy of existing social arrangements Moore attributes to the extent of practical cooperation and mutual trust within a social group, to the degree to which this group retains some real control over its own work, and to the degree to which, and the abruptness with which, its acquired expectations are violated. Customless and disaggregated collectivities have virtually no power to act (p. 266). Because what it has to adapt to is persisting social experience, culture characteristically looks backward rather than forward. In the

82

main what culture *is* is a display of 'the perilous capacity for getting used to things' (pp. 69 and 476). To Moore the consciousness behind proletarian insurrection where this does appear is in a sense genuinely heroic (p. 89), as the more decisively revolutionary consciousness of dissident intellectuals frequently is not (pp. 482, 501). But its admittedly infrequent appearance is no less socially explicable than its preponderant absence.

Within these broad sociological presumptions the history of German manual workers is interpreted, very much as a history (pp. xvi, 119, etc.). At the core of it, as in a sense the individual explicandum of his book, is the structually intelligible history of a cultural world. The desideratum of the inquiry is a direct insight into the life situations of the inhabitants of this cultural world and a direct insight is defined in terms of how *they* thought about and felt about their situations (pp. 119, 140, 174, 193, 269, 322, 411, 457, etc.). Moore seeks such insight for two main reasons. In the first place he clearly holds, however cautious his statement of it may be, a bluntly 'realist' ontological view of human history as the product of human actions.[33] And in the second place he conceives human action as being determined in the first instance (within the objective constraints of external historical possibility) by the dynamics of human consciousness, culture seen from inside the individual or set of individuals. Bluntly rejecting economic determinism (p. 469), Moore thus judges culture, a precipitate of past social experiences, to be irreducibly causally important in determining present action. It is here that his clash with Skocpol's methodological intransigence is sharpest and here that he most obviously aligns himself with another political scientist, James C. Scott, who also acknowledges a debt to the Marxist historian E. P. Thompson. It is because socially incurred beliefs, values, and attitudes causally modify the way in which men act in particular situations that to treat culture as a wholly dependent variable in explaining compliance or resistance is necessarily in error (Scott, p. 160).[34] At least as importantly for Moore's purposes, it is an error which has particularly damaging implications in the analysis of revolution. He sees revolutions, just as much as Skocpol does, as conjunctural outcomes of state crises, crucially influenced by the failure of military control (pp. 369, 375); and he sees the role of urban revolutionary uprisings within them as brief and fragile (p. 482). But he also sees political will and energy as real causal factors and potentially crucial causal factors in determining their outcomes (p. 393)[35]. Because the revolution which he is considering is a revolution which failed and because he both regrets some aspects of this failure and cannot bring himself to regard all of these as inevitable, it is critically important for him why the German proletariat acted exactly as it did when it did. What Moore wishes for is an explanation which does not superstitiously impose inevitability upon the past, not out of any frivolous aversion from causal understanding where this is genuinely to be had, but because of a principled rejection of the conflation of achieved causal understanding with an axiomatic retrospective fatalism.

In practice, because of his view of the cultural capabilities of proletarians, revolutionary intellectuals and party bureaucrats and of the nature of revolutionary situations (pp. 472–82), Moore's analysis of responsibility for the failure of 'the suppressed alternative possibility' in the German revolution is shared out between the relatively rational conduct of the forces of reaction and the defective political judgement of all segments of the socialist leadership. His vision is one which readily ascribes discretion to professional politicians but which shrinks for example from Engels's cheery charge that 'Once again the proletariat has discredited itself terribly ...'[36] The political appraisal of revolutionary outcomes or their suppression as being, not infrequently, 'a damned close-run thing', a natural concomitant of recognizing them to be passages of violent political competition[37] makes it far less politically attractive to consider revolutions distantly and en bloc from the outside. Strong explanatory rubrics and a politically adequate understanding of historical causality may well be incompatible in the a posteriori analysis of revolutions; and the adoption of strong explanatory rubrics may even be politically misleading in the a priori analysis of revolutionary possibility. As noted earlier, judgement and choice are terms which Skocpol may expunge determinedly from her theoretical approach; but (like nature) they do come insistently back in when she gets to the analysis of the historical cases. Part of the explanation of actual revolutions simply *is* that particular human beings judged and acted in particular ways.

Both Moore and Skocpol engage throughout their works with the central issue in the understanding of social causality, how to conceive the relations between possibility and necessity in historical determination. Because Skocpol has a less insistently 'realist' sense of what she is attempting to explain and because, perhaps in consequence, her explanatory hopes are higher, she in fact addresses the question less directly than does Moore. She would, of course, have no difficulty with the idea of alternative possibilities suppressed by the deliberate and successful application of force. But it is fair to say that there is nothing in her approach to assist anyone in considering the question whether men in revolutionary situations can or cannot sensibly be said to have made or failed to make the best use thus far of their historical opportunities. Moore worries away at this last question with tenacity; and he makes a good defence in passing of the impossibility in any social analysis (including history) of avoiding at least tacitly counter-factual theorizing (p. 377). But by the end of his book it is still wholly unclear how it is appropriate to see the relations between causal theorizing about the historical process, the epistemic and ontological status of counterfactuals and the viewpoint of human practical reason. These are, of course, as Jon Elster's work has recently brought out, extremely deep and puzzling questions.[38] It is scarcely surprising that the pragmatic sociological intuitions of even the most skilled social scientists should be hard to relate clearly to this level of cognitive ambition. But what the juxtaposition of Moore's and Skocpol's power-ful and imaginative works does do is to make it apparent that, at least in the face of explicanda which are as intricate in their constituents and as causally untransparent as revolutions, even the most skilful pragma-tic sociological understanding will necessarily falter in the end unless guided by a wholly coherent and explicit intellectual intention.

What this implies in practice for the theoretical explanation of revolution is still rather unclear. But it is possible to offer at least three related suggestions.

First, 'revolution' as a name for a type of historical episode is a term irretrievably elastic in application and its well-judged and appropriate application will in practice vary through time in the face of historical experience. If this is a well-founded judgement, it will make rational agreement on how to specify revolution as an explicandum extremely hard both to achieve and to maintain.

Second, since revolutions are, as Skocpol and Moore both make clear, composites of very different sorts of processes, each of which furnishes a subordinate explicandum of its own, explanations of these component processes that are at all powerful are unlikely all to be available in the same theoretical idiom and thus unlikely to be at all neatly theoretically additive. Again, if this judgement is correct, while both of the two approaches initially suggested (the naively inductive and the theoretically stipulative) were sensible enough as initial approaches to the study of revolution, it is now rather easy to see that neither of them stood a chance of proving overwhelmingly successful.

Thirdly, and still more contentiously, the attempt to improve the sensitivity of our political understanding of revolutions[39] requires the vigorous deployment of both Moore's and Skocpol's styles of approach: the distant and strongly external assessment of the structu-ral genesis of revolutionary possibilities and the intimate and anthropologically delicate assessment of collective human responses in particular cultures at particular times and of the judgement of political leaders in situations of extreme crisis. The main tradition of professional revolutionary practice in the twentieth century, the tradition of Lenin, has tried extremely hard to integrate these perspectives; and, issues of good intention and talent aside, the extreme difficulty which it has experienced in doing so should by now have cast some theoretical light on why it is so difficult to improve the sensitivity of our political understanding of such episodes.

Because of the sheer heterogeneity of revolutionary episodes and the variety of ways in which they impinge practically upon human values the view that a single approach to them might legitimately claim to monopolize their understanding is necessarily mistaken. It would be foolish to presume that there are not other – and perhaps very different – styles of approach to them which could contribute as handsomely to our capacity to grasp their character and to judge their prospective course. But what one can say with some confidence at present is that anyone seriously interested either in social theory or in understanding revolutions now needs to read both *Injustice* and *States and Social Revolutions* and to ponder their implications very carefully indeed.

Chapter 5

Totalitarian democracy and the legacy of modern revolutions: explanation or indictment?

ON Tuesday December 15th 1981, in a televised press conference following the declaration of military rule in Poland, the leader of the Italian communist party, Enrico Berlinguer, acknowledged bluntly (and in some respects for the first time) the heavy burden which the political character of the Soviet Union and its satellite powers had long placed on the prospects for socialism in the West.[1] In the subsequent weeks this acknowledgement was extended and amplified (if in some measure hedged) and it has been essentially sustained ever since. In itself this belated recognition of the catastrophic political character of existing communist regimes is not especially impressive. But the occasion which elicited it and the stress laid by Berlinguer himself on the profoundly un-democratic character of the Soviet state do mark an ideological turning point of a kind. They also perhaps highlight the marked ideological precariousness and instability of the very idea of totalitarian democracy and the continued practical importance of explaining adequately and validly why the Soviet experience has proved politically so repellent.

Both of these preoccupations were plainly of central importance to the late Jacob Talmon. His famous study of the ideological origins and internal dynamics of the tradition of totalitarian democracy – up to the time at which state power was first taken and retained under its aegis – fills three large volumes and its publication stretches across almost three decades. In its first and briefest volume, *The Origins of Totalitarian Democracy*, very much a work of the early 1950s, he offered an influential and pointed diagnosis of the political discontents of the advanced capitalist world in the aftermath of the Second World War. It is not necessary in this setting to emphasize the striking qualities of the trilogy as a whole, the extraordinary range of learning which it exhibits or the human vitality and sense of drama which shines through every page and which in more personal relations enabled Talmon to capture and retain the deep affection of scholars whose political

87

sentiments and judgements differed very sharply from his own. But timely and impressive though it certainly was, there have always been major reservations about the validity of its central contentions.

I take these to be essentially two: firstly, that totalitarian messianic democracy (for current purposes, the political character of a communist regime) is to be disjoined from liberal empirical democracy not by its institutional forms (and certainly not by its structure of ownership and economic control), but, rather, by its distinctive attitude towards the *scope* of politics.[2] And secondly, that its attitude towards the scope of politics is, in turn, a product of a single metaphysical and dispositional error, an error which unites a simplistic moral absolutism and rationalism with a gratuitous trust in the self-regulating capacity of the historical process. In this sense, the contrast between modern Marxist politics, for example, and the politics of ancient republicanism in the Machiavellian tradition[3] would not lie in the former's preference for community over individual nor in its somewhat evasive union of moralizing asceticism with promises of future largesse but rather in its striking optimism about the future viability of the well-ordered polity, once this has been well and truly founded. The ancient prudence, as a heroically forceful and ingenious apparatus for postponing an inevitable decay and corruption of the body politic, is now succeeded by a modern prudence – the Marxist-Leninist doctrine of state – for which the possibility of political decomposition from within through the normal workings of natural forces simply cannot arise. (For a communist regime to succumb to internal decay – unlike a classical republic – can in its own eyes only occur through great folly or a great crime – though some qualification on this point is probably, or at least *was* probably, in order in the case of Maoism.)[4] It is worth emphasizing this contrast between ancient and modern prudence because, at least to some degree, it is common to the two traditions of political understanding which Talmon counterposes. For John Adams or James Madison[5] the question of the future viability of the American republic was complex and necessarily open. But the presumption of the intrinsic and indefinite internal viability of the American polity is at least as deeply ingrained in the political presumptions of most Americans as the analogous presumption in relation to the U.S.S.R. appears to be amongst Soviet citizens. Polities today vary very widely in the extent to which their citizens regard them as well-ordered; but it is not clear, even at the level of ritual pronouncements, let alone at that of practical reproduction, that rigidity of constitutional form or socio-economic structure is a prerogative of the totalitarian democrats. Total rigidity of either can hardly be sustained for long amidst the intense and turbulent interplay of economic and ideological forces which marks the late twentieth century; and political pronouncements are necessarily a poor index of the scale of change or persistence in any form of society.

It is probably fair to say that the main criticism which has been offered of Talmon's work (apart from the simple reversal of political preferences between liberal empiricism and Marxism) has centred on the propriety of the method which he followed for understanding the history of ideas. There is certainly some substance to these criticisms. A contrast between the *Origins of Totalitarian Democracy* itself and, for example, John Lough's careful, if somewhat pedestrian, study *The Philosophes and Post-Revolutionary France*[6] or George Taylor's analysis of the ideological content of the *Cahiers de doléances*[7] of early 1789 does bring out a certain methodological airiness and insubstantiality to Talmon's claims for the coherence of the philosophe programme and for its causal impact upon the revolutionary process. But at some level Talmon would have had every reason to regard such criticisms, whatever their individual cogency and textual foundation, as largely beside the point. Since what he wished to understand was the development of an entire mode of political perception and sentiment and since he explicitly wished to understand it because he saw it as the causally indispensable imaginative prehistory of a hugely important modern idiom of political practice, the finer points of scepticism as to the causal role of particular authors or particular texts were of comparatively minor interest to him. Even if the actual political role of the ideas of Rousseau, for example, was largely one of radical misunderstanding amplified by hearsay at third or fourth remove,[8] it might still be appropriate to include their author as prominently as Talmon did in representing the shaping and reshaping of the traditions of belief and sentiment which he wished to depict.

What is less easy to endorse, however, is the intellectual judgement behind the shape of his trilogy as a whole. For the key question raised by his entire enterprise concerns the relation between the imaginative prehistory of communist regimes (seen by Talmon himself as overwhelmingly a European history) and the causal properties of these regimes themselves. What Talmon chose to study was, to quote from the opening page of *The Origins*, 'a systematic preparation for the headlong collision between empirical and liberal democracy on the one hand, and totalitarian Messianic democracy on the other, in which the world crisis of today consists'.[9] Looked at from thirty years later, however vivid one's distaste for the Soviet Union, that formula suggests a narrowly self-serving and theoretically inept conception of the causation of the Cold War, identifying its sources firmly in the distressing confrontation of our own rational and well-founded system of beliefs with the deranged, hysterical and menacing political presumptions of our enemies, the Soviet Union and its allies. Now it would be absurd to presume, even outside the context of a world crisis (whatever that may be) that the doctrines of state of the Soviet Union (or of any other state) have literally *no* causal implications for the manner in which its state power is intentionally exerted or even for the ways in which its social, economic and political structures do in fact over time develop. But it would be even more absurd to presume that the predominant determinant of the intentional exercise of state power or the principal effective controller of the structural development of a polity, economy or society could be a unitary system of beliefs and sentiments shaped elsewhere and at some other time.

The first question posed by Talmon's approach is therefore simple enough. What are the exact implications of Marxism or Leninism's becoming a ruling doctrine of state? Talmon's answer to this question is a bold one: that it spells inevitably a nasty fusion of ritualized hypocrisy and practical oppression[10] – precisely because of the absurd metaphysical hubris on which its claims to authority rest. It is clear by now to anyone open-mindedly interested in the question (and anyone of any political decency must be interested in the question and attempt to retain some open-mindedness in the face of it), that there is something in Talmon's answer. The link, for example, between metaphysical hubris and ritual hypocrisy does appear to be internal and logical and not merely external and contingent. And the link between both of these disfigurements and oppressive political practices has been too constant for it to be sensible to regard it as just a sorry chapter of accidents. But there is something drastically misconceived about the character of Talmon's position, a presumption of a quite unwarrantable degree of determinacy to the question's answer. One can see this most economically perhaps by considering the case of totalitarian democracy's ghostly and for the most part also eminently material enemy, the tradition of liberal empirical democracy. It would not, of course, be accurate to construe the empirical component of this tradition as an explicit feature of the doctrines of state in which it eventuates. (We do not, in anyone's understanding, owe allegiance to Her Majesty the Queen, or even to the British electoral and parliamentary system, because around here we take *facts* so seriously.) And there is some strain (and not merely one generated by constitutional heterogeneity) even in construing either the liberal or the democratic component of this political assemblage as necessarily a part of its doctrines of state. There is some real plausibility in lumping together the range of Marxist regimes, however cantankerous their mutual relations may now have become. But there is less felicity, either constitutionally, ideologically or substantively, to seeing their political adversaries as united by much more than a common object of their loathing. The political challenge of regimes of Marxist inspiration is domestically rather feeble in France or Britain or Israel, let alone in West Germany or Japan or the United States of America. But it is very considerably less feeble in such countries as Brazil or Argentina, South Africa or Indonesia; and its persisting salience in these settings (however thin on the ground it may at times have been rendered in practice) has prised the liberal and democratic velleities crisply away from the demands of the empirical. It has done so, too, not merely through and for the citizens of these countries but at least as dramatically for the purposes of the United States government in relation to them. In the face of the menacing seductions of Marxist absolutism, the liberal and democratic, outside its heartlands, has been abandoned wholesale for reasons which in themselves appeared, at least to its deserters, to be both empirical and virtually impossible to deny or elude. These deformations can and should be blamed in part on the opportunistic ruthlessness of the internal political demeanour of the Soviet Union and other communist states since their respective inceptions. But it is hard to see how the political protagonist of liberal empirical democracy can hope to avoid sharing this blame and indeed doing so in respects which blot its own escutcheon very unbecomingly indeed. And even that measure of blame which appropriately falls on the opportunistic ruthlessness of Soviet action must be balanced imaginatively by the realization of a corresponding responsibility on the part of western powers for the nervous sense of menace in its more domestic purlieus in Eastern Europe which explains so much of the most grossly obnoxious of Soviet conduct. Some aspects, at least, of the collision which Talmon hoped to understand simply cannot be understood by considering its ideological history but must be grasped, if they are to be grasped at all, in terms of the ideologically disobliging pragmatics of a politically riven but strongly interrelated world. I do not wish to suggest that Talmon himself was in any sense foolish enough to deny this explicitly. But it is fair to say that the character of his work as a whole is less than imaginatively sensitive to its significance.

There is every reason to share Talmon's view of the political character of communist regimes as an unremitting historical disaster and a disaster whose practical consequences for the rest of the world are acutely but as yet unfathomably menacing. But there is also good reason to remain more than a little perturbed in many ways by the political character not merely of some of the allies of liberal empirical democracy (Iran under the Pahlavis, Argentina under the Generals, South Africa, Indonesia) but even at times of some of its least contestable exemplars: the United States, Great Britain, Israel. And since there is good reason to remain somewhat perturbed in these ways, it remains of very pressing intellectual and practical importance (as well as being morally salutary) to attempt to understand the causal properties of communist regimes with no less and no more prior commitment of sentiment than that with which we understand (or seek to understand) those of our own governmental traditions and practices. It may seem both an unadventurous and a banal proposal to attempt to attain a common causal perspective on the variety of state forms which deface or adorn the world today. What political scientist could acknowledge any *other* ambition? But in practice the will to any such impartiality of causal imagination is for most of us extraordinarily feeble and fitful; and in consequence it is effortlessly overborne by other desires and fancies which are altogether more importunate. And it seems to me self-evident that an effective commitment to such imaginative detachment in the first instance will be (and has been) subverted beyond hope of recapture if we do presume the contrast between communist regimes and our own to be a contrast between regimes which generate and depend upon political beliefs which are intrinsically deranged and vicious in their epistemic foundations and regimes which, instead, form their political beliefs in circumstances and by methods which are cognitively beyond reproach.

I return therefore to the entirely real and pressing question (perhaps still the central historical question of the hour and the question which, it seems to me, Talmon sought so doggedly to answer for himself and for others): why exactly *is* the political character of communist regimes such an unremitting historical disaster? Part of the answer manifestly does lie in the sort of considerations on which Talmon himself focused. But even this part cannot be very clearly understood in the sort of terms which he offered. And other – and in my view causally weightier – parts of the answer depend on quite different sorts of considerations. In particular they depend upon a careful assessment of the processes of political and social disorganization which have in every historical instance up to the present preceded the effective and durable establishment of a communist regime capable of protecting itself and upon an equally careful assessment of the political and military challenges to any such establishment and the expedients thus far essayed for meeting these challenges victoriously. One huge component of their political character, that is to say, comes simply from the mode of their inauguration through civil war or foreign conquest by force of arms, the brutal and disorientating exigencies of the politics of revolution.[11] A second and perhaps equally massive component comes from their common commitment, however various the forms in which this is realized, to organizing their economies on the basis of common rather than private ownership.

It is difficult in principle to separate out in a convincing fashion the relative weights of these two considerations because we have no reasonably clear examples of either unaccompanied for extended periods of time by the other. A confident sense of their unsunderable causal union or ready political disjunction must therefore rest on political faith rather than on direct experience. Those who see the Marxist tradition as a tradition of democratic socialism will necessarily wish to stress the mishap of attaining power not merely (as always emphasized) in poor and somewhat barbarous countries but through a process of struggle of such condensed and erratic violence that all democratic niceties speedily go to the wall. (This emphasis, of course, is more cogent in some instances than it is in others – in Russia, China and Vietnam, for example than in Czechoslovakia or Cuba.)[12] Those who see the Marxist tradition, as Talmon saw it, as a form of messianic rationalism will see such mishaps themselves as natural outcomes of the political vices of the tradition as a whole. Those (like myself) who see the Marxist tradition (and even in some measure the thought of Lenin himself)[13] as inherently ambivalent and unstable in its commitments, both on the claims of democracy and on the criteria for objective historical opportunity, will see the range of political possibilities which make up the tradition as broader and less determinate. They will also see the process of determination of which possibilities are in fact actualized in the future (and which possibilities have already been actualized in the past) as historical and mediated by the beliefs and judgements of human agents, severally and in groups[14], and *not* as theoretically pre-guaranteed and controlled by either purely material factors or the strict logical or political implications of a system of false belief. To put the matter very crudely indeed, they will see the key determinant of the historical impact of the tradition not in strictly materialist or narrowly idealist terms but rather as a Machiavellian pragmatics in which the causal balance between *virtù* and *fortuna* on any particular occasion can only be ascertained in principle *a posteriori*. No serious analysis of the role of Marxist politics in the twentieth century can be excused from the need to explain convincingly just why it is that, at least in its Leninist transposition, Marxism in this century has proven such a dramatic and dynamic culture for the genesis of political *virtù*.

In this respect the hubristic rationalism of its theoretical convictions (the sheer enormity of its pretensions) is scarcely a sufficient clue to its practical potency. No doubt it is politically invigorating to know oneself to be the solution to the riddle of history,[15] though one may doubt whether the extremity of that cognitive presumption really makes it easier to sustain in conditions of adversity. No doubt, too, Leninism in the course of violent conflict does offer some aid in psychic identification and thus in sustaining a strong ethos of solidarity. But here again the psychic sustenance does not necessarily derive predominantly from the epistemic pretensions. Considering the impact of the Falkland Islands upon the politics of Great Britain or the characteristic response of the state of Israel to imminent military peril, it does not appear to be true that the projective solidarity of human groups in the course of struggle depends upon a prior dogmatism and indeed dogmatism itself is often less of a precondition for such solidarity than a consequence of its display. Where the clue to the potency of Leninism does lie, rather, is in the eminently Machiavellian insight that nothing succeeds like success and that success can in practice excuse all manner of prior intellectual irregularities just as it can elide all manner of earlier crimes. What has made Leninism politically so formidable (with rather little direct assistance from the thought of Marx himself) has been above all its skilfully cultivated sensitivity to the political vulnerability of different types of regime in the present century;[16] first of all to that of the European and Asian dynastic monarchies and empires, then, and in a sense more remarkably, to that of colonial rule and lastly, and thus far somewhat erratically, to the confusing variety of neocolonial and postcolonial units which form the majority of members of the present international state system. This sensitivity, of course, was in no sense an instance of prior causal knowledge. Lenin's own anticipations and at least the expressed anticipations of all his successors have thus far grossly overestimated the political vulnerability of mature capitalist societies; and the post-revolutionary states of the Marxist confession have repeatedly inflicted severe damage upon themselves by premissing their actions on these gross miscalculations. But, decade by decade since 1940, more and more states have joined the Marxist confession and political leaders and organizations have won power over them through interpreting the political opportunities presented by their societies in these terms and by acting boldly upon their interpretations. The sense of incremental assurance which has come from this process, assurance of the essentially military efficacy of a particular mode of understanding society and history, contrasts increasingly sharply with the distinctly less assured sense of practical control over the internal properties of society and economy held by communist rulers over the same period.

It is not as yet clear how best to separate out the components of causal understanding which figure in this process from the rewards of blind courage or effrontery. More than four and a half centuries ago the great Florentine historian Guicciardini explained why with exemplary economy: 'The pious say that faith can do great things, and, as the gospel tells us, even move mountains. The reason is that faith breeds obstinacy. To have faith means simply to believe firmly – to deem almost a certainty – things that are not reasonable; or, if they are reasonable, to believe them more firmly than reason warrants. A man of faith is stubborn in his beliefs; he goes his way, undaunted and resolute, disdaining hardship and danger, ready to suffer any extremity. Now, since the affairs of the world are subject to chance and to a thousand and one different accidents, there are many ways in which the passage of time may bring unexpected help to those who persevere in their obstinacy. And since this obstinacy is the product of faith, it is then said that faith can do great things.'[17]

Now this is an analysis of which Talmon might well have approved. The political rewards of obstinacy can rest foursquare upon faith. There is no need to distinguish the rewards of fanaticism from those of opportunism since a steady and energetic opportunism (which is what has enabled political revolutionaries in this century to alter so drastically and irreversibly the history of the entire globe) is itself merely the political expression of a prior fanaticism. I have to confess that I used to regard this as a deft and sophisticated judgement myself. But further reflection (aided by subsequent developments in the causal understanding of revolutions by political sociologists like Theda Skocpol)[18] suggests that it requires some amendment. At the most general level, for example, it is clearly an objective causal property of some modern states and some modern counter-state political organizations that concerted political action by the latter can in some circumstances overthrow the former and replace them. As an objective causal property it obviously grossly underdetermines rational political conduct for revolutionaries or incumbent regimes in any actual instance and, of course, it also differs rather sharply from the style of allegation about the causal impact of political action which Marx himself favoured and on which many Marxists on many occasions, now as in the past, have trustingly relied. But however discordant with moral pretension and however hazily related in detail to practical rationality, it is hard to deny that this vulnerability to direct assault does constitute a real causal relation between incumbent regime and contenders to replace it. The most striking example of such causal understanding – and an example in which Lenin was plainly dramatically in advance of his time – was the Comintern apprehension of the extreme structural fragility of colonial rule as a system extended across the whole globe.[19] Putting the point in slightly different terms and inspecting the trajectory of state forms since 1914, we might say that however crassly dependent upon faith the Bolsheviks may have been in that year, their obstinacy by now, as contenders for state power, can rest more comfortably upon an accumulation of rational causal belief. However self-serving and evasive their grounds for regarding themselves as fit to exercise state power, they have certainly earned by now an epistemically plausible title for supposing that, in historically propitious circumstances, they may well possess the capacity to take such power and very possibly to retain it also for the readily imaginable future.

Leninism, then, has prospered (where it has done so) because in some respects and by some criteria it works. But it has, of course, hardly had the sorts of consequences which Marx himself initially advertised as the social, economic and political fruits of anti-capitalist revolution. Some of these anticipated fruits – the absence of any profound structural conflicts of human interests in the societies which emerge from anti-capitalist revolution – may fairly be regarded as messianic expectations. Others, however, like the presumption of the possibility of benign revolutionary transformations of advanced capitalist societies or of the potential economic efficiency of socialist economies, have less the flavour of misplaced theology than that of somewhat erroneous causal belief. Erroneous causal beliefs are no prerogative of socialists or rationalists. (Indeed it is precisely the common hallmark of devotees of liberal democracy and empiricism that they should fully acknowledge their own fallibility in this respect.) What we most need to see more clearly, therefore, is the systematic relations (if such there be) between more or less proven pragmatic efficacy and errors of causal belief which are plausibly systematic in character. For only if we can grasp these in an intellectually convincing fashion can we seriously assess how important causally the residual messianic commitments of the Marxist confession have been over the last three quarters of a century – and, more crucially, how important they still remain today and will be likely to remain for the imaginable future.

As an initial sketch of the relevant pattern, it seems best to represent the locus of proven efficacy of Marxist revolutionary practice (as already suggested) in its sensitivity to the political contradictions of capitalist reproduction. This may be little more than a matter of heuristic energy and alertness; and, over the one hundred and forty or so years since 1843, it has certainly misled its optimistic exponents far more often than it has guided them to success. None of its major theoretical expressions – Marx's initial conception of Germany's distinctive revolutionary susceptibility in 1843,[20] the casting of the 1848 risings within a materialist theory of the historical process as a whole,[21] Lenin's understanding of imperialism, or the doctrine of the weakest link – has combined analytical power and precision with much claim to validity. But this persisting epistemic vagueness or error has proven, through time, far less important than its capacity to sustain a consistently and eagerly Machiavellian political sensibility through thick and thin. Modern prudence may have some quite Polybian absurdities as a political goal within the cycle of regimes. But its capacity to nurture *virtù* certainly beats the fantasies of James Harrington into a cocked hat.[22]

Identifying the principal locus of error is more controversial. Most political analysts, whether friendly or hostile towards Marxism, still perceive this as lying principally in the idioms of revolutionary or post-revolutionary political practice: in the practical ineffectiveness of open and democratic socialist struggle in advanced capitalist societies or in the nefarious consequences of all too effective covert and authoritarian political ventures elsewhere (and perhaps in the fullness of time even in an advanced capitalist society). This is a necessarily vexed set of questions, turning as it does on the choice for an explanation of the gap between political advertisement and political experience between blind faith in the benignity of the historical process or unyielding animosity towards the political morals of one's opponents. We can consider briefly below how far it is possible to elide the crudity of this choice. But what needs first to be emphasized (and it is the central thesis of this essay) is that to concentrate on the political vices or political misfortunes of Marxist political practice is to lay the main weight of explanation in quite the wrong place.

In the work which effectively commences the tradition of political struggle to impose communist institutions by force of arms, Buonarroti's famous account of the Conspiracy for Equality, the author describes the political essence of the French Revolution as 'the explosion of the ever-present discord between the partisans of opulence and distinctions on the one side and the friends of equality or the numerous class of workers on the other'.[23] The ideological form taken by this conflict was that of a struggle between partisans of what Buonarroti called the order of egoism or aristocracy (the English doctrine of the economists)[24] and those of the order of the equality which he associated above all with Rousseau.[25] The English (or, more properly, Scottish) doctrine of the economists made the prosperity of nations consist in 'the multiplicity of their needs, in the ever growing diversity of their material enjoyments, in an immense industry, in a limitless commerce, in the rapid circulation of coined metals and, in the last instance, in the anxious and insatiable cupidity of the citizens'.[26] Marx, of course, modified this prissy attitude towards desire as such, promising a future in which the productive advantages of the order of egoism could be dependably combined with the avoidance of its hitherto attendant psychic and moral costs. But as matters have worked out, this synthesis has proved elusive.

It is above all just this proven elusiveness which explains the residual viability of capitalist state forms over a huge portion of the globe, in some measure even in poor countries but above all in the wealthy countries of the West. It is the economic contradictions of socialism which have above all offset the comparative advantages which socialism might otherwise have drawn from its historical juxtaposition with the economic and political contradictions of the miscellany of capitalist states between 1917 and the present day.

This is not to say, of course, that there are no deep tensions or incoherences in the political traditions of Leninism, still less that the tensions which there certainly are in theory can be reasonably expected to fail to emerge in practice. Both the main types of criticism pressed against Marxist-Leninist practice remain, men being taken as they are, eminently cogent. The conditions for the establishment of a socialist state power in revolutionary struggle may not dictate *a priori* an abandonment of all civil and political liberties and all vestiges of democratic responsibility. But they certainly make these ugly outcomes overwhelmingly likely in practice; and, of course, once their practical probability has been not merely established by experience but also deliberately *espoused* in advance, the chances of any less odious form of regime emerging effectively vanish. Political oppression can be put to good use for a time in poor countries (though that is not to say that it very often has been or is being put to good use there). What is wholly unclear is that it could offer the least benefit in societies which are comparatively wealthy and whose level of material well-being depends upon a complex system of production and exchange. Modern revolution may not guarantee the establishment of a politically oppressive regime. But we have as yet no example of its failing to furnish such a regime in practice and the causal pressures which favour its doing so are by now extremely easy to understand (if, that is, one wishes to understand them).

But, except trivially and tautologously, there is no political reason why a socialist regime should require a revolution for its establishment. A Eurocommunist regime for example might perfectly well arise by purely peaceful means and might sharply modify the political economy of a capitalist state without succumbing to domestic subversion or suppressing civil and political liberties. At present Eurocommunism enjoys a bad repute in most quarters. Rightwing commentators suspect the ability of the leopard to change its spots; and commentators from the left, by contrast, fear that it really has done so, thus transforming itself into a toothless reformism with no greater capacity to establish a viable socialist order than the by now extremely tame battalions of European social democracy. But the main grounds for distrusting the more insinuating advertisements for Eurocommunism, the combination of distributive equity and commitment to popular welfare with political civility and civil liberties, are no more than that: grounds for distrust, not guarantees of impossibility. Marxism as a doctrine of state or as a guiding tradition of political reason for a political party affords (by its rationalism and its naive equation of the political rejection of capitalism with the eventual establishment of the politically unproblematic) overwhelming ideological resources for partisans of political monopoly. As a doctrine of state within an already highly oppressive state form, one might expect these resources to be so overwhelming as to preclude the liberalization of the regime from within. But a number of experiences since 1956 in Eastern Europe have shown this expectation to be false. Since a Eurocommunist regime will not arise under the aegis of the Warsaw pact, it need not adjust its political calculations directly to Soviet susceptibilities; and within its own territory the considerable political costs of the will to monopoly might well offset its intrinsic charms to the possessor and its ideological appeals within the ranks of the faithful.

In Marxist parties or governments (as elsewhere) the relation between doctrine and agency is not one in which the former directly dictates the latter.[27] Rather, aspects of the former assign different costs and gains to different possible courses of action. Assessment of their relative weights by competitors for political power and authority leads these to espouse one possible course rather than another; and the accuracy and realism of these assessments is proven in practice by the outcome of their competitive efforts over extended periods of time. The political ecology of a Marxist regime or party heavily favours an overwhelming monopoly of authority; and, political effectiveness always being limited in reality, it favours also a correspondingly harsh style of rule. But no political ecology *dictates* a monopoly of authority (which is always, whatever else, a feat of skill). And a combination of taste, prudence, courage, adroitness and luck might well succeed in avoiding such a monopoly more or less indefinitely. Of course, taste, prudence, courage, adroitness and luck is a lot to ask for in a political leadership at any point; and too much to depend on confidently for lengthy periods of time. But of course, too, the republican tradition has always acknowledged an unnerving degree of dependence on levels of political virtue. Capitalist democracies simply *are* politically less hazardous, less accident-prone, forms of life than socialist states.

If we remember what originally prompted Marx to the opposite view of the comparative vulnerability of these forms of socio-political organization (and if in addition we consider the often unsavoury record of capitalist states in the present century in the face of acute economic and political crisis) it should be easier to see the drastic importance of the purely economic contradictions of socialism. Capitalist economies certainly remain susceptible to crisis. But it is increasingly hard to see their record (from almost any angle except perhaps the distributive) as *inferior* to that of socialist economies. The Stalinist growth strategy (electrification essentially without Soviets) did for a time provide a startling rate of economic growth for one huge economy with highly distinctive factor endowments. But after the construction of a heavy industrial base, neither it nor the relatively wide range of expedients subsequently essayed in one or other of the socialist countries looks very promising as a long term economic project. The well-known micro-economic inefficiencies of non-market economies remain to some degree compensated by macro-economic advantages, so that comparatively well-run socialist economies (of which there are few – with Hungary, East Germany and North Korea being the most frequent contenders) can continue to combine the welfare advantages of very low unemployment with fairly low rates of inflation and even some residual economic growth.[28] But the juggling act increasingly requires luck as well as skill. There is increasing understanding, particularly amongst Eastern European economists,[29] that socialist economies, too, possess their own laws of motion and that these are little more subject to rational control by human will than those of their capitalist confrères. And the radical absence of political charm in their regime form and the persisting difficulty of uniting luck with skill in their administration, make their intrinsic economic inefficiency a source of dramatic vulnerability.

The Polish case makes these points particularly graphically. Poland is, to be sure, a highly idiosyncratic country, with a past and a cultural self-consciousness which have been of key importance in sustaining the resistance of civil society to the Communist regime.[30] But even in Poland, with its overwhelming and somewhat archaic Catholic commitment, its large peasant residue and its intensely anti-Russian nationalism, it is clear that popular opposition focuses not on an essentially socialist organization of production as such[31] nor on a set of distributive policies, but on the political monopoly of an incompetent, subservient and repressive regime. What turned Solidarity into a major mass movement was the catastrophic economic performance of the Gierek government, the reckless *fuite en avant* of its ill-considered growth policy and the hardships which the utter failure of this policy was always bound eventually to impose upon the Polish people.

Amongst the Comecon economies it has been in many cases economic failure which has generated political challenges to the regime. (And there is certainly every reason to believe that the efficient running of a highly complex modern socialist economy with its devastating dependence on the availability of full and accurate information is wholly incompatible with a high degree of political repression.) But the key relation, perhaps, runs in the opposite direction. If we ask why some capitalist states can continue to avoid political repression for long periods of time (at least domestically), it is hard to avoid the judgement that the principal source of their capacity to do so has been the considerable success of their economies. Existing socialist states built on the Marxist-Leninist model might be unlikely to disestablish their ruling apparatus of their own accord and without harsh prompting from their irate subjects. But existing socialist states are in any case too tightly interrelated to take such decisions one by one. And for the moment it is perhaps more important (because more fundamental) to insist that a diminution of political monopoly by rational choice on the part of the monopolists requires some level of confidence on their part. A rationally planned command economy, after all, *requires* an effective central authority. Such authority might in principle sustain itself, for a time at least, purely on its merits. But what is clear, both in West and East, is that no one at present knows how a socialist economy can and should be organized and administered through time in such a way as to deserve the trust and applause of an entire population. An incumbent government faced with a choice between attempting to legitimate itself by persistently executing a feat which no one really knows how to carry off or filling in for its executive deficiencies by additional and readily available increments of coercion is unlikely to choose the former course with much consistency. The political viability of a capitalist state depends covertly and slyly upon a measure of success of its capitalist economy for which it manages to take only a limited degree of responsibility. But the political viability of an unrepressive socialist state would have to depend solely upon the degree of success of a socialist economy for which it could hardly hope to elude full responsibility. Until socialist rulers, potential or actual, learn how this responsibility can be discharged effectively (if, indeed, it is actually possible to discharge it effectively at all), the economic contradictions of socialism and the political contradictions of capitalism will together guarantee a long future for totalitarian democracy.

The moral which I wish to draw from these reflections is an old one; but its relevance is perennial. What we confront in the historical encounter between what Buonarroti called the orders of egoism and equality over the last two countries is *not* the combat of wisdom and folly or vice and virtue. Such combats never take place over very long periods of time and very wide expanses of territory. Human history is not like that; and to elect to see the world in those terms alone is imaginatively infantile and in the long run ineluctably self-destructive. What we do in fact confront is simply the ineradicable queasiness and the drastic human weight of politics in general – a domain in which understanding is necessarily agonizingly limited, in which self-righteousness is almost always misplaced, and yet in which the most vital human interests are constantly and inescapably at stake.

What we need today (and need in *every* land, in Baghdad and in Nablus, in Tyre and Beirut, in Yamit and in Moscow, in Washington, in London and in Port Stanley) is to learn to live with more suppleness and with greater agility both with the contradictions of socialism and with those of capitalism. What we need is not more practice in endlessly recycling the routine pieties of the orders of egoism or of equality, but instead the genesis of a decidedly more modern and more *prudent* prudence, a matter above all for our wits. For unless we learn to live more skilfully and wisely with the practical political contradictions of our world the alternative which we face is simply in the short or longer run that of dying with them, nation by nation or in one mad spasm together.

Chapter 6

Unimagined community: the deceptions of socialist internationalism

AT THE HEART of Marx's conception of the historical liberation, the slow but eventually decisive self-emancipation of mankind, stood a very simple contrast. On the one side there lay a necessarily distressing and overwhelmingly exploited human past: on the other, a potentially (and at best perhaps necessarily) triumphant and unexploited future. The temporal and geographical dimensions of the zone of transition between these two were very vaguely demarcated; and there is every reason to believe that Marx's own estimates of them fluctuated rather erratically in the face of immediate political experience.[1] Subsequent scholastic commentary on this issue, both apologetic and denunciatory, has proliferated extravagantly – and quite appropriately so, since in the choice of political action under Marxist auspices issues of timing are of central importance. But the most important question about the contrast concerns not the timespan over which it should be expected to take place, but the essential validity of the contrast itself. Here it is plainly not the first term over which the difficulty arises: the judgement that at least in human societies subsequent to primitive communism (or, less scripturally, at least in agrarian societies and their successors) human productive cooperation has historically required a degree of institutionalized coercion and the practical use of a substantial proportion of the labour of some adults for the benefit of others. What is much less convincing, however, is the presumption that the second term, the prospectively triumphant and unexploited human future, has ever been very clearly or coherently conceived. (What cannot even be coherently conceived certainly cannot rationally be *expected* with much confidence.) It is in relation to this equivocal but stirring promise that the theme of Marxism's own national experiences and internationalist hopes most urgently requires consideration.

If we ask why it was that Marx expected the human future to represent such a decisive improvement upon the human past, the key to the answer lies in the account which he offered, particularly in the

103

German Ideology, of the historical achievements of capitalism: the massive increase in human productive powers and their transformation into an international system of extraction and exchange extending over the whole globe, through the brutal but creative energies of the bourgeoisie.[2] The creation of a world market was at least as significant a capitalist achievement as the huge increase in human productivity in a limited number of societies which had accompanied it. The increase in man's productive power was the central theme in human history and the dynamic which relentlessly refashioned all the elements of social and political organization (and the systems of meaning associated with these) to fit its own imperious demands. It is still controversial how far it is theoretically correct to see Marx's theory of history in the last instance, as Jerry Cohen has done,[3] as a functionalist articulation of the requirements of expanding productive forces. But whatever the historically most precise formulation for his theory may be (and it is entirely possible, in representing the thought of Marx as with any other human thinker, that theoretical clarity and historical accuracy are not wholly compatible objectives),[4] what is entirely clear is the degree of Marx's own confidence, in 1845–6 as in the late 1850s and early 1860s, that the forces of production do in the end have the capacity to impose their demands upon the recalcitrant imaginations, habits and power structures of particular human societies.

Capitalist societies had come into existence because of their vast productive superiority over their feudal predecessors; not, of course, by magic but through human praxis in particular historical settings, making use of the advantages which could be derived from such superior efficacy. But like these predecessors, their structural logic sets certain long term limits to the possible expansion within them of human productive powers. Their internal political vulnerability in the face of an exploited proletariat was in part a consequence of their cultural, social and political polarization and of the short term economic instabilities of the trade cycle. But it was also in part a consequence of these eventual long term limits which capitalist relations of production impose on the expansion of productive forces. The anarchy and waste of capitalist production could be (and therefore would be) supplanted by an alternative socialist mode of production, the rational superiority of which would in due course become self-evident. Because it would not be based upon discriminatory ownership of the means of production, it would not require (or, would not long require) to be protected against potential enemies (as discriminatory ownership always does require). The internal dynamics of capitalist development create a proletariat which is, by definition, exploited and which becomes steadily more difficult to repress as it increases in size and gains in corporate self-consciousness and political experience. (Capitalist societies are the first societies in history in which the labouring majority of the male and female population have a distinctively *political* experience thrust upon them.) But except within capitalist ownership relations there is no longer any need for this proletariat to be either exploited or repressed. Hence, in due course, the expropriation of the expropriators.

Neither in the *German Ideology*, where the main outlines of his conception of history were first set out, nor in the *Communist Manifesto* in which they were first offered to a substantial audience as the basis of a programme of immediate political action, nor indeed at any later point in his writings, did Marx offer much guidance on how exactly the proletarians of the world were in practice to unite to appropriate human productive forces on the world scale on which human production was already increasingly coming to be organized. There is, of course, ample doubt (as subsequent history has dismayingly confirmed) as to how far it is actually possible, in any but the most formal and nominal of terms, collectively to appropriate productive forces (and to keep them appropriated) even with the territory of a single national state. But, whatever may have happened subsequently, it has at least proved possible on occasion within particular national territories for a particular proletariat, in Marx's words, to 'settle matters with its own bourgeoisie'.[5]

On the world scale, however, the idea of the collective appropriation of human productive powers by the vast exploited majority of the human population appears thus far to be entirely fanciful: a socialist or communist fantasy every bit as Utopian as the wildest flights of Fourier. One possible explanation of this important misadventure might simply be that Marx's thought (like that of most of us on political matters which keenly concern us) was an uneasy amalgam of the genuinely social scientific and the rationally Machiavellian with large traces of pure wishfulfilment: the unity of the world proletariat, then, being an especially pure instance of the last. There is in my view nothing in fact wrong with this verdict: but as it stands it is unacceptably indolent and superficial. A second type of explanation, considerably less indolent and in some ways less superficial, would be furnished by a careful historical tracing of the vicissitudes of Marxist, and indeed anti-Marxist, political practice since early 1848 throughout the world as a whole, explaining why classes and parties and governments and political leaders acted as and when they did, in the narrow confines which history made available to them and with the wretchedly dim understanding of what they were doing which human historical agents necessarily possess. This historiography is, of course, prodigiously intricate; and the terms in which it is set out are as heavily contested politically as they are inevitably politically contentious. But for those who genuinely wish to understand its broad contours, these are by now, in my view, reasonably easy to discern. It would be absurd to try to summarize them briefly here.

More importantly, it would also for our purposes be grossly insufficient to do so. What has been historically important about Marx's thought up to now can perhaps be considered as the very partial realisation and the fairly gross failure to be realized, over the next century and a third, of a mid-nineteenth-century prophetic vision. But except for the most manipulative and short-term political purposes, it is ludicrous to regard this as what is most important about Marx's thought for us now. For us what matters is how far a Marxist conception of the historical possibilities for human social, economic and political organization is or is not fundamentally sound. For this issue the historical failure of proletarian internationalism cannot be seen merely as a string of particular historical disasters: August 1914,[6] the restabilization of capitalism in Europe after 1918 and in Western Europe after 1945, the postwar political and military order in Eastern Europe, the Sino-Soviet squabble, the war between Vietnam and Kampuchea. It is also, and more crucially, a theoretical puzzle which requires a theoretical solution. It is also, plainly, a practical problem, both for Marxists and for others; and as such it requires a practical solution. Insofar as it is theoretically insoluble, we may be confident that it will prove at least equally insoluble in practice. What matters for us is not that prophecy has failed (as in this instance it very manifestly has) but whether the outcome prophesied could even in principle be realized.

I do not believe that anyone at present possesses a very cogent answer to this question, partly, at least, because for very obvious reasons it is seldom posed very bluntly. When it is posed, too, it is almost always presented in the guise of a rhetorical question, importunately soliciting the assent of a listener to the judgement that no decent person (no true socialist etc.) could doubt it, or that no sane person (no political realist, or person possessed of elementary common sense) could expect it. True socialism, in this setting, is a category of pure desire; but it is much less evident that its antithesis, putative political realism, is a category of pure reason. The basic outlines of an explanation of the failure of prophecy can in this case be given rather easily.

It is no great intellectual feat, that is to say, to make this failure retrospectively unsurprising. But what the explanation shows is how formidable the impediments to realizing the prophecy have always been (and, by implication, how intellectually insecure were the grounds of its initial affirmation). Once the explanation itself is given, what follows is very much less determinate and very much more a matter of political taste and disposition. But at the very least it is reasonable to suppose that the explanation identifies challenges which any intellectually serious and honest exponent of Marxist politics is imperatively obliged to face and to seek out to meet.

The central premiss of Marxist internationalism was, as already noted, the recognition of capitalism as an integrated system of production and exchange operating at a global level; not, of course, in the sense of a unified conspiratorial practice directed by a single rational will, but in something much closer to the normative inversion of the classical theory of international trade, Adam Smith's invisible hand misliked. It was this historically constructed system, and the human aversion which it evokes which, as Marx insisted in the *German Ideology*,[7] has converted a preoccupation with the construction of egalitarian societies founded upon common ownership from an age-old fantasy of philosophic moralists into the realistic prospect for human social organization everywhere on earth. The history of capitalism has forced upon the human race the understanding that, as a single species, it shares a single world for its habitat and that the destinies of all its members for the rest of human history are therefore relentlessly intertwined. From what had often been a high degree of cultural and historical privacy, the myriads of discrete human communities and language groupings have been forced into baffled and uneasy fellowship with each other. As Marx himself expressed it in the *German Ideology*, this brusquely enforced emergence, blinking, into the full glare of a global history had perhaps a misleading flavour of simultaneity to it. It is true that his relatively concrete political views, in the case of Germany in 1843 and early 1850,[8] as in that of Russia in 1877 and 1881,[9] were sometimes focused quite keenly on the implications of uneven political, economic and cultural development: the advantages of backwardness. But it was not really until Trotsky's elaboration of the theory of permanent revolution, particularly in the pamphlet *Results and Prospects* and subsequently,[10] that the conception of combined and uneven development became central to a Marxist conception of political strategy for the world as a whole. The theory of combined and uneven development is perhaps a trifle nebulous; and it is certainly elastic in its practical implications. (A more polite way of expressing the same point would be to note its highly dialectical quality.)[11] But whatever its limitations as a *theory*, it has at least proved more compatible with twentieth century historical experience of the geographical and temporal incidence of the political collapse of capitalist societies and the inception of socialist economies than Marx's own political expectations have proved to be. Trotsky's stress on the global integration of world capitalism was emphatic: 'Binding all countries together with its mode of production and its commerce, capitalism has converted the whole world into a single economic and political organism.'[12] But his estimate of the political consequences of severing the weakest link in the world capitalist chain, made under the impact of the events of 1905, has proved severely overoptimistic: 'The political emancipation of Russia, led by the working class . . . will make it the initiator of the liquidation of world capitalism, for which history has created all the objective conditions.'[13]

Now, since 1917, and more particularly since the invention and military mobilization of nuclear and then thermonuclear weapons, it is quite true to say that the 'political emancipation of Russia', eked out with American assistance, has created all the objective conditions for the extermination of the human race (an event which would certainly be a sufficient condition for the liquidation of both world capitalism and of socialism also, wherever this is to be found). But two thirds of a century of a presumptively politically emancipated Russia, the collapse of western European and American colonial empire throughout the world, and the establishment of socialist government in the most populous country on earth, taken together, have proved an extremely long way from furnishing all the objective conditions for liquidating world capitalism; let alone establishing a plainly superior mode of productive organization in its stead. There are, to be sure, many factors which help to explain this. As it has in fact emerged, the political, social and cultural realities of the Soviet Union make the phrase 'political emancipation' appear at best euphemistic, while the residual, strictly economic, vitality of world capitalism has proved quite remarkable. The early 1980s are not one of capitalism's more auspicious phases; and the economic and political policies of the Reagan administration should guarantee that this remains so for some little time. But thus far the record of Marxist political economists in predicting the rhythms of the world economy is, at any rate, not markedly superior to that of economists who anticipate an unlimited future for capitalism; and there does not appear to be any surviving intellectual basis in Marxist economics for a presumption that capitalist production cannot continue to expand indefinitely in the total value of goods and services which it produces and exchanges. Whether it will survive, of course, will depend on many other matters, political and military as much as economic: not least, the avoidance of full scale thermonuclear war between the great powers. The political defects of the Soviet Union – an arbitrary structure of government in no way responsible to those over whom it rules, a brutal and politically unrestrained coercive apparatus, and so on – have been clearly in part a result of the backwardness which made the Russian empire vulnerable in the first place to political revolution led by a party of the proletariat and committed to the establishment of a socially owned economy.[14] (On this issue, therefore, the honours between Trotsky and the Mensheviks come out roughly even. He was right to insist that a socialist economy could be constructed in Russia as the outcome of proletarian political revolution. But they were right to insist that the political preconditions for constructing a socialist economy in this way would obviate most of the social, cultural and political goals of socialists more or less indefinitely.) Some of the political defects, of course, can be attributed also to more contingent and personal factors: decisions by Lenin, Trotsky himself, Khruschev, Brezhnev and, most abundantly, Stalin. Marxists may hope (and seek) to explain what it was about the objective conditions which rendered the making and implementation of particular political decisions possible. They can even hope to explain what made such decisions appear attractive to those who took them. But they are no better placed than anyone else to explain exactly why the decisions were in fact made as they were.[15] Hence, of course, the tendency of Marxist explanation of phenomena like Stalinism to shift away in the last instance from material factors to the espousal of a false theory or the display of a reprehensible disposition (or some amalgam of the two) by an offending political agent.

It is certainly important that the history of socialism, like the rest of human history, is in some measure a history of crimes and blunders. (At the very least it underlines the point that socialist modes of political agency and economic organization must not be seen as magical talismans enabling their disciples to dispense with the permanent human need for virtue, intelligence and practical skill.) But it is not sufficient to rest content with an explanation of the mishaps of twentieth century socialism or communism which attributes these to the contingent cultural retardation of the sites of socialist political triumph, or to human error on the part of socialist political leaderships and governments. It is particularly unsatisfactory to do so once a serious attempt has been made to explain the geographical incidence of twentieth century revolution and that attempt has eventuated in some version or other of the theory of combined and uneven development. If it is, as thus far appears to be the case, only the weaker links in the chain of world capitalism which are apt to succumb to socialist revolution then it is reasonable to assume that the forms of socialist reconstruction which emerge as a result of severing these links will represent something of a travesty of nineteenth century socialism or communism's claims to constitute a world historical solution for the human race as a whole: the riddle of history solved.[16] (The judgement, incidentally, that it is only the weakest links which do in fact sever rests on a combination of equivocation and tautology, since the evidence that the sites in question are in fact the *least* robust elements in the world capitalist chain is provided retrospectively in each instance by the occurrence within them of anticapitalist revolution.)[17]

If the distribution of socialist revolution in the modern world has so far been (and if indeed it will necessarily remain for some time) geographically and historically patchy — and if its outcomes thus far have been to some degree misshapen, this necessarily has strong implications for the future prospects of socialism. The political survival and military strength of the Soviet Union have vastly enhanced the prospects for the survival of anticapitalist revolution, in Asia, in Africa and even in the immediate vicinity of the greatest capitalist power, the United States of America. In the nineteenth century most of Marx's assurance over the eventual triumph of socialism rested on his sense of the palpable and ineliminable odiousness and irrationality of capitalist production from the point of view of most of those whom this affects. The rationality and eligibility of socialist production, by contrast, were essentially taken on trust. Critics of Marxism have often concentrated their fire on Marx's estimate of the ineliminable demerits of capitalism, arguing either, for example, with Hayek and von Mises,[18] that these are not truly demerits because they in fact represent preconditions for economic efficiency, or that insofar as they are or were defects, they can be or largely have been eliminated by political remedies, and pointing out with relief, where these arguments prove unconvincing, that in practice the majority of the populations of advanced capitalist societies appear to find little difficulty in tolerating their society as a whole, however irksome or irrational they may see some aspects of this as being. In the late twentieth century, however, only the wilfully self-deceptive can any longer see socialist production as unproblematically endowed with a set of merits which reverse the defects of capitalist production. The experience of twentieth century socialist economies is marked, at particular times and in particular settings, by major achievements, especially in the Soviet Union, the People's Republic of

China, Hungary and East Germany. It certainly does not suffice to establish that socialist production is ineliminably odious and irrational. But anyone who chooses to study it in even the most cursory manner is by now well aware that the historical experience of socialist production has proved a deeply problematic one. The continuing weakness of Soviet agriculture a full half century after the trauma of collectivization, the effective decollectivization of Chinese agriculture in the last few years, the persistently unimpressive capacity to produce goods which consumers actually *wish* to use,[19] the poor record of technical innovation outside the sphere of military requirements in even the strongest socialist economy,[20] the weakening or cessation of economic growth in virtually all socialist countries in the face of the present world recession, quite apart from the blatant faults of Soviet or Chinese or East German political institutions,[21] all show that socialism too has its stigmata. When the populations of advanced capitalist societies reflect upon the discontents of their own daily lives they do so now in a context in which they also have presented to them (as evocatively and tendentiously as the capitalist media can contrive) the very evident discontents which socialism too can offer. The most effective emphases in these instances are seldom those of greatest intellectual cogency. There is perhaps no more intimate connection between Pol Pot and the threat of socialism than there is between Adolf Hitler and the menace of capitalism; but even here there is quite certainly no *less*. And on the central question of socialist economics, how far socialist planning in practice can yet succeed in realizing a continuing rational design in the workings of a real economy, the lessons of socialist experience are not at all encouraging:[22] especially for economies already as intricate as those of advanced capitalism. It is particularly important here to stress that the limitations of socialist planning procedures are *not* largely produced by political oppression and could not therefore to any very substantial degree be remedied merely by the establishment of more benign political relations. What causes them is deep and intractable intellectual difficulties in the design of institutions, structures of incentives for human agents and systems for eliciting, distributing and responding to information.

I have said rather little so far about internationalism – and almost nothing about nations. All I have tried to do is to suggest that Marx's identification of the constitution of the world market does mark out the relevant frame for analysing modern political problems, but that his presumption that the global system of production and exchange established by capitalist expansion already was (or is even now) available for socialist appropriation gave him an exceedingly poor sense of the concrete nature of these problems. The theory of combined and uneven development fathered by Trotsky with a little aid from Parvus, by contrast casts at least some illumination on why the twentieth century, unlike the nineteenth, has seen the establishment of socialist economies over large areas of the world but has not seen these in the more advanced of capitalist countries. It also casts some light, though not on the whole as deployed by Trotsky himself, on just why the political orders which have presided over the construction of these socialist economies have been so plainly regressive in character, even in comparison with capitalist representative democracies. But what is far more fundamental in explaining the limitations of socialism as this has been established is the simple failure of a socialist mode of production to show itself *productively* superior to a capitalist mode of production. Socialist states on the whole make more vigorous attempts than do capitalist states to improve the lot of their poorer members. They may or may not be distributively more equitable. But even after six and a half decades of would-be socialist rule in Russia, it is quite unclear that over lengthy periods of time a socialist productive system can be expected with any confidence to improve the real living standards of the majority of a population more handsomely than a capitalist alternative would be able to do. The thinness and flimsiness of Marx's own conception of socialist production has proved to be overwhelmingly important. His sense of the ineliminable political vulnerability of capitalism may have been a little overexcited; but it still retains considerable force. At least the judgement that the 'bourgeois point of view' had become 'problematic'[23] even in Germany by 1843 has held up very well. But what has prevented this point of view from becoming self-evidently 'antiquated' as well has been essentially two factors: the continued capacity of world capitalism, however erratically, to expand, and the failure thus far of socialist countries to develop an economic system which is plainly productively superior to that of a capitalist economy (or perhaps one should just say, which isn't plainly productively inferior).

How is it most helpful to see the implications of this contretemps? Not, I think, in the first instance as grounds for intoning a litany of abuse directed at those socialist protagonists who have misunderstood the possibilities or dangers of different lines of political conduct on one historical occasion after another. Nor, more definitely, as a motive for drawing a veil discreetly over the extent and severity of the political reverses of socialism in the course of the twentieth century. What would be more helpful, I suggest, is to turn once more to the political problem which Marx himself first identified, to express it as clearly and simply as possible, and to reflect again more soberly and with all the wisdom that hindsight can offer, on just what resources socialism does possess for resolving this problem. When we do so, the disturbing relation between the historical fiction or historical reality of nations and the imperative need for, and apparent unattainability of, substantive internationalism shifts immediately to the centre of the picture.

What Marx identified was the creation of a field of massively significant causal interaction between virtually all the human beings who happen to be alive at a single time on earth. In the mid-1840s this field of interaction was considerably less dense and, for most human beings, existentially far less salient than it has since become. There is no guarantee that it will persist or grow in density in face of the two main dimensions of vulnerability in the expansive capacity of the forces of production: the threat of purely physical destruction in thermonuclear war or the increasingly pressing danger of accumulative poisoning of the human habitat by industrial pollution and the plundering of irreplaceable natural resources. There is no guarantee, as Marx of course vehemently insisted (and as many classical political economists agreed), that the capitalist mode of production can expand indefinitely. But there is also no guarantee, as already noted, that a socialist mode of production with superior capacity to sustain the expansion of human productive powers will, or even could, be conceived and realized by human intelligence and design.[24] The reality of the ecological and thermonuclear threats (and the manifest inability of socialist political orders to respond to these any more prudently and adroitly than capitalist political orders) certainly indicate that theoretical confidence in the capacity of historically developed productive forces to secure, through human praxis, the social and political preconditions for their reproduction (let alone their continued expansion) is simply mis-placed. We may manage to improve the opportunities for human flourishing on earth or we may not. Perhaps it is still on balance *slightly* more probable that we *shall* (taking the world's population as a whole) manage to do so than that we shall not. But nothing in the accumulated historical experience of the human species gives any kind of guarantee that we *must* be able to do so.

If, however, the capitalist mode of production does continue to expand for some time (or, to be a little more sensitive to the immediate present, if its expansion recommences and continues for some time), or if it does become transformed into a socialist mode of production which is genuinely productively superior, then human life will continue to be overwhelmingly interdependent. World capitalism is a political as well as an economic system. Its political arrangements at present are in rather blatant disarray; but there is no reason at all to assume them ever to have been very well adapted to its systemic needs.

What has been generated by the creation of the world market, and what would survive even the simultaneous political triumph of socialism everywhere on earth, is a frame of human interaction between persons who understand (and as yet wish to understand) rather little about each other and who enjoy wildly unequal opportunities for material enjoyment and self-development. In large measure these persons have no humanly real alternative to cooperating with each other. The historically given choice which they face is simply a choice of the terms of which they are to cooperate. The liberal view of world capitalism sees this as a system of cooperation in which the terms are (or at least ought ideally to be) those of uncoerced exchange of goods, services and labour, either directly or through the passive instrument of money. It requires, to be sure, a high level of selective inattention, even within the categories of capitalist ideology, to presume that these are the terms which in fact apply. Since to see these terms as conceptually connected at all with the requirements of justice it is necessary to take history at a particular time tacitly as given, and to treat individual holdings correspondingly as entitlements in the absence of any reason whatever for so regarding them,[25] it also requires a high level of moral equanimity to find them ideologically at all compelling. But at least the liberal model of international trade, from Adam Smith to the present day, has succeeded in presenting a conception of what is and ought to be occurring within this frame of human interaction. Socialism, unfortunately, thus far appears to possess no such conception. Six and a half decades after the foundation of the first would-be socialist state and several decades after the foundation of a putatively socialist framework of international economic cooperation in Eastern Europe, there does not even exist a coherent socialist conception of the appropriate terms for international trade.[26] Nor is this simply a lacuna in the coherence and clarity of socialist *conceptions* of what is to be done. The distortion and inequity of economic interactions between developed and underdeveloped regions or between town and country, in individual capitalist countries or in the world capitalist system as a whole, are replicated in the relations between different regions of particular socialist states (China, Yugoslavia, perhaps even the Soviet Union). There is as yet no intellectually coherent socialist conception of how such distortions and inequities could in principle be avoided in the construction of individual socialist societies, still less in the construction of a credible socialist community of the world's population as a whole.

On these issues the debility of modern socialist thought is over-whelming. Consider, for example, the classical allegation of criminal betrayal of internationalist duty by a socialist political leader: Stalin's construction of socialism in one country. This has been criticized predominantly by admirers of Trotsky on the grounds that it inflicted great and gratuitous damage on the prospects for world revolution in the 1930s, and presumably ever since. This may or may not be on balance a persuasive conclusion. (It is certainly easy to dispute the judgement that any damage which it did inflict was gratuitous; and it is far from clear that such damage as Stalin's strategy and tactics did occasion in particular countries was sufficient to make much difference to the pace and force of anticapitalist revolution on the world scale. To find the conclusion persuasive is, at the very least, to attribute impressive causal weight in determining twentieth century world history to an eminently non-material factor.) But Stalin's decision to opt firmly for socialism in one country has also been criticized as a betrayal of socialism itself since socialism is by definition a more advanced form of production than capitalism, since capitalism has long been very evidently international and since any reversion to an autarkic mode of development must therefore preclude the construc-tion of a genuinely socialist economy, society, or presumably polity.[27] (It is unclear quite how this judgement is to be combined with the now commonplace socialist judgement that effective subtraction of peri-pheral capitalist economies from the world capitalist system is in itself a necessarily progressive development, a judgement very poorly sup-ported by recent historical experience.)[28]

One way of looking at the problematic character of cooperation between human beings who are forced to interact with one another across the whole globe is to consider the terms of exchange on which these interactions might reasonably and validly be regarded by all participants as mutually beneficial. As I have tried to emphasize, there exists at present no account of such terms, conservative, liberal or socialist, with the least claim to intellectual cogency. (The most widely touted recent attempts to specify these – John Rawls's theory of justice[29] or reworkings of classical utilitarianism by Singer, Glover and others, in each case wholly ignore political pragmatics and offer feeble grounds, or no grounds at all, for why any historical human agent should regard their conclusions as giving him a reason to perform any particular actions.) Human beings today, accordingly, are forced willy nilly to interact internationally. But in the absence of a plausible medium for fair exchange or any clear and rational basis for mutual trust to expect them to appreciate this enforced fellowship is wholly unreasonable. Nations, perhaps, are merely the largest demographic units over which the fantasy of enjoying such a medium of exchange or of possessing a sound basis for mutual trust has as yet been successfully synthesized, even fitfully.[30]

A second, and perhaps equally important way of looking at the problematic character of human cooperation across the globe is to consider the actual political entities and organizations within which human beings are at present incorporated and through which such cooperation must in the first instance be implemented. (The imaginative response of socialists to this challenge has taken the form of an unsteady oscillation between imagining wholly different, exquisitely serviceable and almost entirely undescribed fresh organizational agencies and presuming, in the teeth of the evidence, that particular soi-disant socialist states already constitute such agencies.) On this point the abysmal inadequacy in the understanding of political institutions throughout the history of the socialist tradition[31] is a heavy legacy. Any form of economic cooperation which succeeded in replacing the invisible hand of the market with a single coherent rational will, because of its geographical scope and prodigious causal complexity, would require the construction of political institutions utterly unlike anything previously seen in human history. (Is there any reason at all to believe that such institutions *could* be constructed even in principle?) Any attempt to stand in for these institutions in the (necessarily protracted) meantime by acting through existing political agencies, the state apparatuses of existing national units and their international intermediaries, would have to take full account of the causal properties of these agencies and intermediaries. They would, that is to say, have to take account of the precise causal characteristics of the political world in which we already happen to live and to explain how these characteristics can permit relatively unarbitrary and uncoerced cooperation. But, of course, the principal animus of socialist criticism of these institutions is precisely that their causal characteristics structurally preclude any such cooperation.

One of the more intractable obstacles to such cooperation is the existing beliefs and sentiments of much, perhaps most, of the world's population.[32] The form in which this obstruction has most obtruded itself upon socialist attention (apart perhaps from the primal criminality of the comparatively torpid revolutionary zeal of the proletariat in advanced capitalist societies) has been in the political sentiment of nationalism. Nationalism, the sense of membership in and commitment towards particular national units (up to and including the willingness to die on their behalf, if necessary) has often been a political affront to Marxists (though it has also often been a key causal element in the success of twentieth-century anticapitalist revolutions).[33] As an often politically decisive aspect of the imaginative life of twentieth-century populations, however, its main challenge to Marxists ought in the first instance to be one of explanation. *Why* is this, on whatever geographical scale it in fact applies, the way in which the majority of modern populations do in fact choose to define their allegiance at the crucial points of political choice?[34] Nationalist sentiment, where it exists, is an eminently causal part of the social reality of particular human aggregates. It cannot simply be brushed aside by political disapprobation. Human beings always have their reasons for identifying themselves as they do. These may not always, or even usually, be very good reasons but they are none the less causally efficacious for that. In order to emend them and secure their replacement by better reasons, it is first necessary to understand them.[35]

From this point of view the important limitation of Marx's own views is not that he failed to notice the historical differences between nations (a charge which is wholly misplaced).[36] Nor is it even that his method of social and political analysis is incapable of explaining the properties of nations. (On this score the complaint might rather be that, if interpreted with sufficient elasticity, there is virtually no logically conceivable human happening which it could not be held to explain.)[37] Rather it is that his conception of political good (vague enough in all honesty in itself) is very poorly equipped to take account of the political implications of these properties. Here the Marxist insistence on the union of theory and practice is all too apt.

What explains the failures of socialist politics in the twentieth century is not predominantly the gratuitous folly, vice or weakness of will of socialist political leaders. Rather, it is the lack of any clear conception of how, nationally and internationally, there could actually be a political order which permits human beings, in the wildly unequal situations in which history has left them, to cooperate together in rational mutual trust for a genuinely shared good and in an economy which is not based upon private ownership. Still more, of course, the lack of any coherent conception at all of how such a political order could be constructed. (I take it myself as self-evident that such cooperation could never in principle take place in an economy, local, national or global which is based upon drastically differential private ownership of the means of production.) In the absence of such a conception, there is little in principle to restrain the frenzied competitive struggles of modern economics and geopolitics and the remorselessly Machiavellian style of consciousness which these reinforce and arm ever more hideously. But in its absence, also, it is both intellectually and emotionally puerile to see capitalism and socialism as simple moral antitheses which stand to one another in the relation of evil to good (or, of course, vice versa). What has brought modern socialist politics to this impasse is in the last instance a purely intellectual bafflement in the face of questions which socialists have never solved and which their twentieth-century political triumphs have forced ever more relentlessly upon their attention.[38]

Unless this bafflement is dissipated intellectually, unless an intellectual solution is found for the puzzles which provoke it, the future of socialist or communist allegiance is certain to prove even more painful than its past in this century has been traumatic.

Chapter 7

Social theory, social understanding, and political action*

I

EVERY human being who is not in some way fundamentally cognitively damaged is at least an amateur social theorist. To acquire a human culture at all and to perform human actions both require social understanding. Being human is not something which we simply *are* but rather something which we learn; and much of learning it is learning how to understand the social relations in which we find ourselves. Because this is such a central truth for all human beings, it is not merely the case for each of us at an individual level that we are perforce amateur social theorists to a person, but also true at a social level that every human society embodies a more or less coherent 'official' social theory or set of social theories. But the term 'social theory' in modern speech, of course, does not in general refer to these relatively universal commonplaces of official doctrine or of the grammar of social membership. Instead it points, a trifle waveringly to be sure, to something more distinctive about the social relations of today, in Britain or in Zaire or in Chile or in North Korea. Social theory is what we have with which to close the gap between our individual social understandings and our experience of modern history, to reconcile, perhaps, the real with the rational. For us it is the intelligibility of what we know to be a largely unintelligible human world, the acceptability of an always potentially intolerable condition, a true opium of the intellectuals. Like opium, however, it is not merely addictive – in that we have come to rely more and more upon it, to find it less and less dispensable – but also diminishingly effective, requiring ever larger doses to sustain its desired impact, and increasingly disastrous in its side-effects.

* I am very grateful to Susan James for her thoughtful criticisms of the initial text of this lecture, particularly since lack of space and incapacity have prevented me from meeting so many of them.

Expressed in these terms, this may appear a somewhat hysterical judgement. But it is not a judgement which is at all difficult to defend. What I attempt here, in crude outline, in order to make the judgement seem a trifle more real is, firstly, to explain how this condition of ideological intoxication has arisen; secondly, to suggest how we could realistically seek at least to initiate the slow process of detoxification; and thirdly, to indicate how directly and how painfully these issues obtrude in the present condition of the politics of Britain.

II

To take the explanation first: it will be apparent at once that this is a complicated matter. At one level, in order to explain at all adequately the place occupied by social theory in modern thought and modern experience, it would be necessary to tell, more or less concisely, most of the history of the human race. But being less ambitious, and simplifying wildly for the sake of intelligibility, we can see it in the first instance simply as a direct product of the secularization of modern culture. Within an explicitly secular culture the actual social understandings of the individual members of a society can in principle be joined onto the official social theory or doctrine of the society to which they belong only by an elaborate normative theory and an apparatus of causal beliefs. The history of modern social thought has seen extensive squabbling about the theoretical terms of trade in this conjunction. Methodological individualists and exponents of some varieties of utilitarianism, for example, have seen the sensory states and the actual social understandings of individual human beings at a particular time as the sole locus of human reality at that time and treated the social relations in which individual human beings find themselves simply as inventories of resources to be exploited by each of us, on the basis of optimal causal understanding – as effectively as possible – for our personal gratification. This is not a distinctively modern view. Indeed, eloquent statements of it can be found among the thinkers of ancient Greece. But there is an extremely strong historical relation between it and the self-understanding of capitalist economies; and in historical perspective, the vulgarization and dispersion of this view throughout the population of modern capitalist societies is by now as decisively a characteristic of these societies as the levels of material consumption which have been attained within them. A culture, in this view, is simply something which individual human beings happen to acquire – and to do so more or less thoroughly, depending upon the contingencies of reinforcement. Methodological holists, by contrast, firmly reverse the perspective, seeing culture (within a variety of causal frames) as constitutive of human reality (as the site of being human at all) and seeing individual human beings accordingly as instances which cultures happen more or less thoroughly to acquire.

The fact of socialization, of course, and its real, if limited, efficacy in the case of most human beings, is not something which any serious social theorist could have sound reason to ignore. But it is not a fact which bears its own meaning on its face. It is not in any sense self-interpreting. To appear susceptible to socialization, to seem its willing victim, is on the whole a prudent investment for anyone. But to be too susceptible to it in actuality might well prove an existential disaster. Empathy may be a good servant to the ego. But it may also be a harsh master. A subtle attention to the expectations of others and an insight into their feelings may, in the cool and self-controlled, be a considerable aid to getting one's own way. But a degree of moral self-repression and an incapacity to avoid feeling for the feelings of others can be a nasty obstruction to realizing one's own desires. How does it really make sense for human beings to live?

In an explicitly religious culture this is a question which could at least anticipate an answer drawn from outside the space of human social existence altogether. In a secular culture, however, if it is indeed a question which can expect any answer at all, that answer must certainly be drawn from inside the space of human social existence. For most of us today, the space of human social relations is all the evaluative space there is. The answer might not, of course, draw its central theoretical term directly from *social* experience as such. Utilitarianism for example, at least in some versions, puts its trust as directly as it can in materially given sensory states. But even the most crudely hedonic versions of utilitarianism sanction the promotion of the highest aggregate of preferred sensory states, however distributed, which they deem to be socially possible. Social possibility is a real causal constraint on the sensory states in which human beings can in practice find themselves. This is not the context in which to assess utilitarianism as a theory of the human good. But even if utilitarianism is theoretically determinate in principle (which I doubt) and even if it can be related convincingly to the theory of individual practical reason, it is hard to see how it can be *read* clearly at all as a *social* theory, a theory of the relationship between individual existence and social reality. Within the constraints of a particular culture, no doubt, it may serve well enough as an idiom of loosely prudential advice. Consequences certainly do matter and it is as well to watch out for them as best one can. But as a theory of what sort of culture human beings have good reason to seek to fashion for themselves and their descendants, or as a theory of what sort of human beings it is desirable in principle for cultures to contrive to form, it is extremely hard to believe that utilitarianism in fact offers any clear direction at all apart from a certain mild disparagement of what David Hume called the 'monkish virtues'.[1]

But if the answer which utilitarianism offers to the question of how it really makes sense for human beings to live is a trifle feeble, because of its virtual silence on the nature of social relations, at least utilitarianism does possess an answer of sorts to the question. It is far less clear that the same holds true for its most important modern competitor, Marxism. As a conception of how we have good reason to live, utilitarianism is theoretically sincere but humanly unconvincing. (No doubt each of us enjoys the pleasures which please us; and we certainly prefer our own preferences. But are either of these really very deeply directive thoughts?) Marxism, by contrast, at least within capitalist societies, is often humanly rather compelling on the matter of which side it is more creditable to be on in a particular brawl (or at the very least which side it is better not to be on). But on the issue of how human beings do have good reason to live, Marxism is both deeply incoherent in its fundamental tastes and profoundly evasive in its tactical pronouncements. ('Be good enough to leave that question till later. No decent person would ask it now' – and so on. And later, when it *is* too late, 'Well, that's all just blood under the bridge now, isn't it?'). Marxism may be cogent enough at times on the moral and practical implications of the immediate social context of action. But as a comprehensive conception of how human beings do have good reason to live their lives, it is theoretically disingenuous to a truly staggering degree. Now it is possible (though not in my view correct) to dispute the claim that Marx himself ever conceived his own views as a comprehensive conception of how human beings have good reason to live; and it is relatively simple to acknowledge that it would have been intellectually more prudent in any case for him to have repudiated any such ambition. But what cannot plausibly be denied is that the claims to political authority of Marxism as a theory of practice are deeply involved with this essentially spurious semblance of comprehensiveness in scope, and that the full menace of this intellectual hubris can be legitimately read off the deformations which it has undergone in its modern historical career as a doctrine of state. At the very least the terms in which Marx lived his own intellectual life gave, from the point of view of his subsequent auditors, altogether too many hostages to fortune.

It is, of course, a familiar enough theme in conservative polemic to insist that Marxism has sacrificed its promise as an analytic approach to the understanding of society and history to a superstitious and morally illicit claim to political authority and political power. But, although there is a good deal of truth in this conservative judgement, it is not my wish here simply to reiterate it. Indeed, I should like instead to suggest that precisely such an elision between analytic understanding and political pretension is a standing peril for all modern social theories. It is the single key characteristic of any serious modern social theory as such that it must in this manner seek to close the gap between our individual social understandings and the official doctrines of particular societies, affirming, negating, qualifying, or simply inter-preting the latter. To close this gap would be to stretch across a space which there is no guarantee in principle that human imagination and understanding can in fact bridge. Insofar as the gap is in fact closed by veridical understanding in a particular society at a particular time, this analytic insight is in no way guaranteed to retain such a status in any other setting and at any other time. In a sense, most of modern social theory, where it does not simply consist of the more or less dreary reiteration of devout tautologies, is predominantly a forlorn hoarding of scraps of past understanding, reminiscences of fugitive episodes or passages of comprehension, recollected sometimes in tranquillity but often in rising anxiety: in Thomas Hobbes's phrase, 'decaying sense'.[2] To be sceptical about the truth status of modern social theories is not an exacting intellectual project. Considered as technical devices for understanding the reality of the societies in which we live and the extraordinarily complicated causal ecology within which these soci-eties subsist, the full resources of modern social theories (despite in some cases their formidable intellectual intricacy) are no more than a pitiful array of intellectual knick-knacks.

But, if to feel authentic scorn for the achievements of modern social theory is a pretty effortless feat, a mood of more or less complacent personal contempt is hardly today a satisfactory surrogate for a theory of society. The place of social theory in the material reality of modern societies is not simply a random mishap. If there is one thing which is as certain about our lives today as the intellectual impossibility of taking modern social theory wholly seriously, it is the absurdity of hoping simply to dispense with it.

The ideological synthesis of political authority or of the subjective plausibility of collective political projects in modern societies (Great Britain, Poland, Uganda) is certainly both intellectually and morally a perilous venture. (When was it ever not?) But if such synthesis is not even attempted in intellectual and moral good faith, it will simply be substituted for by even larger increments of pure violence than those to which we have already become accustomed. If a measure of social integration and compliance is not secured in societies today through opinion, it will simply be imposed by force, since the conditions in which we live today are practically unacceptable to almost all of us without such a measure of social integration and since, where this minimum is indeed under active threat from inside a society, anyone who can muster sufficient force to guarantee it will also muster a minimum of political consent. The reasons why the Argentine was still governable in 1981 and why the Soviet Union is still governed by the Communist Party today have more in common than would be likely to appeal to the political leaderships of either country.

The choice which is open to modern societies – and, more importantly, the choice which is widely *known* to be open to modern societies – is a choice between the extent to which their social integration rests simply on opinion and the extent to which it rests directly on force. There are no explicit social theories of any importance extant today which happily endorse the resting of social integration solely on force (and perhaps, under reasonably close inspection, there have not been many such theories in the past either).[3] But if social integration today is widely recognized as materially necessary and if, at least in secular societies, it is also expected ideally to rest its weight on secular opinion, one key question in modern social theory is how far such opinion can be sanely hoped to consist of true beliefs and how far it must be resignedly expected to consist of beliefs which are in fact false. Now this, of course, is a very old question in political theory and one which has on occasion been discussed even in the distant past with quite disconcerting frankness. But Plato's Noble Lie and Machiavelli's good laws *and* good arms (an Industrial Relations Act *and* the Special Air Services) were formulae addressed to societies too different from at least the industrial societies of today to be very helpfully directive to a modern social theorist. The modern social theorist who has made the most extensive and adventurous effort to think through this question is probably Jürgen Habermas.[4] It would be convenient to be able to present my own conception of this issue in his terms. But to do so would require a clearer understanding of his views than I can muster. Accordingly I pose the question instead in more homespun fashion for myself. It is not, it must be confessed, at all an easy question to pose without inadvertently begging it.

The key question is what one takes to be prior constraints on any valid social theory.[5] If, for example, one presumed, as methodological individualists in general would presume, that what must be taken theoretically as given in social theory is the consolidated existential substance (the experienced reality) of individual human lives, then society as such would be conceived as the pragmatic interrelations between such existences, externally, contingently, and causally. Social theory would be a purely causal mode of thought and the question of how false and how true politically relevant opinion in modern societies has to be or could be would be merely a question in natural science. It would not in fact be a question to which we would ever in practice be likely to know an accurate answer. But there would be nothing intrinsically bemusing about what type of question it was. For a more robust type of holist, by contrast, what is theoretically given would be located very differently. Substantive human reality would be society considered as a causal system and individual human lives would be just the medium in which its causal properties were implemented. And because reality in this conception lies elsewhere, and because human beings in general as self-conceived do not recognize it to do so human lives as self-conceived would in essence be nothing more than tissues of more or less deeply felt illusion.[6]

There is some disagreement, naturally, within this view as to whether all forms of human society are necessarily constituted by deluded persons or whether there could, or even will, come to be in some settings a type of society which would be veridically transparent to its members and would have its causal properties veridically mirrored in the consciousness of these members and rationally endorsed (or even chosen) by them accordingly. This question also can be (and indeed at times has been) conceived as a question in natural science, the science of history. But it is worth noticing how hard it is even to formulate it without employing fairly blatantly ethical terms. Thus expressed, these two broad theoretical conceptions, the individualist and the holist are diametrically opposite. But they do have something massive in common. Each of them is in one respect deeply alienated, seeing a constitutive aspect of human existence resolutely from the outside and implicitly dehumanizing it by doing so. Methodological individualists see human sociality as an external and contingent attribute of human beings and holists return the compliment by seeing human individuality as the fantasy of a creature constitutionally unable to apprehend its rigidly social location.

Now, each of these perspectives can and does disclose important features of the human situation. And since each can and at times does do so it is tempting in the first place to opt for the anodyne resolution that they should be seen not as antithetical but instead as complementary. This may appear a characteristically commonsensical Anglo-Saxon compromise, trading off a little mild intellectual scruffiness for the advantages of a broad and undogmatic view. Its only major inconvenience, perhaps, is that the two conceptions do at first glance appear in fact to contradict one another – and more importantly that this apparent contradiction does not, on closer inspection, dissolve effortlessly, displaying the irretrievable superficiality of the Anglo-Saxon understanding and its brute insensibility to the truths of dialectics. The reason this is so is extremely important. What lies behind the explicit contradictoriness of theories, each of which is founded upon what might well – and indeed should – seem an indisputable attribute of human beings, is a fundamental choice as to how to cast the theories in question. The motivation of this choice is a very obscure matter; but it is plain that what it goes back to in the history of Western epistemology is the project, fathered particularly by Descartes, of seeking to specify and comprehend what Bernard Williams has termed an 'absolute conception of reality',[7] a conception of possible objects of knowledge – the world and all that is in it is – which is in no way relativized to the causal contingencies of human experience. Whether or not this is a coherent project in relation to any possible objects of knowledge – mathematical, natural scientific, and so on – there are very good reasons for not regarding it as coherent in relation to many of the attributes of human beings.

Convinced methodological holists and convinced methodological individualists both seek a fundamentally external view of the character of human beings in society, not simply as a pragmatic and temporary intellectual convenience (a choice which would be easy enough to defend) but rather as a presumptive precondition for attaining *knowledge* about human beings in society. On a holist view individual self understanding is simply a factual given and a genuinely epistemic status is only open to it insofar as it furnishes an accurate apprehension of an individual's objective social location. On an individualist view such self-understanding is also potentially a factual given. But it is a factual given precisely because, in some not very clearly demarcated respects, it is epistemically incorrigible in principle; and social causality is conceived as operating around its edges, externally to it and in response to its causal weight.

Now, human beings certainly do possess self-understandings. Human self-understanding is existentially actual. We all do have our own understandings of ourselves, however vague and prevaricatory and externally grotesque these may be. And the self-understanding of all human beings is deeply interwoven with their understanding of the social settings of their lives, with, that is to say, their amateur social theories. (Amateur social theory has always been, and will always remain, partly constitutive of human existence.) But although it is clearly appropriate, reckoning in the idiom of more or less brute fact, to take the self-understanding of human beings simply as existentially actual, it is also quite clearly inappropriate to confine oneself, in seeking to conceive such self-understanding, to an idiom of more or less brute fact. Human beings understand themselves the way they do and not differently. But they notoriously do not for the most part understand themselves especially well. (You may understand yourselves perfectly. But I must confess to finding much of myself a fairly impenetrable mystery.) And because all persons' self-understanding is predicated in part on their amateur social theory, on their conception of the meaning and pragmatic character of their more or less intimate or distant relations with many other human beings, this opacity in self-understanding is not just something crudely internal to their own minds or bodies, a matter of the deep penetralia of the unconscious or some theoretical surrogate for this. It is, in addition, a relatively simple function of the limits of their social vision, a direct mark of the limitations of their amateur social theories and the miscellaneous contingencies of their personal social experience.

Putting the point still more crassly, it is not possible satisfactorily to defend the view that the way to understand human beings is to think of them as creatures whose properties stop at the edges of their own bodies. For a long time this view drew powerful support from an interpretation of the epistemological implications of the scientific revolution. But today its popularity is plainly on the wane and it is hard to see it ever being resuscitated simply on grounds of intellectual plausibility. The main individualist alternative to this view, that we should think of human beings above all as creatures whose properties stop at the edges of their own minds, also draws support from an interpretation of the epistemological implications of the scientific revolution; and, unlike the view that human beings are in essence simply physically bounded creatures set within a physical universe, this more mentalist conception is today véry much on the advance – and indeed wreaking some little havoc even within the philosophy of natural science itself. But what is important for my purpose is not the adequacy or precision of such a mentalist conception of the human individual, still less its current intellectual popularity, but rather the fact that even if it is in principle adequate and can in practice be made precise (two very optimistic assumptions), the edges of our minds today stretch so far spatially and temporally that they take in, however fecklessly and ineffectively, a large portion of human experience as a whole. This is not, of course, to say that each of us in any sense understands human experience as a whole, a notion which, if intelligible at all lacks any shred of plausibility. What it means, rather, is that our self-understanding today is predicated upon, incorporates references to, forms of human social interaction which stretch across the entire globe and forms of temporal awareness which take in many past generations and at least some hoped for (or feared) future generations. Our self-understanding today has this bewildering (and indeed bemused) spatial and chronological extension, of course, because of the extent to which, and the pace at which, the world as a whole has changed – and changed over the last century in particular. It is important, too, to realize that this overextended consciousness which today we have no choice but seek somehow to incorporate into our conceptions of ourselves is not a prerogative of, or a burden confined to, intellectuals at major universities, but, rather, a fate incumbent on the vast majority of human beings now alive.

Even in the furthest recesses of the Ghanaian rain forest today illiterate cocoa labourers know quite well that the social causality within which their lives must be lived out is bounded not by the hamlets in which they reside nor by the forest itself nor even the territorial borders of the state of Ghana (which many of them have crossed in order to secure a cash income at all) but rather by the world cocoa market and the consuming tastes and habits and capacities of the populations of very distant and alien countries. No doubt most of them understand this vast and intricate causal field very poorly indeed. (Don't we all in our own case? You and I, Sir Keith Joseph, and Mr Tony Benn? International economic exchange is the major witchcraft zone of modern experience.) But what matters is that even in the depths of rural Africa modern selves, the selves of today, *must* incorporate into their amateur social theories, in however gingerly a fashion, a conception of how global social and economic causality bears upon their own lives.[8]

All of this, to be sure, is only a fact about modern history. In itself it may cast a little doubt on the practical wisdom of picking individuals as the explanatory units of social theory merely on grounds of their palpable determinacy; but it implies nothing at all about the fundamental terms in which human beings have good reason to understand their societies and their selves. Once it is recognized as a fact about modern history, however, and once we have drawn the implications which it presents for the forlornness of the major extant traditions of social understanding, we can perhaps reconsider the possibilities for social understanding in a somewhat humbler and more patient mood.

And perhaps, if we are lucky and persevere, we may even eventually engender a form of social understanding which is less heavily toxic in its impact.

I have tried in outline to trace the process of intoxication to two very different sorts of factor, one clearly an aspect of the history of thought and the other more crudely an aspect of the history of society. The peculiar and menacing arrogance of modern social theory is a product, I have tried to suggest, of grandiose epistemological pretension and of the place of university teachers and secular intellectuals more generally in the modern division of labour.[9] Neither of these factors is arbitrary or irrational. But it is a simple and sober judgement to make by now that, at least in the field of social theory, each has greatly overreached itself. Social authority in the modern world (at least when explicitly taking the initiative) takes its stand on the presumed cognitive prowess of intellectuals: Lenin or Hayek, Milton Friedman or Stuart Holland. It does so insofar as it both needs, and recognizes the need, to understand what it is doing. And intellectuals duly respond by casting their beliefs as to what is desirable or possible in a cognitively professional idiom, modelled as best they can on the sciences of nature.

III

It would not, needless to say, be a better idea to seek instead to found social authority today on explicit whim, or to replace the advice of secular intellectuals in its entirety by that of astrologers. But it certainly would be an improvement, a lengthy stride towards detoxification, for professional social theorists to learn to express their guesses as to what is desirable or possible in a more intellectually democratic and a less cognitively pretentious idiom.[10] In social theory at least, the charms of the absolute standpoint have been strictly those of an illicit title to authority. The eyes of God offer a viewpoint which may well have been a necessary condition for the very idea of the absolute conception. But human beings cannot see themselves through the eyes of God and not even social theorists are well advised to claim to see their fellows from this vantage point. Pragmatically considered through the eyes of God, the space of human existence in its entirety, perhaps, should be taken simply as a homogeneous causal field and one which is not ontologically broken up into discrete units at the level of individual or society. But we, as human beings, certainly have no idea of how to conceive it as such; and we have at present no good reason to believe that to succeed in conceiving it accurately as such lies within the scope of human cognitive powers at all. To design social theories to meet such an epistemological standard is in itself merely to fantasize an imaginary cognitive potency for ourselves. But by doing so we risk worse consequences than that of simply making fools of ourselves. In particular we risk coming to believe in our possession of such powers and coming to feel a resulting entitlement to thrust aside the amateur social theories of others (and the professional social theories of our rivals) in order to implement the epistemic insight which we ourselves supposedly possess.

It could not, of course, generally make sense to will our society to be organized and governed on the basis of ends which we do not favour and causal beliefs which we suppose to be false. Even the most professional social theorist is an amateur social theorist under the skin. In the first instance, at least, one amateur social theorist, one vote. And, within the relevant social circles, to will defeat for the presumptively false professional social theories of our rivals is simply a criterion of sincerity for our believing our own social beliefs. But the relation between our own professional social theories and the amateur social theories of others is a good deal more delicate. Any purely causal social theory will have to treat much amateur social theory in a decisively external way. But no human being (professional social theorist or not) has any right because she or he regards the beliefs of other human beings from a causal point of view simply and exclusively as matters of fact and from an epistemic point of view simply as false beliefs, to treat them from a practical point of view as politically illicit and lacking in weight.[11] Or if, for harshly Machiavellian reasons, any human being does have such a right, she or he possesses it not *qua* professional social theorist but *qua* amateur social theorist, doing the best she or he can in the face of the odious importunities of politics. *Salus populi suprema lex.* The worst temptation in social theory, greatly exacerbated by academic professionalization and by the increasing political prominence of social theory in the practical reproduction of modern societies, is to treat a social theory as an external and technical device for augmenting the political entitlements of the self or depleting the real identities of other human beings.[12] To resist this temptation at all effectively it is above all else necessary to try to form a conception of the relations between identity and social causality in human beings which can be trusted to remain fairly stable when applied both to other human beings and to one's own self.

In relation to ourselves we certainly cannot afford to regard social theories merely as wholly external intellectual devices because we in fact conceive ourselves and fashion ourselves partly through the social theories which we form. (On a behaviourist vision of human nature this might seem a somewhat murky thought; but on a more mentalist view it could scarcely be more blatantly obvious.) No more can we afford to conceive human beings (including ourselves) as entities epistemically external to the vagaries of their actual consciousness. We cannot afford to do so, not for reasons of compulsive narcissism – because to do so would inflict such painful wounds on our self-esteem – but because to do so would jam human practical reason across the board. Human beings could not act at all without possessing some conception of themselves as agents; and they could not have good reason to act without possessing conceptions of themselves as agents which they have good reason to possess.

Social theory is a branch of human practical reason and its obsession with epistemology over the last three centuries, however historically intelligible, has made it serve the requirements of human practice very poorly indeed. Only if we learn to expect very much less of it do we stand a reasonable chance of refashioning it so that it can serve us rather better. At least one constraint on any humanly acceptable social theory is that it should not impair the adequacy of the conceptions which its exponents hold either of themselves or of other human beings, *as* human agents. It should, that is to say, at the very least exclude unjustified contempt or sentimentality *throughout* its conceptions of what human action is like and of why this occurs as it does. The importance of closing the gap between the understanding of the self and the understanding of others is obvious enough here; and it requires no great feat of the imagination to grasp the potential political implications of the persistence of such gaps. (To take only a single example: one can be confident that human beings cannot in practice dispense with a conception of themselves as agents. If therefore they adopt a social theory (such as that of Professor Althusser) which repudiates such a conception in its entirety, what they will in fact be left with is a wholly external (and implicitly contemptuous) vision of the agency of most human beings and a vision of themselves and perhaps of their more intimate political associates in which this external and contemptuous vision is compulsively suspended, to be replaced by one which could scarcely avoid sentimentality and self-deception.)

Within political practice, very broadly considered, the role of social theory over the last two centuries has been at least as much one of assigning blame as it has one of guiding political action. In itself a purely causal and instrumental social theory (if such could be discovered) might at first glance seem well enough suited to the guidance of political action. But one need not be surprised that such social theories mutate fairly drastically, under the pressure of the demand to assign blame for the more unacceptable aspects of history as directly encountered. Powerful theories of whom to blame soon construct strong categorical distinctions between trustworthy selves and untrustworthy others; and by doing so they augment their sparely causal contentions with expressively more implicating facilities for human identification. The initial pressures towards this mutation may be instrumental and clear-headed enough. But their consequences rapidly cease to be so. Causal understanding and corporate political self-righteousness become steadily harder to disentangle. What begins as a means for understanding the world and for recruiting followers to share this understanding becomes in due course a hysterical compound of projective suspicion and analytical confusion, in which political entrepreneurs are every bit as deeply mired as those whom they have previously persuaded and in which political self-righteousness drastically impairs causal understanding.

IV

Here, plainly enough, we come to the politics of today, albeit very briefly and in no very constructive spirit. (If I wanted to get anywhere at all to which I could genuinely wish to make my way, I would certainly not start from here and now.) There is little dispute today that this country is in a very bad way and rather little expectation that it will avoid soon being in a decidedly worse one. The causes of a great deal of its predicament are by now rather well understood. Many of them, indeed, are frequently mentioned in public discussion. A few even appear in the political debate between the present government of the country under Mrs Thatcher and its only politically viable alternative – those bits which fit fairly effortlessly into a justification of the demented policies of this government and, by contrast, those bits which can serve to highlight some of the more reckless acts of vandalism which it has perpetrated. The disparity between the extent of available understanding and the paucity of this understanding which is politically espoused and deployed is extremely striking – and all the more striking because the intensity of the social crisis which we face, both immediately and in the longer term, is no longer seriously denied by any political actors. No doubt the degree of omission and caricature in these political interpretations of what is to be done here and now is a fairly direct product of the intensity of the crisis. In routine political conditions a largely undirective official social theory or one which simply endorses a stolid persistence in current practices is easy to accept. In conditions of crisis the view that something in particular needs to be done is harder to resist. The two candidates for official social theories at present (the political visions of the dominant groups in the two major parties) accordingly each prescribe very drastic actions. Each promises in effect to the amateur social theorists who make up the electorate (and indeed the labour force) that if it is permitted to act as it wishes (to make its social theory the official social theory and implement this through the machinery of government) and if the citizens behave as it enjoins them, the predicament of the country can be successfully eluded. In each case the social theories offered insofar as they are determinate, clearly owe much to the past labours of professional social theorists: in the case of the Thatcher government, whose policies are in a number of ways unusually determinate (if not particularly coherent), to some variety or other of monetarist economics; in the case of the Labour Party at present to a more nebulous range of intellectual sources. In neither case do the social theories as publicly proffered possess a shred of intellectual plausibility as a means for dealing with the present difficulties of the country, let alone with the problems which it is likely to face in the future.

It is easiest to discuss the main defects of the present government's vision since it is so hard to get clear answers about anything from the present leadership of the Labour Party and so difficult to be confident where precisely the leadership of the Labour Party should now be deemed to reside. (All that can perhaps be said on the last score is that it is extremely hard to believe that a combination of high tariff barriers, extensive nationalization, and freezing existing labour allocation in an economy administered by the man who gave us our impressive fleet of Concordes is a promising guarantee in even the medium-term future for the existing living standards of the British working class.) About the Thatcher government, however, it is easy to say all too much. I will confine myself to making two points. The first is about the incoherence of Mrs Thatcher's economic views as a *political* doctrine. The view that high interest rates and a commitment to lowering public expenditure would in due course force down the level of wage settlements because of the huge rise in unemployment it would threaten is quite incompatible with the general theory of economic motivation to which Mrs Thatcher is committed.[13] On this theory, for the level of unemployment to act as a threat in any particular wage negotiation it must be the unemployment of the workers negotiating which is directly in question. As a political threat, therefore, the menace of unemployment can only hold down wage levels rapidly and generally if the working class shows an extraordinarily high level of class solidarity – a level of class solidarity which is utterly incompatible with the theory of economic motivation on which all Mrs Thatcher's policies rest! It is, of course, true that to obliterate the British economy will have a substantial effect on wage settlements along with the rest of our lives. But it is important to try to remember that the Thatcher government's policies began as a comparatively rational (if misguided) attempt to change British economic activities and not simply to end them.

The second point is a little less crude. It involves in the first instance inquiring innocently why it was that Mrs Thatcher (and Sir Keith Joseph[14]) ever expected the organized British working class to exhibit such extraordinary class solidarity. The explanation, it seems likely, lies in the extreme simplicity of Mrs Thatcher's social vision and the extent to which she did genuinely perceive the organized working class as a single bloc adversary, in the short term at least a unitary political enemy. Within the legally somewhat underpoliced zone of civil society, the zone of family life and of production but also of flying pickets, the past votes and the industrial power of the working class had established conditions in which profitable production was impossible. But the past votes of the working class were of course civic actions, actions directed at the order of public law and the state; and within the order of public law and the state the British working class since 1945 has attained a reasonably high and stable level of class solidarity. An economic policy which could lower real wages and a political thrust which could transfer civic dutifulness and a long-term sense of collective interest from an undeserving social democratic state to a very abstract conception of rational conduct in the labour market, taken together, might do wonders. Class solidarity, at least amongst the working class, could be evicted from politics where it could only do harm and transposed deftly into private economic conduct where it would take as its goal the long-term public good of restoring profitability through the economy, instead of the short-term private good of maximizing individual wages. This plainly is the politics of fantasy – and at least as much so as the celebrated views of Mr Benn.

Few, perhaps, would accept the justice of this description of the premisses of Mrs Thatcher's policies. But however ungenerous it may seem as a description of the Prime Minister's better intentions, it does, I trust, bring out the potential perils of taking stray bits and pieces of professional social theory and pretending, at first to others but then no doubt rapidly to oneself, and these stray bits and pieces do genuinely articulate the causal dynamics of the extraordinarily complicated space which extends from all of us as amateur social theorists to the structures of the nation state of which we are citizens and the international economy on which we haplessly depend for our livelihoods.

What requires emphasis is not the peril of uniting such shreds and tatters of causal understanding with power, a union to which there may in any case be no real causal alternative, since full causal understanding of society may be naturally impossible for human beings and indeed the very idea of such understanding for human beings may simply be internally incoherent. What must be stressed, rather, is the practical political importance of seeing whatever shreds and tatters of causal understanding a government can muster in direct relation to the amateur social theories of ordinary citizens. To see what, if anything, is to be done here and now is to see on what terms and for what purposes we could rationally cooperate with each other. To implement such a vision in practice (supposing it to be accurate) would be above all to discover how in practice we could learn to trust one another to cooperate. Because what is in question is what is to be done, the historical constraints on the second (roughly, the class history of the country) are also constraints on the first. Perhaps in fact over any lengthy period of time there simply *are* no such terms, or no such terms which include even the great bulk of the population – in which case the actual future of this country is likely to be grim. A hazy sense of these points is in fact rather prominent in the public pronouncements of Mr Benn, though it does not appear to be accompanied there by any serious respect for social causality at all. Neither Mrs Thatcher's sincere refusal to listen to the people, nor Mr Benn's insincere eagerness to be instructed by them, exemplifies a very satisfactory conception of the role of social theory in political action; but each does express a real feeling for the major blemishes of the other.

V

I have tramped a number of times round a rather small cage and I certainly cannot promise in conclusion any neat way out through the bars. But what I would like to do in conclusion is to consider once again very briefly the relations between amateur, professional, and official social theories and political action and to do so in the context of the very old-fashioned questions in political theory and ethics of how we have good reason to perceive ourselves and how it makes sense for us to live our lives. We may take these last two questions very much in the mood of the Platonic dialogues particularly the *Gorgias* and the *Republic* – not, of course because the theoretical answers which Plato offers to them in those dialogues are either clear or convincing – but because the questions themselves have never been expressed with more urgency. If the way in which we have good reason to live our own lives is, as Socrates argues against Callicles not as more or less discreet brigands[15] but rather with the principled trustworthiness which is a precondition for friendship and community, then the same should hold good for other human beings too. And if this is not the way in which we have good reason to live our lives, then we cannot reasonably expect others to presume it appropriate for themselves either. Civic dutifulness and a genuinely egoistic maximization can be fitted together, both in theory and in practice, only by a measure of intellectual inattention.[16] And this is true over time either way – whether we adopt sentimental or moralistic views of ourselves as moral agents and cynical views of others, or espouse our own cynicism self-referentially and yet expect that others will pay the costs of the moral expectations which we solemnly proffer to them. On the whole professional social theories take the first form, while official social theories (since they have to solicit the cooperation of subjects or citizens and since governing is so troublesome) more frequently take the second. Professional social theories are very much theories cast in the third person. (You and I, we're good friends – and perhaps even good citizens if we choose to be so – but they – they're egoists to a person: just in social life for what they can get out of it.)

If we return once more to the political predicament of this country and ask again for what purposes we could rationally cooperate with one another – and trust each other to do so in actuality – the dangers of this split in our human vision become very apparent. Taking the class history of the country and the present organization of production within it as given (as for the moment we must) it is not very plausible that there are many purposes for which everyone does have good reason to cooperate with one another, and the possibilities of rational trust extending all the way across this space seem slimmer still. The intrinsic difficulties of making capitalist production as such an object of allegiance are immense and probably insuperable. If we consider in the first instance for what purposes we might rationally cooperate with one another as a question of what it makes sense for us politically to do, it is apparent that any third-person theory is ill-shaped to take the choice for us. Third-person theories can certainly draw our attention to important causal considerations – in particular to impossibilities and probabilities. They can tell us (or at least try to tell us) what might work and what certainly cannot be brought about. But there is not, and could not be, anything else to tell us politically what to *do* but the amateur social theories which we possess as ordinary agents[17]. Collective political and social life (even the reproduction of the capitalist mode of production) is not something which can be done for us by a government or a party. It is the *living* of *our* lives. The living of our lives is something for which professional social theory has (and perhaps can in principle have) very little respect. And at least when politically applied from above (when espoused as official social theory) what professional social theory does is to expropriate the existential reality of individual lives. As official social theories, as doctrines of state, all professional social theories are wildly undemocratic – whatever formal role they may allot to the term democracy in their public self-justifications. Democracy is simply the political form of fraternity, the recognition that the species to which we belong is a species comprised of amateur social theorists and that rational cooperation and trust for its members must always depend in large part upon their actual beliefs and sentiments. Fraternity is a very varying historical possibility. But it can only *start* where professional social theory leaves off.

It is not that there is something misguided or vicious in the attempt to understand social causality – or indeed that there is any alternative to making such an attempt as best we all can. Still less is it the case that social causality is potentially to be eluded or is somehow unreal. The view that there is no such thing as social causality could not in fact form part of the amateur social theory of anyone at all. One could not hold it and live a human life. The fantasy of a wholly causally transparent social world, a world so clear that life within it would have neither need nor opportunity for trust, is simply a political sedative. Men, as John Locke said, *live* upon trust.[18] They behave as they behave and act as they act on grounds which are necessarily for the most part insufficient. Rational political cooperation amongst them requires a great deal of courage and good will. But they cannot be offered any rationally superior alternative to political cooperation. Political authority today in most countries has for the most part given up the sacred. But to replace this, where it retains any ideological pretensions at all, it has clutched to itself instead a style of social theory which in epistemic terms is merely a pale shadow of the sacred. It has done so, in effect, in order to retain the key prerogative of authority, the entitlement to speak *de haut en bas*. It is certainly a government's business to attempt as best it can to understand social causality. But it is equally certain that any government's success in understanding social causality will be extremely limited. All a public authority can offer its citizens, at the level of intention, in this respect is the sincere attempt to understand social causality and the frank avowal of such understanding as it does hold. Rational cooperation between citizens and government will necessarily depend upon how cogently this understanding meshes with and modifies the amateur social theories of the citizens at large.

Political authority can certainly be heuristic. But it cannot appropriately and in general be didactic, because there is nothing determinate for it to teach. Collective social and political life is not a classroom, with masters (or mistresses) and pupils. In the end there is simply *us*, trying to decide as best we can and on the basis of necessarily limited powers, what we have good reason to do. It is this more modest and democratic vision of the nature of modern political authority which we would have learnt by now if we truly understood the history of social theory. It is this to which we need individually and collectively to discipline our imaginations. And unless we in this country do manage collectively to learn it and learn it very fast indeed, our political and social future here is likely to be excessively ugly.

Chapter 8

Identity, modernity and the claim to know better

IN his exciting and imaginative recent study *Philosophy and the Mirror of Nature*,[1] Professor Richard Rorty attempts both to trace the historical constitution of and to dissipate the intellectual authority of a particular conception of academic philosophy, that institutionalized in university departments of philosophy in the English-speaking world. From the viewpoint of the rest of the world this may appear at first glance to be a theme of somewhat parochial relevance. But any such semblance, is, I think, essentially deceptive. For, to take the most important institutionalized adversary culture in the modern world, the official Marxist theory of communist countries in all its current variety, the conception of the nature of *Marxist* philosophy (the true theory of the nature of knowledge of nature and of society) which it presupposes is simply one of the minor branches of the intellectual lineage traced by Rorty. (Minor, of course, that is to say, in degree of conceptual deviation, not in degree of political importance.) And in those countries in the world today whose official culture eludes to any significant extent the hegemony of either the academic culture of the Anglo-American world or of one variety or other of official Marxism, their residual cultural autonomy is seldom particularly – and perhaps never wholly – assured in the alternative account which it succeeds in offering of the status and meaning of the cultural core of modern academic philosophy in the West, the sciences of nature.

The story which Rorty tells is intricate and protracted, and virtually every element in it is open to vigorous dispute. At its centre is a picture of the relations between human thought and non-human as well as human nature in which human thought ideally can – and should seek to – capture these in a mental and linguistic idiom which reproduces them perfectly. The goal of 'Western philosophy' as Rorty conceives this, a particular academic ideology of the nineteenth and twentieth centuries identifying itself in the perspective of the entire history of Western thought, is the perfect vision which Plato imagined so enticingly. (Hence the metaphor of the mirror in Rorty's title.) What philosophy aspires to do is to *mirror* nature. When it succeeds in so doing in its own eyes, what it does, since philosophers do not in fact paint pictures or compose photographs, is to describe nature the way nature wishes to be described. It is the idea that nature has any particular preferences between human descriptions on which Rorty lavishes his most graphic scorn.[2] In contrast to this conception, he offers an alternative, also drawn from a number of sources within the institutional history of philosophy as an academic 'discipline' in Western universities, from Wittgenstein and Heidegger but perhaps most importantly from the distinctively American tradition of Pragmatism and especially the thought of John Dewey. Pragmatism explicitly acknowledges the wilfulness of human thought: not merely its creativity, as any historically sensitive philosophy of natural science must necessarily do, but also the abundant discretion which human thought enjoys, and which it cannot without self-deception elude, in its characterizations of reality. The limits to the legitimate wilfulness of human thought, Pragmatism supposes, are set by its incapacity to avoid distressing surprises from nature, by crude predictive failure. And these limits, of course, are precisely those which any state-articulated corporate intellectual culture (not to say any operating state apparatus) will do its utmost to acknowledge. No one today aims their weapons at random on the fond assumption that if God wishes the targets to succumb, He will secure His end irrespective of deliberate human mediation and, if He does not so wish, no human performance will cause them to do so: least of all those who belong to either of the two main sides in the protracted Holy War of Iran today. The pragmatic efficacy of modern natural science and of the technology which it renders possible enjoys virtually universal cultural recognition, if widely varying cultural enthusiasm; and the distribution of hostility, ambivalence, and zest towards it differs today at least as markedly within particular national societies (like Great Britain) as it does between them. But within particular national societies it has a somewhat different significance to that which it bears between them. The relations between technique, theoretical knowledge, and military and economic power was a major and bemusing theme of nineteenth-century imperialist advance.[3] The problems which it posed for societies outside the West, both locally[4] and nationally, were very obviously cultural from the outset. The intellectual history of China, to take a crucial example, turned for nearly a century on the question of how to secure the practical advantages of Western technique without undergoing the cultural blight which threatened to accompany it.[5] In due

course, and perhaps inevitably, the balance of intentions tipped decisively and a growing proportion of Chinese intellectuals in effect
deserted the solidary culture of a China which had millennially dominated its own private world[6] and affiliated themselves instead with the
invasive culture of the barbarians.[7] The obvious alternative to 'Chinese
essence, Western accidents' was a cultural version of the Quisling
solution.[8]

This story continues to cast a long shadow. There are few societies in
the world today (Japan, perhaps, being the most prominent of them)
whose intelligentsias can plausibly be claimed to have solved the
problem of how to master those aspects of Western 'rationality' which
engender economic and military power without inadvertently finding
themselves to have become in part cultural 'running dogs' of imperialism. The experience of economic and military power at the receiving
end is intimately involved with the experience of cultural subjection.
And, because of the role which control over technical progress continues to play in sustaining the political and economic viability of the
advanced capitalist societies against increasingly effective political
pressures to indigenize the control of production and to increase its
local benefits,[9] the relation between the cultures of societies which
dominate the process of technical invention and the more practical
prerequisites for their continued domination will also continue to be
experienced by the intelligentsias of other societies with bewilderment
and dismay.[10] At some level, economic and military power in the world
today just does rest on a very practically vindicated claim to be better at
knowing; and it can be effectively restrained, insofar as it can be
restrained at all, only by seeking to meet it within its own cognitive
idiom. The extent and limits of the claim to be genuinely better at
knowing are not merely central issues in the academic tradition of
Western philosophy; they are also central issues in the political and
cultural life of the modern world. What is at stake in them is not merely
cultural meaning; it is also power and economic welfare.

The central motif of modern philosophy, as sketched by Rorty, is the
primacy of epistemology, of the theory of what it is to *know*, in
contrast with simply to believe or to presume. It is not necessary here
either to question or to endorse this account as an exercise in the
history of ideas, let alone as a theoretical critique of a mode of
philosophy centred on epistemology. What is important for present
purposes is the boldness with which Rorty brings out the singularity of
the role of epistemology within modern philosophy and the skill with
which he expounds the contradictions to which this cognitive adven-
ture has given rise. He is, of course, by no means the only important

Western thinker to have emphasized this issue in recent years. Jürgen Habermas and Charles Taylor in social theory and Alasdair MacIntyre and Thomas Nagel in ethics have all in different ways underlined the alarming (or invigorating) instabilities in conceptions of knowledge, rationality, moral identity, and human values which have been engendered by this scientistic conception of epistemic validity and by its more or less hysterical (and dialectically related) rejection. These instabilities are not simply a product of intellectual feebleness or indolence. They are intrinsic to deeply grounded and resilient structures of modern belief, structures profoundly adapted to the logic of capitalist production (as of its at least formally socialist competitors) and heavily marked by the revolutionary advance of the sciences of nature. Modernity is the cultural condition which results from the prevalence of these structures, the highly uneven but extremely vigorous impact upon the beliefs of contemporary populations of modes of perceiving and inquiring which have been nurtured in carefully insulated and exceedingly distinctive social settings. In cultural terms, the motors of modernity are the advancement of science and the competitive dynamics, within the varying tolerances of different societies, of institutionalized academic cultures. The key dilemma of modernity for those who do not belong merely by birth, primary socialization, and intellectual formation to some version or other of the hegemonic culture of the modern world, whose initial social identity is not itself constituted out of this culture, is how to distinguish those aspects of the culture which genuinely exemplify the capacity to know better from those which instead exemplify only its brazen and deceptive claim to do so. For it is the ability to draw this distinction which alone makes it possible to discriminate an extension of cognitive capacity which no human agent or human society could have good reason to reject in itself from a cognitively arbitrary erosion of personal or social identity by the action of alien force. (The rub comes, of course, when, as is perhaps usually the case, culture as directly encountered in this context contains unmistakable elements of both.)

What philosophers aspire to do (and for the most part presume themselves corporately able to do) is, as Rorty sneers, to know 'something about knowing which nobody else knows so well'.[11] Whether or not this is, as he supposes, an absurd professional self-image – because there simply is nothing general of the kind to be known – it is just such an equation of a particular culture with superior epistemic power which is paradigmatic for the political struggle for cultural hegemony in the modern world. This paper sketches the extremely strong grounds which have emerged in two or three fields of recent Western thinking for regarding any such equation with deep scepticism and suggests that the internal antinomies which have become apparent in these fields of Western culture require a quite different image of the relations between cultures from the occidental arrogance of American modernization theorists of the 1960s or their crude antithesis, the idiot relativism of presuming the cultures of all national units (and thus presumably of no sub-national units) to deserve an equal and untrammelled degree of credal respect. The fields which I shall principally mention are those of moral theory, of the theory of personal identity, and of social theory. In each of them I will trace, in the sketchiest and crassest of outlines, the impact of the epistemological obsessions of Western philosophy upon existential values, presenting its outcome as an instance of the self-contradictions of purely instrumental reason and arguing that this latter conception is no longer coherent even as a philosophical conception of the sciences of nature and hence that it is radically incapable of justifying an authority over the existential substance of human lives, whether those of single individuals or those of entire societies. A Darwinian struggle between cultures is intrinsic to the political and social life of a world as practically integrated as our own, however unnatural the selective mechanisms which sometimes determine its course. But some of the principal intellectual devices which are deployed within this struggle today pretend to an intellectual weight which is almost entirely bogus. Cultural struggle is guaranteed by the material organization of the world in which we live. (There is simply no set of possible collective actions open to mankind today – short of destroying the ecosphere – which could give to such struggle its quietus.) But the intellectual weapons which prove most efficacious within it are neither materially guaranteed nor self-legitimating in any automatic fashion. Here, and especially as intellectuals, we retain a wide range of real choice; and the choice to discard some of the more malign and deceptive pretensions of occidental rationality can at least open up a more democratic and potentially sustaining dialogue between cultures. (In a less insulated and institutionalized sense, the embracing of this possibility parallels Rorty's plea[12] for replacing a foundationalist by an edificatory conception of philosophy.) The task to which Rorty summons an academic philosophy, purged of self-deception and sensitized to its own historical formation, that of opening the imagination to the immense range of possible valid understandings, is no less appropriate an ideal for cultural relations of a less specialized character.

Perhaps the most graphic vignette of the antinomies of an alienated conception of human reason has come in Alasdair MacIntyre's remarkable study *After Virtue* (1981). In his book MacIntyre resumes themes with which he has long been concerned and which he has already treated with great force and imagination in his *A Short History of Ethics* (1967) and *Against the Self-Images of the Age* (1971). But *After Virtue* is a bolder and somewhat more systematic volume than its predecessors, and its argument offers a striking complement to *Philosophy and the Mirror of Nature*. What it does is to set out the impossibility of grounding human values rationally within an epistemological viewpoint which distinguishes radically, with Kant, between fact and value, and to trace with subtlety and power the working through of this impossibility not merely in the history of ethics as an academic discipline but also in the phenomenology of popular moral consciousness, at least amongst the relatively highly educated classes in the Western world. A necessary outcome of the philosophical legitimation of the view that human values are not and cannot be grounded in fact, MacIntyre argues, is the technical meta-ethical theory named 'emotivism', associated with the American philosopher C. L. Stevenson and, more uproariously, with the youthful A. J. Ayer of *Language, Truth and Logic*. Emotivism is now a somewhat passé doctrine in academic philosophy. The breeze of fashion has long passed it by, though some of its theses have reappeared more recently in a richer and more guarded form in the writings of such moral philosophers as Bernard Williams. The central tenet of emotivism was (and is) that moral statements do not describe any aspect of reality and do not report what is true or false. They simply express the sentiments of those who utter them. There are well-known philosophical objections to this view: that such reports of their feelings are certainly not what those who make moral statements suppose themselves to be saying; that conceptually strong formulations of disapproval do not necessarily emanate from those who themselves do authentically feel strongly (or even trouble hypocritically to pretend that *they* feel strongly) about the matter in question; and so on. But logical objections to any form of 'descriptivism' (to use the term favoured by R. M. Hare), if these are to be accepted and not rejected as MacIntyre urges, do encourage a fundamentally emotivist vision of the nature of moral discourse, even if they do not necessarily lead their proponents to regard emotivism as at all an adequate theory of the meaning of moral propositions. And MacIntyre is certainly in order in asking whether, in the light of the chaotic heterogeneity of normative concepts touted in Western moral arguments, an emotivist account does not indeed describe with considerable fidelity what most frequently occurs nowadays in such arguments: the direct conflict of wills and sentiments, lightly cloaked by the invocation of standards, the authority and conclusiveness of which is now entirely bogus.

This disjunction can be looked at (and indeed is in part considered by MacIntyre himself) from two very different angles. One angle is offered by the practical realities of Western social organization. Seen in this light, the array of moral categories which are at work in Western moral dispute today (rights, utility, justice, liberty, etc.) do not merely happen to conflict logically with one another in their demands. Many or all of them are also now sundered from the cultural traditions and social contexts which gave them in the past a certain determinacy and authority and cast loose in a social setting with which they are irremediably at odds.[13] MacIntyre himself appears to regard this state of affairs with surprise as well as dismay. But it may well be doubted whether it really is at all an unusual cultural predicament in which for human beings to find themselves. From this angle, emotivist moral discourse is a form of discourse necessitated by an existing set of cultural contradictions, themselves in turn no doubt in part a consequence of structural contradictions in social and economic (and perhaps political) organization. The second angle is very different. It would treat the alienated conception of practical reason (which is a precondition for regarding every version of descriptivism as necessarily false) as a product of the epistemological trajectory of Western thought since Descartes and the scientific revolution and would present the logical chasm between fact and value as the appropriate consummation, the true triumph of Western philosophy, as though a mode of analysis of non-human nature which fondly hoped that it had succeeded in describing this as it itself deeply desired to be described could somehow enforce upon human beings a practice of describing themselves and each other which no human being could authentically and comprehendingly accept in relation to himself or herself. Behind this epistemological trajectory of Western philosophy there lies a single idea, perhaps formed partially in the first instance by Greek philosophers but set forward most strikingly and influentially in the seventeenth century by Descartes, that of an absolute conception of reality[14] – a conception of how the world is which is in no way relativized to human perceptual powers or human cultural categories. The absolute conception of reality is a conception from which all anthropocentric properties have been purged, a mode of describing and explaining nature in terms which fully acknowledge its independence of human will and desire. Teasingly, but perhaps also naturally, the forward thrust of this conception, which has served so decisively to separate the human from the natural and to disenchant the world, has been closely accompanied by the extension of the technical and social control of man over nature. So that a species which has established itself to an astonishing (if precarious) degree as the controller of nature has become at the same time bizarrely imprisoned within a conception of itself which grossly slights its own creativity and capacity for agency.

MacIntyre's tentative riposte to this débâcle is to seek to resuscitate an Aristotelian conception of the virtues as potentially life-long projects which link the self-understanding of an individual's life, the moral and emotional energies which this makes available for self-development, and the social setting within which any human life as a whole must be seen if it is to be coherently fashioned and realized. In advancing this alternative, what he particularly assails is the epistemic basis of the split between fact and value and the grossly alienated and disseminated representation of the substance and setting of moral agency suggested by modern utilitarianism. (It is reasonable to see utilitarianism not simply as a natural ideological counterpart to capitalist production, an idiom purpose-built for the celebration of capitalist rationality and one which exercises extensive imaginative influence upon the self-understanding of would-be socialist states, but also as a natural extension into moral philosophy of the image of man until recently presupposed by the great bulk of Western philosophy of natural science. This affinity is present in both of the main readings of utilitarianism – as a crudely aggregative hedonism founded on the idea of calibrating materially given sensory states and as an altogether more sophisticated and flexible behaviourist ordinal reckoning of preferences.) The core of MacIntyre's message is that the way in which the theory of how to know better has developed in the West in recent centuries has disintegrated at a theoretical level all our conceptions of how men can have good reason to strive to live well either as individuals or as members of society.

There are at least four perspectives in which this claim may helpfully be considered and which, taken together, should make it easier to grasp the character of the division between power and understanding in the shaping of modern cultures. The first, which may be noted very briefly, derives from the recent history of Western epistemology. Following principally from W. V. O. Quine's historic assault on the analytic/synthetic distinction[15] and from the controversial implications which have been drawn from this attack both by Quine himself and by others,[16] the underdetermination of theory by evidence and the indeterminacy of translation – the entire conception of a foundationalist epistemology has fallen into severe discredit. A complementary, though not altogether harmonious line of thought, developed most insistently by Jürgen Habermas, has insisted on the inexpugnability from any 'factual' characterization of segments of non-human as well as human nature offered by human beings of distinctively human evaluations. It is important to emphasize that neither of these two lines of thought is in any sense irrationalist. Each depends for its cogency on extremely complex and sophisticated arguments and, in the case of Quine's theory at least, on arguments which are also worked out with very considerable precision. Habermas's writings have exercised a shaping intellectual influence not merely on more or less politically disenchanted analysts of capitalist society but also on intellectually ambitious and energetic philosophers of natural science like Mary Hesse. A revanchement from the imperious cultural style of positivist philosophy of natural and social science in the 1950s is in no sense just a form of lumpen-intellectual *ressentiment* at the unflattering presentation which it offered of human nature. Rather, it arises from deep and increasingly blatant contradictions within the Western epistemological tradition, contradictions which are far from being confined to their manifestations to the writings of Quine, Habermas, and their respective epigoni.

It would be idle at this point to pretend to see very clearly precisely what implications do follow validly from either of these recent traditions of academic thought. But what they do clearly suggest, when taken together, is the forlornness of any image of a culture *founded* upon epistemic rationality, any culture in which the external and objective *dictates* to the human and the existential how in general the latter has good reason to be. There have, of course, been plenty of other versions of the attempt to set up the external and objective (nature) as a univocal norm for the human and the existential, many of them earlier and many also far from being confined to the Western world. Virtually all such attempts do possess, too, in addition to their other qualities, a real prudential force. (We had better, as Thomas Carlyle observed, accept the universe; and in consequence we had better, as far as we can, learn to take accurate account of its causal properties.) Not a few of these attempts have had their roots in explicitly religious beliefs, as they did in a very conspicuous fashion in the thought of the philosophical progenitor of the European Enlightenment, John Locke. We can see the ambiguities which followed from this origin, for example, at a poignant moment in one of the letters from Locke to his friend Edward Clarke, subsequently incorporated into his influential *Some Thoughts concerning Education* (1693). At this point Locke, reflecting on the apparent cruelty on occasion of small children, expresses his reluctance to regard this dispositional trait as *natural* and offers a suggestion on how 'to *plant* the contrary, or more natural tempers of good nature, and Compassion in the roome of it'.[17] For Locke the presumption that a given nature could and should serve as norm for human culture followed directly from the presumption that nature as a whole and man himself within it were both the precisely intended and the perfectly controlled handiwork of God.[18] Nature could serve as a univocal norm because, mirrored in it, man could read clearly, as God desired him to do, the way which God wished him to be: 'The Candle, that is set up in us, shines bright enough for all our Purposes.'[19] But when he came to think seriously about the question in practice, as the metaphor of planting memorably brings out, Locke sees the formation of culture and social identity as a process of active human creation. In a philosopher like Locke (and in many of his more secular Enlightenment successors) the presumption that nature could serve in this way as a univocal norm for culture was at least frank, if at times a little simple-minded. In the more alienated and instrumental culture of advanced capitalism, the relation between the two has been appreciably subtler and slyer. As its insistence upon the logical chasm between facts and values suggests, the official view enjoined until recently by Western epistemology was that nature cannot serve as norm for human culture, because nothing but a human value can accredit a human value – and least of all the way the world happens to be. Tacitly, however, the vision which it has encouraged has been very different. By its intractable insistence upon epistemic rigour and its expulsion of all judgements intimately linked with sentiments from the epistemic domain, modern Western philosophy has contrived to segregate the epistemically respectable from the cognitively arbitrary and to consign virtually all human significance to the latter category. In doing so, naturally, it has steadily bled human evaluations, both sacred and secular, of cultural authority and lavished this instead, with reckless servility, on the supposedly given properties of nature. All conceptions of man and what matters to him which are not cast in the idiom which has proved so powerful in the scientific understanding of nature are stigmatized more or less explicitly as superstitions. Modern culture, accordingly, as rendered in the idiom of academic philosophy, is divided up into the epistemically serious and respectable (broadly, science) on one side and, on the other, the epistemically empty (the existential flotsam and jetsam of the great bulk of human self-understanding). It is precisely this crudely stigmatizing disjunction between the culture of natural science and the rest of human culture which has given Rorty the opportunity and motive to develop his spirited antithesis, the levelling rejoinder that all that natural science can be is simply one family of cultures amongst a myriad of other cultures, that its writ runs no further than its own boundaries, and that the fond pretence of its boot-licking lackey philosophy to establish its rational hegemony over human experience as a whole is nothing but the most comical of self-deceptions.

A second perspective in which to consider the balance between power and understanding in the shaping of modern cultures is offered by the history of attempts to analyse the basis of individual identity. The technical problem of personal identity in Western philosophy was invented by Locke in an addition which he made to the second edition of the *Essay concerning Human Understanding*,[20] seeking to answer the question of what it was which made every human being 'to himself, that which he calls *self*'.[21] For Locke personal identity was 'a Forensick Term appropriating Actions and their Merit',[22] and the continuity which he wished to explain was a continuity of individual responsibility. The problem was posed, as Leibniz disapprovingly noted,[23] by Locke's rejection on epistemological grounds of the ontological conception of substance shared in some form by the great majority of his philosophically interested Christian predecessors. For the ascription of personal responsibility, Locke's primary concern, the self-referential continuity of consciousness seemed at first sight to offer a reassuringly solid foundation to the identity of persons. But the conceptual relations between the continuity of an individual body and the continuity of an individual consciousness soon raised on this point,[24] as they have continued to raise subsequently,[25] embarrassing conundra. With the powerfully sceptical epistemological critique of personal identity advanced in the first book of David Hume's *Treatise of Human Nature* (1738) a half century later, it became harder to resist theoretically an altogether more disseminated conception of personal identity. Much more recently, in the writings of the Oxford philosopher Derek Parfit[26] a less sceptical but morally much more intrusive conception of personal identity has reshaped the question quite drastically.

The technical detail of the philosophical discussion is not important here. But Parfit's powerful and scintillating thinking does show forcibly how far, in the two centuries and more since the *Treatise*, the advance of an epistemology closely linked to the practice of natural science has contrived to move outside the existentially inert confines of Hume's study into the most fundamental aspects of human self-understanding in the midst of real life. What Parfit argues, very crudely put, is that human identity should not be thought of as unitary across the life cycle but rather as modifying more or less constantly throughout this timespan, and that forms of human self-commitment across time should rationally be adjusted to the real discontinuities which arise with these modifications. An individual life consists of a set of temporally extended component selves, the identity between which is severely relative and the relations of responsibility between which should rationally be adjusted to the real discontinuities which arise with these modifications. Morally rational action for an individual agent is best adjudicated by utilitarian calculation across selves or from the viewpoint of the current self and not at all in terms of the commitments of a past self, except insofar as these linger actively on in the current self's consciousness. In the conflict between present passion and past commitment dramatized in George Eliot's great novel *The Mill on the Floss*, Parfit sides in effect with the claims of present passion. Her ringing proclamation of the claims of the past are undercut by the corrosion of the socially situated and life-long self on which their significance depends:

'We have proved that it was impossible to keep our resolutions. We have proved that the feeling which draws us towards each other is too strong to be overcome: the natural law surmounts every other; we can't help what it clashes with.'
'It is not so, Stephen. I'm quite sure that it is wrong. I have tried to think it again and again; but I see, if we judged in that way, there would be a warrant for all treachery and cruelty – we should justify breaking the most sacred ties that can ever be formed on earth. If the past is not to bind us, where can duty lie? We should have no law but the inclination of the moment.'[27]

If Parfit is right on the question of how a human individual has good reason to regard their own life, then not merely are the accents of Maggie Tulliver sociologically under attack today (as we all know them to be) but in addition the culture of the world which they (no doubt very selectively) evoke must be judged always to have been a culture predominantly of illusion.

A third perspective on the formation of modern cultures which helps to identify the balance of power and understanding in their formation is afforded by considering the distinctive role of social theory in the reproduction of modern societies.[28] No society, of course, lacks an official social theory of some kind, though societies vary rather widely in how far their official social theories are insulated from, or even at odds with, the mass of prevailing popular belief. But in the past the official social theories of almost all societies have been heavily impregnated with religious beliefs, and sacred and secular dimensions of authority have been hard to distinguish fully. Most modern states are formally secular, and, even in those which are not, the great majority of political authorities seek to legitimate their power in essentially secular terms of welfare or defence or the righting of territorial wrongs. Both what political authorities attempt to do in the heavily governed societies of the modern world and how their subjects perceive them are heavily marked by the social theories officially adopted, while the effectiveness of modern governments radically depends upon the degree to which their subjects find these official social theories normatively cogent and causally credible. The formal democratization of political authority in the modern world,[29] the ideological process which Marx identified when he called democracy 'the resolved mystery of all constitutions',[30] registers this dual dependence. But it does so in a singularly forlorn and bemusing manner, foisting off upon governments the duty to know what they are doing both morally and practically to a degree that the realities of social and economic organization unmistakably preclude and demanding that they vindicate their title to rule by displaying (or pretending to display) an epistemological prowess and an ethical authority the very idea of which is probably incoherent.[31] Between a degree of democratization which no longer privileges the consciousness of rulers over that of their subject fellow citizens (which might well irretrievably corrode the capacity to govern at all) and the assertion of what is often an essentially fraudulent claim to cognitive superiority, causal or ethical, there is no happy intermediate resting place. Every human being who is not in some way irretrievably cognitively damaged is at least an amateur social theorist and has to be such in order to learn a language and understand his or her fellows at all. In epistemological terms any secular official social theory is merely an amateur social theory backed by coercive power. And the obdurately professional social theories so painstakingly developed by the institutional intellectuals of the modern world, carefully decked out with their epistemic pretensions, are likewise, in their final claims to cognitive authority, grounded no more securely on a reality independent of their proponents' desires and external to human culture. The idea of a secular authority grounded outside and above the beliefs prevailing in a particular population no longer makes sense today. And because it no longer makes sense, the proportions of power to understanding within that causally enormously important segment of modern social process affected by the exercise of governmental power are necessarily deeply disturbing.

This is not something which many today see very clearly – and perhaps in some respects mercifully so. For to see the causal weight and the cognitive arbitrariness of governmental commitment in these terms is to identify the politics of a very disenchanted world indeed. In this perspective, discomfitingly, a sense of the hazards of cultural distortion through the application of power, aptly aroused by the experience of imperialist pressure, must rationally extend also to the possibility of precisely the same impact of external force upon existential meaning occurring through the agency of Third World state powers, just as through the agency of the state powers of the First or Second World. Such political clashes in the modern world between the amateur social theories of citizens (their conceptions of the meaning of their own lives and of the relations between this meaning and the activities of the state to which they belong) and the official social theories of governments (today in almost all instances a more or less crisply adapted version of one of the professional social theories spawned by modern intellectuals inside or outside the academy) are necessarily painful affairs. It is simply populist sentimentality to presume that the populace standardly (or perhaps even often) has better taste than its rulers. But what is quite generally true is that it is almost never given sufficient reason to respect the claims of its political superiors to possess superior cognitive authority and that the latter no longer dare to acknowledge openly their lack of any such authority. Directly enountered, the 'ideological state apparatuses' of the modern world discharge the function theoretically allotted to them – that of ensuring by hook or by crook that those who directly exercise the power of the state are felt by their subject population to do so with its own authentic consent – very poorly indeed. Hence the increasing recoil by confessedly conservative intellectuals in the West,[32] but also perhaps by many decidedly less willing to acknowledge themselves simply as conservatives,[33] from seeing the secular rationalism of the Enlightenment as a sound source for a political authority unacknowledged by those subject to it. Enlightened despotism looks less attractive when the very applicability of the idea of enlightenment to social existence as such has been firmly called into question. Its intrinsic arrogance becomes harder to miss and its prospective causal benefits become more difficult to credit.

Here, doubts concerning the epistemic status of social theory can be linked directly to a major movement of sensibility, spawned within the Enlightenment and in part reacting to it,[34] the historicist insistence that any sound conception of what is rationally of value for man must see this as grounded firmly in the lived sentiments and attitudes of a particular population, in the form of life which it feels to be its own. This stress on the centrality of cultural loyalties to both social identity and existential rationality has many dubious potentialities. But it is a deep and, on the whole, a very compelling theme in modern moral consciousness. In contrast with the 'vigorously corrective' theories of existential rationality[35] advanced not merely by an extreme moralist like Kant but less explicitly and clear-headedly by many theorists of social and political value – liberal, utilitarian, or Marxist – it insists on the absurdity of forgetting what the lives of human beings are really like and of treating them as though they were simply artefacts of the theorist's own ethical predilections. A complementary stress, within a far narrower and more professionalized idiom of thought, has been the attempt by recent moral philosophers to analyse the relations between moral claims and human rationality not as categorical, as Kant saw it, but rather as hypothetical, as resting simply on the degree of interest which particular human agents happen themselves to feel in moral considerations.[36]

Each of these views is open to destructively nihilist interpretations; and it is hard to regard the latter as adequate at all. But each offers a viewpoint from which to assess the implications of recognizing the truth that nature cannot dictate a single human culture and the still more puzzling truth which follows from this that there is no place outside human culture from which this can be judged by human beings. The imaginative response encouraged by the history of Western epistemology impels us, almost irresistibly, to see its implications as nihilist. But in a somewhat broader human perspective,[37] there is no reason to see it as anything of the sort. If both the force of human value and the cogency of human argument are necessarily intra-cultural in the last instance, it is a blatant enough truth about the world in which we live that the cogency of either in some settings is much better able to survive a dialogue with other cultures than that in other settings. Some cultures (the culture of natural science, for example) have immense elasticity and absorptive power. Others have extremely little. There is no guarantee that in the dialogue between cultures the better culture will win, since the encounter between them, as we all know, is so far from being 'free and open', so often and sometimes so drastically distorted by power. But over the decades the merits of different segments of culture can make these into sources as well as victims of power. We do not live in a providential world, but neither, as a species, do we have either occasion or excuse for despair. The claim to know better is flourished menacingly at identities, personal, cultural, and political, from the outside as much as it has ever been before in human history. But today – more clearly than ever before – we know that it can be vindicated only within identities, that the only authority which it can possess is a human authority, an authority *for* human beings not an external domination over them. What it is to be modern is not to conform to the parochial ideological proclivities of the United States a decade or two ago– or of any other society now or subsequently. It is simply to face up to this knowledge.

Chapter 9

The future of liberalism

CONCEPTIONS of political value are permanently at risk in two sharply distinct dimensions. Like any human attempt at understanding, they are epistemically at risk – potentially in error in their assessment of what is the case. And like any human attempt to assess what is of value, what is good or right, they are ethically at risk – potentially in error in their assessment of the *moral* force of a particular conception. But also, and in a markedly different manner, they are at risk in their exposure to the vicissitudes of economic, social and political history. The future of a congeries of political values like liberalism depends, and depends in very different ways, on the epistemic grounding and moral force of the values themselves and on the structural propitiousness of the socio-political context within which the values must be actualized, if they are to be actualized at all.

This contrast, a contrast at bottom between the ideal and the practicable, is necessarily sharper in the case of political theory than it will be in the case of a view of ethics centred, as most Western philosophers still habitually conceive this, on purely private life. In an ethic of purely private life, a contrast between the ideal and the practicable is in the first instance essentially a challenge to the moral prowess of individuals, an external ethical pressure on what is conceived as an ethically defective will. But because of the asymmetry between individual agency and the workings of political institutions, in political theory a gap between the ideal and the practicable is always potentially (and usually in practice) a challenge in the first instance to the epistemic adequacy of the conception of the ideal. If an individual human being happens to be (as no doubt most of us in fact are) pretty lethargically responsive to his or her carefully considered conception of the good, then that is, other things being equal, merely their own moral problem. But in political understanding, if a society happens to be deeply unresponsive to a particular conception of the good, it is not an adequate assessment of this state of affairs to see it simply as the moral problem of the society in question. If there is any epistemic force whatever to ethical conceptions, human societies certainly differ in moral merit. (Kampuchea and El Salvador today are worse societies than Switzerland.) But political theory is not principally an exercise in the appraisal and grading of the comparative ethical merits of different societies. Rather, it is a segment of human practical reason. In practical reason, the epistemic standard in question is necessarily a trifle elusive, and even elastic. (It is so because in practical reason the desideratum is not (or at least not directly) that our concepts should match the world or some other presumptively mind-independent reality, but rather that they should specify how the world can be brought to match our concepts.) Since economy, society and polity are so deeply untransparent to human understanding and so fiercely resistant to the imposition of considered human purposes, and since political agency, both individual and concerted, is what political theory aspires to guide, the criteria of validity for political theory are extremely hard to specify even in principle. But, on any plausible reading, they certainly include the proviso that all stipulations of what human beings have good reason to do be at least causally coherent – that they not prescribe the doing of what cannot in fact ever be done. (Of course, in the right culture and at the right time men and women may have the best of reasons deliberately to make martyrs of themselves or die on barricades, to sacrifice their lives, even unavailingly, for their God, or class, or country or even Queen. But no one can have a good reason to be an inadvertent martyr.) It has been an important criticism of liberalism throughout its history, from the sixteenth- and seventeenth-century assaults on the right of religious toleration up to the present day, that it mistakes social, political and religious existence for a form of purely private life. This is an issue to which it will be necessary to return. But for the moment what I wish to underline is not this familiar complaint at the moral inadequacy of liberal understanding of social life, but rather the very sharp disparity, as I take it, between the two ways in which it is necessary to think about the future of any conception of political value, and yet, the emphatic and perhaps dismaying bearing which the second, the ecological propitiousness of the real history of societies, may well carry for the first, the epistemic and hence even the moral force of the conception of political value itself.

This is not, of course, to suggest that the history of theoretical conceptions of value is in any sense a direct reflex of the history of social, economic and political organization. It remains (and is likely always to remain) an extremely complex and puzzling historical question just how one should see the relation between, for example, theories of justice like those of Plato, David Hume and John Rawls and the social settings within which these theories came initially to be formulated by their authors. And, thus far at any rate, the conception of ideology is a good deal closer to furnishing a mere name for the explanatory problem than it is to offering clear guidance on how this problem can effectively be resolved.[1] But opaque in character and historically diverse in content though the relation certainly is, it is hardly one which anyone attempting to consider the future of a congeries of political doctrines can afford to ignore. The idea that moral conceptions can make their own way through history, oblivious to the obstructions presented by the practical organization of societies, is less than cogent; and where the political conceptions in question happen, broadly speaking, to be at present our own, it betrays a particularly unedifying style of political complacency as well as a marked imprudence. Of these two vices, for the purposes of political philosophers – unlike those of citizens or political leaders – the complacency is probably more important than the imprudence.

It may, of course, be true that the future of all human political conceptions is going to be brief and bathetic, if the human race proceeds to crown its not unimpressive career of historical self-modification by taking advantage of the accumulated powers and practices which it has developed to exterminate itself in one fell swoop. This outcome would hardly impair the conceptual status of anyone's theory of justice and, insofar as it certainly would damage the political cogency of existing political traditions (which is presumably very far indeed), there is no reason why it should do more harm to liberalism than it will to socialism, Marxist or otherwise. But what it certainly would do, were it to occur, is to highlight certain evasions and debilities of judgement which are of central importance in assessing conceptions of political value. In particular it would underline the gross folly of conceiving political value as located within or realizable within the bounds of discrete territorial communities, of seeing the problem of imagining and sustaining, improving or creating, a good society as essentially domestic and internal to a particular state. (I don't, of course, mean to contrast this presumption unflatteringly with the presumption – now little short of demented – that the workers of the world can readily unite or, for that matter, with President Reagan's belief that the international capitalist economy can look after itself, without the capitalists of the world or their respective governments making the least effort to concert their activities effectively. I simply wish to underline the judgement that a conception of political value which sees this essentially in terms of domestic welfare, distributive justice and free cultural exploration will be shown to be pretty callow if the human world happens to end shortly with a bang.)[2] There is of course an element of overkill in any such thought – for in the face of a prospect as appalling as that, what conceptions of human value may not be shown up as a trifle callow? But there is a major difference between the realization that human values have been rendered forlorn and the realization that the particular way in which they have been conceived has always been inadequate. And since liberalism explicitly presents itself as a conception of human value (and since there are serious grounds in relation to at least some versions of it for supposing that it adopts the pretensions of a political doctrine without seriously acknowledging the responsibilities which follow from this status), it remains an issue worth pressing. There could, no doubt, be purely external débâcles to which liberalism succumbed which would leave its practical prospects poor without doing much damage to its theoretical credentials. A world ruled from Moscow, for example, would be a world which had been made highly unsafe for liberalism; but it would not necessarily impugn a purely domestic conception of political value, since even the most optimistic of liberals acknowledge the possibility in principle of external interference with domestic welfare and with cultural and political liberty, and supplement their conception of political value accordingly (though, it must be said, pretty mechanically) with what they judge to be an appropriate conception of defence policy. All a world ruled from Moscow would show about liberalism, therefore, (it might be argued) would be that liberal statesmen are capable of practical misjudgements in choosing defence policies. In itself this is a pretty sanguine view; but even if it were more powerfully convincing, the contrast with the possibility of full-scale nuclear war would remain instructive. Certainly, drastic misjudgements in defence policy are likely to have to be causal antecedents for a humanly depopulated world, should this be effected in the near future. But they would hardly be the only inadequacy in liberal conceptions of political value which the eventuality would disclose.

Of course if liberalism were simply a philosophical conception, an abstract standard against which human social and political institutions were to be appraised, but one which there was no practical possibility of their ever contriving to reach, if it was an explicitly utopian conception, it would stand in a less interesting relation to the historical time of human societies. A consideration of its future, like one of its past, could be satisfactorily divided up in broadly Platonic terms into an epistemic analysis of its status, a theory of the psychosocial mechanisms of inhibition which facilitate or obstruct its perception, and an estimate of the degree to which future, like past, societies might vary in how far they fostered these mechanisms. But if the relation between political value and political possibility is internal and logical, rather than external and contingent, then both eschatological broodings and sober assessments of past and future changes in the character of human societies can and will bear very directly upon conceptions of political value.

Consider, for example, the account of the nature of liberalism offered by R. G. Collingwood in his trenchant preface to the English translation of Guido de Ruggiero's *History of European Liberalism*:

Liberalism ... begins with the recognition that men, do what we will, are free; that a man's acts are his own, spring from his own personality, and cannot be coerced. But this freedom is not possessed at birth; it is acquired by degrees as a man enters into the self-conscious possession of his personality through a life of discipline and moral progress. The aim of Liberalism is to assist the individual to discipline himself and achieve his own moral progress; renouncing the two opposite errors of forcing upon him a development for which he is inwardly unprepared, and leaving him alone, depriving him of that aid to progress which a political system, wisely designed and wisely administered can give. These principles lead in practice to a policy that may be called, in the sense above defined, Liberal: a policy which regards the State, not as the vehicle of a superhuman wisdom or a superhuman power, but as the organ by which a people expresses whatever of political ability it can find and breed and train within itself. This is not democracy, or the rule of the mere majority; nor is it authoritarianism, or the irresponsible rule of those who, for whatever reason, hold power at a given moment. It is something between the two. Democratic in its respect for human liberty, it is authoritarian in the importance it attaches to the necessity for skilful and practised government. But it is no mere compromise; it has its own principles; and not only are these superior in practice to the abstractions of democracy and authoritarianism, but, when properly understood, they reveal themselves as more logical.[3]

The question about this doctrine which both Collingwood and de Ruggiero wished to pose in 1927 was a severely practical question: that of its future: 'Is it destined to disappear, crushed between the opposing tyrannies of the majority and the minority, or has it the strength to outlive its opponents?'[4]

In 1927 there is no doubt that this was a good question, whatever one may think of the terms in which it was formulated. In 1985, while the tyranny of the majority is hardly much in evidence, even perhaps in the city of Teheran, it remains an excellent question. In reflecting upon it, it is important to avoid being too hypnotized by the experience of the recent past. In a number of respects, and until relatively recently, the history of postwar North America, Western Europe and Japan has been the most remarkable practical triumph in the history of liberalism, bringing levels of effective civil and political liberty to the great majority of their adult populations for which there were no historical precedents and accompanying these with levels of material well-being, again for the great majority of their populations, for which there were also no historical precedents and which no socialist economy has yet contrived to match. A necessary condition for these impressive feats was the longest running single boom in the history of capitalism. This, of course, has now emphatically come to an end; and very few bankers, or industrialists, or economists – and not many even amongst political leaders – really expect it to recommence in any future which they can concretely imagine.

At present it is still hard for us to identify clearly the relations between the intellectual history of the postwar West and its economic, political and social experience over the same period. And it is certainly far too early to judge with confidence what the intellectual impact of this abrupt reversal in economic expectations over the last ten years or so is likely to prove. But some developments do stand out quite starkly. One is the huge expansion, in the course of the boom, in the attempt to understand economic, social and political phenomena on the model of the sciences of nature. This has not been a private cultural fad of the academic world, but has intruded itself extensively into the activities of exponents of 'skilful and practised government' and even of bankers.[5] More recently, however, and particularly since 1973, this expansion has been halted and in part reversed. The intrinsic intellectual limitations of a scientistic conception of the human sciences have elicited an expressivist and humanist backlash within the academy, and the cost and ineffectiveness of attempts to practise 'skilful government' have provoked a more sceptical (or sometimes just a harder-hearted) attitude amongst contenders in the political arena.

A second major development of the last three decades, elusively related to the first, has been a vigorous revival of concern amongst philosophers with issues of political value. Not all of this, of course, has been explicitly liberal in its substantive political affirmations. But a remarkably large proportion of it, particularly in the United States, has been based upon liberal individualist conceptions of the nature of human value which are set out with a confidence and amplitude (and perhaps often also with a sociological innocence) which in a European context had become hard to sustain even by the days of L. T. Hobhouse.[6] The major American works in this revival of political philosophy, those of Rawls, Nozick and Dworkin for example, all present their favoured conceptions of political value very much as applications of a determinedly non-utilitarian ethics, while the somewhat less emphatic British version of the same revival[7] has been ideologically more variegated, far less hostile to utilitarianism, and rather less strategic in its lines of attack. No doubt the contrast between the two settings – political and social milieux which plainly are divided by a good deal more than a common language – ought not to be overdrawn. But it does raise the question whether there is not some relation between the comparative advance of the social sciences in the United States in the 1950s and 1960s and the efflorescence of a strongly moralizing liberal political philosophy in the 1970s and early 1980s. Scientistic social science, in this perspective, would offer a natural modality of self-understanding for an advanced capitalist society in full expansion, and a strongly moralizing a-priori critique of social relations (from one political viewpoint or other) an equally natural form of cultural revulsion on the part of its edificatory intelligentsia from the moral anarchy and instrumentalist dehumanization which this expansion in due course engenders. From this point of view there is surprisingly much in common in the imaginative motivation of the major works of modern American liberal political philosophy and such an utterly distinct style of cultural lucubration as the late Herbert Marcuse's *One-Dimensional Man*. It is perhaps fair also to insist that, while these share the judgement that America today is gravely defective as a cultural or political setting within which persons can enter into the self-conscious possession of their personalities through lives of discipline and moral progress, they differ very sharply indeed on the degree to which the remedy for this state of affairs can or should be entrusted to the American polity. And none of them offers much hint as to how its edifying considerations might in political reality be brought to bear more than marginally upon the character of the American state. It is still unclear, therefore, whether the revival of political philosophy in the United States has much significance outside the edificatory self-consciousness, the defensive fastidiousness (or to put it more rudely, the moral narcissism) of a largely impotent status group of cultural functionaries.

Except in conditions of dramatic political instability, the future of the moral narcissism of a largely impotent status group is unlikely to be of much *practical* importance. But it might, nevertheless, also be the future of a uniquely full and valid understanding of ethical truth. If Plato's conception of the Form of the Good had offered an authoritative account of the character and content of human value, neither its epistemic nor its moral force would necessarily have been in any way impaired by the subsequent history of Athens or Syracuse or Greek society in general. The more philosophically ambitious defences of a

Kantian alternative to the utilitarian rationalization of modern capitalist society may succeed simply in expressing aversion for the direction of historical development, rather than contributing actively to its shaping. But since there is usually much which merits aversion in the direction of historical development, inefficacy as such offers no grounds for doubting the ethical validity of the predominantly Kantian intuitions of recent American liberals. Utopia may now just be the natural theoretical form for North American moral thought. (As such, there is no reason why it should not prove an illuminating genre through which to explore the nature of the good or intrinsically desirable, however slender the contribution which it can hope to offer to the assessment of what men have good reason in practice to do.)

If we are to try to assess the future prospects for Utopian liberalism, it is not, I think, helpful to concentrate on its gross unsuitability as an approach to understanding the operations of the world market, the international state system or the social and cultural convulsions which these engender.[8] Certainly as an approach to the moral rationalization in practice of the world in which we all live Utopian liberalism is utterly vapid; and even as an understanding of the character of social and political relations as such the works of Rawls, Nozick or Dworkin do display a social and political sensibility which is damagingly and parochially American in its range and responsiveness (in the sense in which, for example, Aristotle's social and political sensibility can fairly be described as damagingly and parochially Greek). But, as with Aristotle, (to whom Rawls at least plainly feels some debt) what will matter for Utopian liberalism in the long run is the epistemic and moral force of their respective conceptions of the good. (By common consent the parochialism of Aristotle's social and political sensibility has depleted the legacy of his political doctrines far more severely than it has that of his general conception of what it is for human beings to flourish.)

It is a very delicate issue indeed at present how one should see the relations between the epistemic and moral force of Utopian liberal conceptions of the good or the right. Rawls, Nozick, Dworkin and Ackerman, for example,[9] have varied considerably in the frankness and fullness with which they have been willing to discuss the meta-ethical foundations of their conception of the good. Following his Dewey lectures on Kantian constructivism, if not perhaps merely from the evidence of his *Theory of Justice* itself, Rawls seems to be clearly committed to the rejection of moral realism. But Dworkin's views now appear to require the presumption of some version of moral realism; and Nozick, whose political theory rests roundly on a conception of men's possession of rights which, as far as I know, he has never condescended either to explain or to defend, has recently espoused an extremely expansive version of moral realism.[10] The validity or otherwise of moral realism is a pretty dizzying issue. It is not always easy to distinguish clearly between complex versions of what Simon Blackburn has called 'projectivism'[11] (the view that what human values are in the last instance is merely human fancies, but fancies of a causally explicable and in some sense pragmatically helpful kind) and the more agile (or evasive) versions of moral realism which insist that, however difficult it may be to explain or defend their authority in general, what true human values are is valid apprehensions of key aspects of what is the case about human existence.[12]

The metaethical issue is important because to deny moral realism is at least to open the door to (perhaps even to require) moral scepticism. And moral scepticism, however much of a hazard one should or should not expect it to present in purely private life, definitely does present a threat to the conceptual stability of Utopian liberalism. It may still be possible domestically within the United States, though hardly on a world scale, to reach liberal political conclusions on utilitarian grounds; and any morally plausible form of utilitarianism will be likely to require an epistemic foundation in moral realism.[13] But Utopian liberalism is markedly hostile to utilitarianism, and far less disposed than the latter to endorse a moral realist view. The view that adult human beings can be and ought to be sovereign over their own lives is a very different view if it is grounded on epistemically well-founded claims about the nature of human rationality and the character of value for man than it can be if it is to be grounded merely in a presumption that there are no authoritative values external to human preference and choice to which the latter have any good reason to defer. The view that what the good for a human individual is is something which it is ultimately and fully and solely up to that individual to see, to judge, and therefore to decide, is corrosive of any conception of external obligation and of society as a frame of non-discretionary responsibilities.[14] No doubt Plato held an overoptimistic conception of the independence and stability of human values. But it was not an unmotivated conception. Without a solid foundation in moral realism it is hard to see how Utopian moral thought can expect either to keep its shape for any length of time or to display the least authority to any moderately inattentive or truculent auditor. To see society as a whole simply as a facility for the provision of individually acceptable experiences and to seek to reconstitute it in imagination so that it can furnish these to the largest possible degree will only be a morally commanding vision where the experiences which individuals happen to find acceptable have already been rendered (through effective socialization) reasonably unrevolting to each other[15] or where the force of human values has been so devastated that the idea of a vision possessing the force of *moral* command has become utterly incoherent. I conclude therefore that for Utopian liberalism in any form to be robust enough to stand the gales of the future, it will require altogether firmer and deeper metaphysical foundations than any which it at present possesses.

It is hard therefore to believe that the weight accorded in the last decade and a half to the Utopian liberal strand in modern political philosophy will be borne out by its eventual contribution to sustaining an intellectual future for liberalism. Unlike its seventeenth and eighteenth-century forerunners,[16] modern contractarianism offers an abstract and philosophically debilitated reverie on how ethical and political value should be conceived – not a relatively powerful account of how human beings have good reason to *act* in the political settings in which they happen to find themselves. In doing so, it exemplifies the uncertainty or implausibility of our present understandings of the rational force of ethical considerations in individual human life, of the degree to which a model of rational systematization is epistemically appropriate to the subject matter of ethics, and of the theoretical terms of trade between individualist and subjective specifications of human value and collective and purportedly objective conceptions of this.[17] Anglophone moral philosophy is vastly more interesting today than it was a quarter of a century ago; but it cannot be said to be in a theoretically very well-ordered and cogent condition. The development of a more commanding form of moral theory would improve the prospective durability of Utopian liberalism; but it would do so, of course, if and only if the values affirmed by Utopian liberalism proved to survive unscathed the criteria of assessment which this form of theory established. At least from the eastern side of the Atlantic at present, it is quite hard to believe that they would do so.

But not all extant versions of liberalism are Utopian in the sense intended; and even if all extant versions at present did happen to be so, there is no reason why future versions should not recapture a crisper and more immediate relevance to the real choices of politics. The most promising approach to such recapture would be to construct a liberal political theory in direct relation to the institutional substance of (and the distribution of power within) existing states: to construct a liberal conception of political value as a theory of modern politics and not as a supposedly timeless mediation on the Form of the Good (or Just).

There are in fact a number of such versions of essentially liberal political theory still more or less extant. The commonest probably, at least in North America, is the somewhat flaccid pluralist political science and political sociology which seek to explain (but which also discreetly applaud) the full range, at least within the law, of organized competitive activity directed at shaping the exercise of political authority in capitalist democracies. But this version is ethically too incoherent or too licentious to convince anyone who did not already accept its morally myopic premisses. If fastidious moral philosophers in the United States, particularly in the closing stages of the Vietnam war, edged away from utilitarianism on the suspicion that its plasticity in use was bound to prove excessively responsive to the internal power dynamics and external misbehaviour of the leading modern capitalist state,[18] it is only natural that they should have recoiled still more violently from a conception of political value which explicitly endorses the subjection of ethics to the working of effective power.

A second variety of liberalism, now showing rather less vitality than in the early days of the Cold War, focuses not on the characteristics of Western liberal democracies but on the disfigurements of their principal political adversaries, the states of the Soviet bloc. The liberal critique of 'totalitarianism' and its metaphysical presumptions (or at least slogans), as set out in the 1950s in rather different ways by Berlin, Popper and Talmon, may not ever have been politically enormously revealing; but it served at that time as effective abuse of an assemblage of political orders which has continued to deserve much, if not most, of the abuse which it has encountered. As a style of social and political theory, it was excessively holistic in approach, and perhaps even a little credulous about the causal role of ideological pronouncements. But after due allowance has been made for such limitations, one of its main presumptions does retain considerable force: that it is often of fundamental importance in political understanding to identify political possibilities which it is imperative to avoid. As a theory of political prudence, Cold War liberalism was shrill in tone and overly selective in the matters to which it gave attention. But, under sympathetic interpretation, it can at least be seen as having put the appropriate virtue at the centre of its conception of political value.

There are at least three other distinguishable strands in liberal theory which have sought to display themselves as applications to political practice of the central virtue of practical reason. The first of these is the classical utilitarian account of the criteria for designing humanly dependable political institutions. The second is the tradition of political economy, stretching from Hume and Adam Smith to Keynes,

Hayek and Milton Friedman, which seeks to assess the practical and moral merits of the market in domestic and international economic life and judges political institutions in the first instance in terms of their capacity to secure its working where this will be advantageous and to restrict it where it is likely to do harm. The third strand is more diffuse and perhaps also at present intellectually less effectively presented – the would-be cosmopolitan appraisal of the comparative political and cultural propitiousness of different modalities of political concern and organization for the promotion and protection of human flourishing. In the last two centuries, plainly, these strands have often been deeply interwoven with one another; and none of them, perhaps, is in fact necessarily liberal in the conclusions which it licenses on each particular occasion.

The utilitarian is the least puzzling to identify. In the form in which it was first elaborated by Bentham and James Mill it offered a simple (if not altogether coherent) defence of democratic political institutions as devices for minimizing the threats which human beings pose to one another.[19] Since the early nineteenth century, however, this simplicity of outline has become increasingly blurred. A broadly utilitarian idiom of political appraisal features in the public pieties of all but the most ebulliently barbarous of modern regimes. The view that utilitarian criteria clearly sanction any particular institutional order, or even perhaps that they yield any determinate account of the content of human flourishing for a given human population at a particular time, has become extremely hard to sustain. And whatever clear directive force in the last instance a utilitarian assessment may be thought to retain depends far more on causal beliefs about the working of economies than it does upon the direct consideration of political institutions or human values. Even a utilitarian as wedded to liberty as John Stuart Mill himself was clear that liberty was unsuitable for backward races;[20] and it is hard to see even an elective affinity between utilitarian appraisals and liberal political conclusions over much of the globe. Of course, because of the inherent vagueness of utilitarian judgements it remains unclear that accurate utilitarian calculations (supposing this conception to make sense) would *not* yield clearly liberal political conclusions over the world as a whole. But there seems at present no reason whatever to anticipate that they would do so.

The second strand, that of political economy, is notoriously in some intellectual disarray at the moment; and it too is less trustworthily wedded to liberal political conclusions than it used to appear. Even in the theories of Bentham and James Mill the prospective contribution of democratically elected representative government to minimizing men's threats to one another depended upon conceiving a market economy and the protection of the entitlements which emerged from its workings as a form of public good.[21] Modern liberal economists like Hayek and Friedman see the issue in much the same terms but are markedly less sanguine about the capacity of democracy to identify the market's workings in their entirety as a public good or to protect them accordingly against the rampant greed or compulsive moral embarrassment of groups who see them very differently. Hayek himself has drawn the conclusion that defending the operations of domestic markets (and the gains in welfare and civil liberty which flow from these) may require some measure of abatement in political democracy,[22] a conclusion emphatically and repeatedly implemented in less happy lands in recent decades. The view that it is natural for representative democracy through time to interfere sufficiently extensively with domestic and foreign market relations to damage their workings severely has aroused some enthusiasm also on the left because it resuscitates doubts over the long-term political and economic stability of advanced capitalist states which the length and scale of the postwar boom had largely laid to rest. The history of Europe between the two world wars scarcely suggests, however, that this enthusiasm is particularly discerning. And whether it is correct to see Keynesian contra-cyclical stabilization policies as rationally coherent and responsible for the length and vigour of the postwar boom or as incoherent and responsible for the depth and prospective duration of the slump which succeeded it, neither their acceptance nor their rejection at present promises a solid political and economic foundation for a continuation of postwar western liberalism or social democracy.

Domestically, therefore, the disarray of political economy poses both a practical threat to the prosperity (and perhaps even to the stability) of a genuinely liberal polity and a theoretical threat to the belief that such a polity constitutes a practically coherent and ethically desirable political order. But the principal damage which political economy has inflicted upon liberal conceptions of political good has been in their international rather than in their domestic dimensions. In the two hundred years since Adam Smith's extraordinary synthesis of 1776, no subsequent defence of the view that the world market is correctly understood as an unequivocally public good for all who trade upon it has carried comparable intellectual authority. And it has by now become the single most embarrassing lacuna in modern political theory, conservative and socialist as much as liberal, that social, economic and political flourishing everywhere in the world depends extensively on international economic exchange, while no one today possesses a clear and intellectually authoritative understanding of how the costs and benefits of such exchanges are to be appraised.

The third strand which I wish to consider possesses a more shadowy outline, though it enjoys an intellectual ancestry of some distinction, going back to Aristotle, Machiavelli, Montesquieu and Tocqueville.[23] Unlike utilitarianism and political economy, it sees the political claims of prudence as not merely of predominant importance but also as permanently elusive: hard even to identify and alarmingly difficult to apply. Of course early nineteenth-century utilitarians like James Mill, as Macaulay pointed out,[24] officially regarded politics as a terrain of intense hazard; but under even cursory inspection this aspect of their views was manifestly in bad faith. But for the more pragmatic and sociologically aware liberalism of this last tradition the hazards to political liberty and human decency in every human society of any merit (any human society which has something to lose) are multifarious and acute, and come from an endless variety of sources.

Despite Plato's hopes prudence is scarcely a sufficient basis on which to construct a coherent theory of the human good. So this form of liberalism is necessarily indeterminate, perhaps indeed necessarily *vague*,[25] in its conception of what the human good actually consists in. But it can on occasion, and without superstition, be extremely confident in its identification of particular evils. In its social theory at present (as in the past) it would need to hold a fine balance between a superstitious sacralization of state, society or particular classes and a wholly alienated and instrumental conception of social and political arrangements.[26] In the theory of value it would need to hold a balance between a depth of veneration for human rationality and freedom of the will sufficient to treat these in all settings and at all times as normatively authoritative and the destructive nihilism which is a natural (if possibly incorrect) inference from modern varieties of moral scepticism and pragmatism.[27] As with any exercise in the balancing of values, it is reasonable to be pessimistic both practically and conceptually on the question of whether any stable equilibrium does in fact exist. But if the exercise is understood not as an overtly Aristotelian espousal of the mean between two extremes, but just as the recognition that human values are often under effective threat from sharply different directions, it need not appear excessively credulous. In the case of social theory, for example, the recognition that social membership is central to the specification of human good but that particular social and political arrangements are frequently singularly lacking in merit does register quite well the sharply contrasting threats of an increasingly frenetic and instrumental individualism and a massive increase in the domestic (to say nothing of the external) coercive power of modern states. Similarly, in the domain of politics itself, the espousal of a democratic conception of the nature of modern political authority, along with a realization of the irretrievably undemocratic institutional workings of modern state power,[28] excludes the twin threats of essentially bogus pretensions to the didactic exercise of state power by those who happen currently to possess it and equally bogus promises that such power could instead be coherently exerted by a modern demos itself. In the field of political economy also, this unheroic penchant for the mean (or revulsion from diametrically opposed absurdities) has at least equal cogency. It would reject the forlorn attempt to represent markets everywhere and always as essentially a public good for all who exchange upon them or produce for them. But it would be at least equally averse to the fatuity of supposing that the production and distribution of all material goods and services by and for human beings, either within particular countries or in the world as a whole, could be secured through an objective identification of the public good and through the authoritative implementation of an instrumentally rational and systematic plan for its realization.

In some ways a liberal philosophy of this character would be profoundly lacking both in philosophical *éclat* and in the capacity to inspire emotion, being grounded as it is not in a giddy rapture at the moral splendours of human liberty and autonomy, but in a more sober and despondent sense of the diversity of hazards to which human collective life has always been exposed and of the profoundly disturbing, if vaguely delineated, configuration of such hazards which it confronts at present. It would be a defensive and nervous, not a confident and crusading liberalism. But if it would be compelled to dispense with elegance of philosophical line and emotional afflatus, it would not necessarily lack intellectual depth. Grounded in the recognition that human social cooperation is irretrievably problematic,[29] as well as morally and practically indispensable, it would conceive the central virtues of political life as virtues to be cultivated, perhaps warily but also strenuously and bravely, not as rights to be exacted. It would affirm the dispositional virtue of tolerance and the epistemic merits of free inquiry rather than the implausibly grandiose metaphysical pretensions of a right to toleration or to freedom of speech. Viewing the creation and maintenance of rational trust as the central challenge to human powers of social cooperation[30] it would refuse to restrict the responsibility for collective prudence to a tiny governing elite and insist instead that most of this responsibility has to be carried, if it is to be discharged at all, by the solidarity, civic virtue and political discernment of the citizenry as a whole. In face of the moral anarchy and the opacity to human understanding of the world economy and of the bewildering menace of human annihilation, the call on these virtues is more urgent than it has ever been before.

It would be optimistic to hope that the home life of our own dear societies will not continue to caricature this conception pretty miserably in practice. But unlike the conceptions of Plato, or John Stuart Mill or Rawls or even Nozick, what such practical caricature would disclose is not an eminently disputable relevance of a set of morally fastidious and socially eccentric ideas to the real collective life of a particular society, but something blatantly shameful in the reality of that society, something the shame of which could be brought home with a little patience or imagination to almost anyone.

There remains, to be sure, at least one major doubt about this pious and perhaps mildly artificial construction. Is the political viewpoint so lavishly commended actually a form of *liberalism* at all? Was Aristotle then a liberal? Was Machiavelli a liberal? In this form the question is of little importance. (Call it what you will.) For insofar as liberalism is not such a doctrine, then its not being so in my contention is precisely what makes it today politically vapid or pernicious. But there is a more pressing version of the same question over which in conclusion I must simply nerve myself to come clean. For one inference which certainly does follow validly from this position is that liberalism so conceived may well in practice in particular societies and at particular times entail a politics which describes itself as either socialist or conservative. Precisely because it casts prudence as the central political value, it is obliged to take its bearings as best it can by assessing the current configuration of hazards facing a society and the existing resources, moral and material, of which that society then disposes and which it must employ to meet these hazards to the best of its abilities. A prudential and sociologically sensitive liberalism, therefore, may well prove distressingly politically plastic; and it will inevitably accommodate itself to the causal properties of existing fields of power. It will do so because these fields furnish the materials with which and through which it *must* work if it is to be able to work at all.

For those for whom moral and political philosophy are confined to the theory of what is intrinsically desirable (the moral radicals perhaps) this will seem a fatal moral stigma. But for those for whom political philosophy is firmly a part of human practical reason, by contrast, such epistemic openness to the bad news is the mark of political seriousness. The dispute between these two viewpoints is at least as old as Plato or Aristotle and it is likely to last as long as human thought itself. What I

169

have tried principally to do in this essay is to register a protest at the modern tendency for all morally engaged forms of liberalism – any form of liberalism supposedly committed to changing the world and not merely to denouncing it – to be appropriated exclusively for the Utopian tradition.

Chapter 10

The future of political philosophy in the West

TO SPEAK with any authority of the future of political philosophy in the West it would be necessary to possess an accurate and confident sense of the prospective course of both philosophy and politics in this terrain over the next few decades. It is unlikely that any human being enjoys such a privileged insight. Certainly I make not the least claim to do so. But I begin with the enormity of any such pretension, not simply from the rhetorical convenience of issuing at the outset a prudentially indispensable disclaimer but rather to stress the discomfitingly dual exposure which I take to be characteristic of political philosophy at any point in its history.

This exposure is certainly not very clearly registered at present in the self-consciousness of political philosophy as an academic trade. It is also at present not at all impressively exemplified in the intellectual force and depth of the recent products of this trade. But the exposure itself is intrinsic to the human condition over the last few millennia of its history and the failure of would-be philosophers of politics to acknowledge it simply guarantees the relative triviality and insufficiency of their work. In some respects Wittgenstein may have been justified in his contention that philosophy leaves the world as it is.[1] But even those who have endeavoured to interpret the implications of his thought for political philosophy have not had the nerve to argue that political philosophy of any real intellectual force could leave the world of politics just exactly as this is.[2] To strive to see clearly the relations between power, evil, justice, duty and collective human achievement is necessarily to grapple with the importunities and deceptions of politics. It may seldom constitute a very efficacious modality of political action. It may well be attempted as propitiously in Ivory Towers as in the *agora* or the Central Committee. But however removed in social style and personal privilege, however intricately mediated, its tacit setting is still the struggle for power and justice, for the organization and shaping of human lives. And because this is and must be its setting, the imaginative discretion or inconsequence of those who practice it can be a very real betrayal; not merely a failure in personal integrity or a display of moral indolence but a squandering of real cultural and political opportunities, a narrowing of the already all too restrictive confines of historical possibility. I will return to this issue, nervously but I hope firmly, towards the end.

First, it will be necessary to look briefly at the recent history of political philosophy in the West and at the changing temper of philosophy as a whole over the same period: to start with the academic trade or trades. It is in fact of some importance that political philosophy should fall within the territorial claims of at least two very different academic trades – philosophy and political science. For a brief period in the 1950s and early 1960s this status posed no particular problems. An eminently scientistic political science and a narrow version of philosophy proper, a curious amalgam of positivism and the analysis of ordinary language, could agree readily on shrinking both the cognitive scope and responsibilities and the intellectual significance of political philosophy. It was at this time that political philosophy was noisily pronounced dead[3] and less brusquely assessed to have come alive again[4] or to be indestructible in principle.[5] (In the case of Sir Isaiah Berlin, who took the latter view, the insistence was intriguingly related to his personal decision to abandon working as an analytical philosopher himself.)[6] At its least promising the academic political philosophy of this era in the Anglo-Saxon world represented little more than the application of a favoured meta-ethical theory, the emotivism of C. E. Stevenson or the prescriptivism of R. M. Hare, to political categories which were treated in themselves as wholly philosophically inert.[7] Its banality thus mirrored the banality of the prevailing style of ethical theory. But, at least in retrospect, this period did not last long; and it is easy enough by now to see that it was never as uniform in its triumph as it appeared to be at the time. A number of political philosophers of a European background – Leo Strauss, Hannah Arendt, Eric Voegelin, Herbert Marcuse – continued to theorize about politics without inhibition from prevailing philosophical fashion, as did a major philosopher of natural science, Karl Popper. Even amongst the ranks of those who saw themselves as analytical philosophers, the early articles of John Rawls[8] and several of the major works of Herbert Hart[9] on the philosophy of law first appeared in the 1950s or early 1960s. But it remains true that, since the death of R. G. Collingwood and with the partial exception of Popper, no modern British or American philosopher has made a serious attempt to elaborate a political philosophy as part of an over-arching general metaphysics, a political philosophy embedded in an overtly expressed epistemology and ontology proclaimed as apt for the purpose. Yet the articulated philosophical context of works such as Rawls's *Theory of Justice* or Nozick's *Anarchy, State and Utopia*[10] and even of less synthetic works such as Bernard Williams's, *Moral Luck*[11] or Thomas Nagel's *Mortal Questions*[12] is far broader and richer than anything attempted by analytical philosophers two or three decades ago. It seems most unlikely, moreover, that this broadening of intellectual ambitions will readily be reversed. In the mid-1950s, briefly, it was easy to judge that serious thinking about politics could not be done in a genuinely philosophical manner and that serious philosophy could have no direct bearing on political values. Today, by contrast, the more immediate danger is perhaps the reverse: a drastically inadequate sense of the breadth and conceptual complexity of the philosophical field which stretches from ontology at one limit to political and aesthetic value at the other.

What holds analytical philosophy together as a movement, lending it self-esteem and corporate solidarity within the unpleasant competitive pressures of a shrinking academic labour market, is not a shared set of doctrines or even an agreed sense of methodological precepts. Rather, it is the common possession of a range of analytical techniques. Like any techniques, these do not dictate at all determinately the manner of their own use, though they naturally place many restrictions on the ways in which they could in principle be employed. Philosophically, there are strong currents tugging them in opposite directions – both towards the deconstruction of philosophy as an academic trade urged by Richard Rorty[13] and towards the reconstitution of a comprehensive conception of practical reason essayed in different ways by MacIntyre, Williams, Nagel, David Wiggins and Charles Taylor and perhaps also from other angles by writers as diverse as Nozick and Hilary Putnam.[14] Rorty's position is perhaps the most spectacular, drawing as it does on a heady brew of Nietzsche, Foucault, Heidegger, Dewey and the later Wittgenstein, along with the work of Sellars, Putnam and Quine. *Philosophy and the Mirror of Nature* is an exhilarating book. But it does not take great sociological acumen to predict that, at least in the medium-term future, no profession under siege is likely to succumb to the seductions of its arguments. Even if Rorty's arguments were convincing in every instance, the deconstruction of philosophy would remain a social project as well as an intellectual conclusion; and, as a social project, it might be expected to reach its terminus only after a substantial lapse of time.

As in the case of Wittgenstein himself, it is easiest to identify the negative implications of Rorty's position. *Philosophy and the Mirror of Nature* is principally an attack on the overweening pretensions of a particular academic guild, on the claims to intellectual authority made by philosophers and on their vision of themselves as members of an epistemic court of last instance, determining the *quaestiones juris* of human understanding. The book's strategy allies intellectual and institutional history with a powerful internal critique of ontological and epistemological reflection in the analytical tradition over the last few decades. It displays academic philosophy as now understood in Britain and North America (and, indeed, in most of Western Europe), an entity defined by a more or less determinate subject matter or range of problems, as a historical invention over a limited period of time which then takes institutional form in the late eighteenth and the nineteenth centuries. The juridical conception of philosophy as competent judge, in virtue of knowing 'something about knowing which no one else knows so well'[15] lies at the heart of this recently devised, if now highly institutionalized, practice. Consequently the practice itself is acutely vulnerable to a scepticism, common to American pragmatism and the later Wittgenstein, as to the existence of conclusive and wholly extra-human epistemic standards. If not merely natural science but even logic and mathematics may be seen not as external authorities over us but as simply highly ingenious and skilful forms of activity which human beings happen to have devised, the special authority of philosophers is plainly cast in doubt. Authority in human cognition drifts away from their hands and settles wherever in more everyday assessment it is currently presumed to lie. This Wittgensteinian emphasis on practices and forms of life as the reality beyond which no human appeal can be made[16] is certainly bracing to the imagination and may well be simply philosophically valid. What remains elusive, however, is just what positive implications it would have, if it were indeed valid, for ethical, social and political values. Rorty's own view of this question seems as yet a little unsteady, stretching from the somewhat fideist orientation towards existing practices offered by a conservative philosopher like Michael Oakeshott to the decidedly more intrepid (if perhaps equally vague) approach of the American pragmatist John Dewey.[17] Since the question of whether an existing assemblage of human practices is essentially appropriate as it stands or whether it requires drastic and systematic reconstitution is at the core of social and political theory, a simple appeal to the authority of practice has no determinate content and is necessarily either evasive, insidious or vacuous. Even Oakeshott's assault on rationalism inflicted some damage on a real target;[18] and there is undoubtedly some moral and prudential force to the brooding conservative preoccupation with the fragility and indispensability of forms of human life.[19] (It is worth noting, too, the substantial overlap which exists between any articulation of these themes which follows self-consciously in the intellectual footsteps of Wittgenstein and the broader range of revulsion, drawing heavily on Marx or even on Aristotle and Plato, to the alienated modern view of human social existence. And at a decidedly less cloistered level it is worth noting also the presence of common sentiments in the massive recrudescence of fundamentalist religion in many different societies in the last decade. But however culturally sensitive or emotionally urgent it may be on occasion, it hardly makes a very adequate philosophical approach to the rational critique and prudent revision of human practices. And, at least in this instance, an adequate philosophical approach cannot be equated with the subjective ideological ease of an intellectual status group, since it cannot readily be distinguished from an adequate approach *tout court*. (One of the least satisfactory legacies of the tradition of Marx and Hegel to concerned modern thinkers is the presumption that, even if human beings do not know what they are doing, history can be trusted to sort itself out.)

Thus far, it seems fair to say, no one sympathetic to Wittgenstein's philosophy has succeeded in giving a very convincing account of its implications for social or political philosophy.[20] The view that these are in fact inadvertently and ludicrously conservative has been pressed from an early date by Ernest Gellner;[21] and, on this score at least, his arguments have never received a cogent answer. The most influential lesson drawn from Wittgenstein's arguments has been the inanity of a positivist social science.[22] Peter Winch's famous work *The Idea of a Social Science* persuaded rather few readers of the validity of its central thesis. But it certainly alerted very many more to the degree to which positivist social sciences are obliged to wallow in intellectual confusion and bad faith. Winch's insistence on the obtuseness of a presumptively non-human perspective on human social existence was extremely persuasive. But his apparent conclusion that social and political causality either does not occur or else lies beyond human ken has naturally proved less attractive.[23] If the lines of inference of Wittgenstein's later writings to their presumed implications for social and political theory were more direct and apparent, it might by now be permissible to treat the interpretations of the latter as a reductio ad absurdum of the former. But at present it is at least as likely that they merely represent less than felicitous guesses as to what Wittgenstein's arguments do imply. More recent attempts to assess these implications – such as those of Pitkin, Danford and perhaps MacIntyre[24] – have a variety of merits. But on the central question of how to envisage a rational critique of practices in a world in which the authority of practices is the final cognitive authority, none makes a clear advance. Here, it does seem likely that it is the extreme scepticism of Wittgenstein's philosophical position which is responsible. Logic and mathematics, it seems, do possess powers of self-organization and self-maintenance which enable them to survive in a multiplicity of distinct forms without external criteria to which to appeal. But, with existential values, the corrosion of scepticism is not merely more painful; it is also practically more destructive. How human beings choose to act depends fundamentally on how they imagine the settings of their lives. If they cannot sense values as authoritative and in the last instance external to the contingencies of their own desires, they are inclined to lose their moral nerve. We do not really have much idea of how to assess the consequences of a protracted loss of moral nerve, though the imaginative literature of individual terrorism and totalitarian repression over the last century and a quarter has explored the question with some courage. But it is in any case far from clear that it is the *external* consequences of a loss of moral nerve on which we need to concentrate. Could any consequence whatever be a greater disaster for the human race than the loss of moral nerve itself? I intend that, plainly, as an ostentatiously anti-utilitarian question.

It is important to raise such questions because of the dominating role played by utilitarianism in moral and political thinking about the world today, very explicitly in the legitimatory and critical politics of capitalist societies and somewhat more surreptitiously in those of communist states. Utilitarianism, sociologically, has long been the moral commonsense of a capitalist culture; and, whatever the fate of the capitalist mode of production, the future role of utilitarianism can be expected to endure as the self-understanding of coercive power in the modern world. Behind this ideological salience there lie two deep and very different foundations, the immemorial pressures of material scarcity in an increasingly overpopulated and contaminated world and the relentless imaginative impetus of reductive mechanical explanation in the sciences of nature and the materialist ontology which these have fostered. Utilitarianism is an unexciting and, in my view, a politically and humanly obtuse mode of thought. But it is unfrivolous in itself; and the pressures behind it, both practical and imaginative, are as urgent as any on earth. It is, of course, the practical pressures which link it so closely to organized coercive power and which do so in a deeply rational manner, through the intimate relations between political power and political responsibility. No government on earth today, however brutal and inefficacious, can afford to be durably indifferent to the material needs of its subjects. The rational organization of production is still, as it has been for some millennia, the central preoccupation of collective human life. Both the productive benefits of market efficiency acclaimed by Adam Smith and the criteria of rational decision-making in a planned economy are most economically and clearly expressed in utilitarian terms. For a variety of reasons, Marxists and even liberal economists may feel a certain fastidiousness at the crude homogenization of human values which is both the blemish and the point of utilitarian thinking. But it is idle to presume that utilitarianism could be discarded and the analytical instruments of economics, in all their distressing debility, be comfortably retained. Since the human settings in which men will live, in any future in which they have not exterminated most of their own kind, will require a higher and defter level of economic understanding than any modern societies have yet attained, the hope of being able to dispense with economics, the systematic analysis of optimal allocation of scarce resources, is just a pipe dream. This understanding is hardest to avoid at the centre of a modern state apparatus, because in that setting it operates so blatantly as a Machiavellian constraint on the retention of power. The ritual execution of the monarch when the harvest fails lacks an elegant modern analogue. But however scruffily and erratically mediated, the prospective outcomes of economic failure for the powerful in any modern state are at least as unpromising. Nor is it only at the centre of state apparatuses, or in the exchange of commodities itself, that this consciousness presides. As the overexcited and imprecise but deeply suggestive vision of Michel Foucault has shown us, it lurks omnipresently throughout the comprehensive reorganization of social existence to accommodate the demands of modern production.[25] The instrumental assessment of human practices and the incessant reckoning of consequences is part of the way in which we have learnt to live and whatever the validity of idyllic representations of the unsullied holism of human societies in the distant past,[26] there is no way back from the warily strategic and tactical consciousness of modern human beings. (Of course, the validity of such representations is not a wholly trivial matter since, if the Hegelian contrast with modern plurality and social antagonism – Schöne Welt wo bist du? – relies on a contrast which never in fact existed – there is literally nothing for us to regret – and the self-consciousness of modernity is not in reality a historical predicament but simply a historical consciousness of a condition inherent in human nature and human society as such.) This last is not a very fashionable

sentiment because of the accumulated intellectual damage done by
Hegelian and Marxist thought to the idea of there being a distinctively
human nature outside history. But unfashionable though it may be, it is
in this form, nevertheless, valid.

As an intellectual idiom utilitarianism is susceptible of more or less
indefinite elaboration. The contrast between the thinking of Derek
Parfit, the most creative utilitarian philosopher in the Anglo-Saxon
world today, and any nineteenth-century predecessor is strikingly
large.[27] The rigour and power of versions of utilitarianism elaborated
by some recent Western economists is extremely impressive.[28] And
even less subtle utilitarian political philosophers such as Glover,
Honderich and Peter Singer have done much to broaden British and
American discussion of the ethical and political implications of
economic exchanges between rich and poor countries, of the rationality of political violence, and of the obligations of the living to future
generations of mankind.[29] The single safest prediction about the future
of political philosophy (if, like we ourselves, it is fortunate enough to
experience a future of any length) is that there will be a great deal more
utilitarian political philosophy and that *some* of it will be extremely
clever.

As it is, utilitarianism continues to bulk large in the treatment of
political topics in the major Western philosophical journals and
especially in those, like *Ethics* or *Philosophy and Public Affairs*, which
concentrate on political and social theory. But neither the most
influential nor the most impressive of recent writing on political philosophy, nor on ethics more generally, has been utilitarian in inspiration.
The cultural revulsion from utilitarian philistinism and inhumanity is
roughly coeval with utilitarianism itself. In the last century and three
quarters in Germany, England, France and the United States it has
received a wide variety of philosophical orchestrations. Some of these
have been more adventurous than others. It is difficult, for example, to
believe that a defence of value for man centred, like Michel Foucault's,
on the defence of bodies and pleasures can be seriously hostile to
utilitarianism in the last instance, however offended it may be by the
particular cultural or political forms which the latter has taken.
Bentham's Panopticon, that stunningly direct historical vindication of
the rationality of our paranoias, was, after all, a historical adjunct of
utilitarian consciousness, not an ineluctable logical implication of its
philosophical premises. Utilitarianism is a self-conscious corrective of
our existing moral sentiments, not an attempt to model the casual
disarray in which history has left these. It cannot, to a clear-headed
utilitarian, be a *serious* criticism of utilitarianism as a theory of the

human good that it affronts some aspects of our existing moral sensibilities.

But, as so often in philosophy, the key question at issue here is who is to bear the burden of proof. On this, utilitarians are as much at risk as anyone else. There are three quite separate pressures behind utilitarian beliefs. One is essentially cultural and rests on the process of commodity exchange which plays such a prominent role in modern social experience and which can be plausibly (if not perhaps altogether adequately) depicted in purely utilitarian terms. The other two are more philosophical in character, though they also draw some of their plausibility from broader aspects of social experience. The first of the two is an appeal beyond cultural diversity to common (and hence presumable biological) dimensions of human experience: from cultural diversity to biological uniformity. The intense interactive pressure between cultures in the world today makes the quest for standards external to a particular culture of some practical urgency. And, whatever its deficiencies as an œcumenical standard, there is no doubting the force of a utilitarian critique of the scale of inequality in material misery and enjoyment amongst the human race at present. The second, philosophically more grandiose and humanly more unnerving, is the materialist ontology favoured by any version of scientific realism which is motivated by the explanatory triumphs of modern natural science. Utilitarians make a bold attempt to answer the bemusing ontological question of where in a material universe value for man can find a place. Of the two major responses to this question since the mid eighteenth century, utilitarianism certainly imposes less frenzied and forlorn ontological demands than does the ethical theory of Kant. It is striking how much of the recent Anglo-Saxon philosophical backlash against utilitarianism in political philosophy remains essentially Kantian in inspiration. John Rawls's *Theory of Justice*,[30] Robert Nozick's *Anarchy, State and Utopia* and Thomas Nagel's *The Possibility of Altruism* and *Mortal Questions* are all profoundly Kantian works. But thus far they offer a Kantian ethics without any convincingly characterized defence of or surrogate for a Kantian ontology. It therefore seems unlikely (quite apart from the cogency or otherwise of their political conceptions) that they will prove markedly more robust than, for example, Alasdair MacIntyre's[31] attempt to resuscitate an Aristotelian ethics without its attendant metaphysics or Charles Taylor's rather less clearly delineated struggle to execute the same task on the even less fissile philosophy of Hegel.[32] It is not, of course, that philosophers cannot, and indeed do not often, get some arguments right and others wrong. But it is hard to resist the judgement, on this issue, that, however unsuccessfully, Aristotle and Kant and Hegel were at least addressing very deep imaginative problems and that to raid their philosophical creations, like magpies, for odd bits of more or less sparkling material to adorn our own less ambitious intellectual domiciles is to display a particularly unreflective intellectual indolence. At the very least, it would be prudent first to consider carefully just what function these items were designed to perform in their original theoretical settings.

If it is right, for these or other reasons, to see the major philosophical strength of utilitarianism as lying in the continuing vitality of one or other variety of scientific realism, only a sapping of the defences of the latter will be likely to undermine its intellectual foundations at all durably. The main incentive for the elaboration of scientific realism is the desire to *explain* the success of natural science, an experience which, if left unexplained, is implicitly seen, as Hilary Putnam has complained,[33] as a continuing miracle. The relationship between modern philosophy and modern science has been extremely intimate ever since the seventeenth century and much of it has turned on the desire of the former to explain the success of the latter. Once the legitimacy and coherence of this demand has been accepted, the charms of a monist ontology become far harder to resist (though the technical problems of rendering one plausible, adequate to human experience and coherent naturally persist). In the longer run the most serious specifically philosophical threat to the dominance of utilitarianism in political consciousness and political philosophy is likely to come from a successful challenge to any scientific realist ontology. The prospect of mounting such a challenge successfully on behalf of subjective moral effort, as Kant attempted, looks unpromising. But the challenge to scientific realism is far more intense on a very different front.[34] The attack by Wittgenstein in his later writings on the ultimate coherence of explanation from beyond human culture (and hence on the very idea of an absolute conception of reality)[35] constitutes one branch of this challenge; and the pragmatist tradition epitomized by Rorty, with its contempt for the chimera of final explanation furnishes another.

If it is right to see the philosophical thrust behind utilitarianism as coming, in this way, from a more or less explicitly monist ontology dictated by scientific realism, its appeals can hardly be separated from the philosophical appeals of the latter. Any weakening in these appeals, therefore, will only expose more cruelly the intrinsic fragility of utilitarianism as a theory of value. The site of this weakness is the relation between value and rational agency. Kant's ethics can reasonably be accused of fetishizing agency. But utilitarians, by contrast, hold a view of agency so detached, unsuperstitious and disabused as virtually to deprive it of significance. The agent figures in utilitarian analysis as the bearer of her or his current tastes (like any other sentient creature). But once having so figured, he or she enjoys, with one exception, no further conceptual privilege. The exception consists in whatever scope for narrowly egoistic choice is allotted to the agent on the contingent grounds that *its* allocation (and no more and no less) will maximize aggregate utility. This proviso is important since it serves as an eminently necessary insurance policy against the wildly counter-intuitive agent-implications of the general doctrine: the charge, for example, that a consistent utilitarian must be committed to thinking of his or her own life simply as a causal resource for the maximization of aggregate utility.[36] It is not easy to think through these allegations to a stable conclusion, since they rapidly spawn an array of paradoxes. But even a preliminary consideration rapidly brings out a most peculiar *shape* in utilitarian conceptions of ethically rational practice, in which at one stage in the assessment individuals are permitted (or indeed required) to adopt a singularly literal-minded and passive attitude towards their own current preferences and at another they are enjoined in effect to see their own life from the outside, from the perspective of the totality of sentient creatures and subordinate their desires rigorously to the interests of this totality. Each of these two perspectives, the unmonitored and unedified preferences of the agent's present and the utility of all creatures capable of feeling at all, involves a remarkably alienated attitude towards one's own life. Since the core of any serious theory of human value must be a conception of why men or women have good reason to *act* as it enjoins, the instability and untransparency of the links between value and agency in utilitarian theory are a fatal flaw.

In moral theory more generally, the most intriguing recent discussions of these links have come in the writings of Williams, Nagel and MacIntyre. These writers differ sharply on such issues as the intelligibility or cogency of moral realism. Williams, for example, takes a far more sceptical and individualist view of the relations between value and reason and individual action than either Nagel or MacIntyre. But the plasticity of the central concepts at issue makes it hard to distinguish clearly between differences of temperamental orientation and those of conceptual necessity.[37] What needs to be emphasized, however, is the extreme difficulty and importance of these issues, and, by induction from the history of political philosophy (Plato, Aristotle, Machiavelli, Hobbes, Spinoza, Locke, Hume, Kant, Hegel, Marx), the radical dependence of any coherent notion of political value in the last instance upon a clear and confident conception of how they are to be understood. It is in the general theory of practical reason, if anywhere, that a well-founded political philosophy must take its stand.[38]

Yet the best-known recent criticisms of utilitarian views in political philosophy itself have been decidedly less well-grounded. Contractarian theories of social justice, like the sharply contrasting works of Rawls and Nozick, have pruned the lush undergrowth of utilitarian evaluation by applying strong theories of rights or the priority of liberty. But not only are these theories, as already mentioned, unanchored in any convincing philosophical account of the status of rights, they are also internally unstable[39] and damagingly parochial in their sense of political possibility and reality.[40] The widespread and deeply felt criticisms of the moral adequacy of utilitarian assessment of legitimate violence in warfare, prompted especially by the American involvement in Vietnam, also rested in the last instance on hazy[41] or unargued[42] ethical assumptions.

Perhaps the most important recent attempt to set out a political philosophy which is adequately grounded both ethically and epistemologically and which tries to take systematic account of social and political reality has been the work of Jürgen Habermas over the last two decades. Habermas's writings have already had a powerful impact upon the philosophy of the social, and in some measure even of the natural, sciences.[43] They have also spawned a massive secondary literature of exposition and assessment. The central Frankfurt School project of a critical theory has recently been summarized with great lucidity and elegance in Raymond Geuss's *The Idea of a Critical Theory*.[44] On the basis of this and other recent evaluations it seems most unlikely that the enduring legacy of Habermas's work will be at all deep. The relations between political perception and philosophical argument in his writings have always been at best vague and optimistic. The vision of highly convergent real interests of historical human beings in the dizzily heterogeneous societies generated by world history up to now looks increasingly arbitrary and ill-considered. And perhaps most pressingly of all, as Geuss brings out in his marvellously fairminded presentation, the link between even the real interests plausibly ascribed to human beings in an ideal social setting and the equally real interests possessed by these beings in their actual social settings is extremely tenuous and it is, once more, wholly unclear what weight, if any, such ideally considered real interests should rationally possess in the determination of their practical conduct. To put it more tersely, even if Habermas's moral and political opinions were less moralistic and more widely convincing, his wide-ranging and dogged investigations have made no progress whatever in resolving the theoretical problems of practical reason with which Williams, Nagel and MacIntyre are now engaged. Nor, on the other hand, has he made much progress in indicating what forms of collective political agency could enable even human beings who agree on the content of their own real interests to realize these in the historical circumstances in which they find themselves today.

I have left until last, in this estimate of philosophical styles, the relation between philosophy and Marxism as a self-consciously adopted intellectual creed. By contrast with most Western political philosophy, Marxism has very obvious strengths. At least in profession (if not always in achievement) it is relentlessly concerned with political causality and with what is to be done here and now. Not only is it directly concerned with practice; it is also committed to the bold ambition of seeing the rationality of the political practice which it vindicates in the broadest possible perspective of human history. Of course in actuality, as we all know, these latter two commitments are more honoured in the breach than in the observance. The flesh is weak and the spirit not always ecstatically willing. But what is important for the future of political philosophy, manifestly, is not the lower reaches of imaginative prowess in a particular intellectual tradition but the best of which it is capable. In the future, as in the past, no doubt most political philosophy, Marxist or otherwise, will be dreary, myopic and at best queasily honest. But what we need to consider, rather, is the intellectual triumphs of a particular tradition, the peaks of its potential achievements.

Here the record of Marxism as political philosophy throughout its history is not very encouraging. There is no doubt at all that the thought of Marx himself constitutes a profound critique (probably, indeed, the most profound critique ever) of the tradition which views the state or political community as guarantor of a common interest and of unambiguously collective values. As a critical political philosopher in effect Marx represents an apotheosis of the theoretical views of Thrasymachus. This is not a line of thought in which it is easy to carry Marx's thought significantly forwards. But it has been explored with little interruption since the 1840s and there is no difficulty in seeing its direct relevance to the quest for political power. In a more detached version, also, it furnishes the central explanatory paradigm of Marxism, the social vision which still illuminates Marxist historiography or social science. On the whole, in recent decades, it has been this more academic version of the tradition which has been intellectually the most impressive.[45]

But the key task of political philosophy is not the task of grasping why power usually deserves to be distrusted (seldom an arduous task). It is that of seeing how power could or can be fashioned and maintained so that it *deserves* trust and loyalty. On this issue Marxism has exceedingly little to offer (a state of affairs which is particularly unfortunate since it is on this issue that it has the strongest political inducements to press its offers upon the widest possible audience). In theoretical form Marxism ought to be above all else a political theory of collective prudence, a theory of how to act so as to enjoy the best chance of producing political effects which are intended and collectively desired. But in strictly political terms, Marxism as an organizing theory of political strategy has been committed, more concretely, throughout its history to more or less radical imprudence. It has been so not so much in its negative assault on existing structures of power (where it has often been remarkably discerning) but in the positive struggle to fashion new and superior structures of power. This weakness goes back directly to the thought of Karl Marx himself which, on this question, remained utopian or fideist or simply evasive from the early 1840s until the day of his death. The refusal to think seriously in advance about the design of socialist institutions (a refusal which, as Norberto Bobbio has pointed out,[46] is singularly unlike the record of bourgeois political theory and practice) has resulted in large areas of the world being governed by the calcified institutional legacy of a series of desperate historical improvisations. It is possible that Marxism as an explanatory paradigm can and does offer an explanation of this outcome more powerful than anyone else can provide. But the power of its explanation presses agonizingly on the residual optimism and good faith of Marxism as a tradition of political practice. If the fundamental aspiration of Marxism is to serve in historical actuality as a theory of human liberation, of the self-emancipation of the proletariat and other historically oppressed groups, it has by the stern standards established in Marx's own critique of historical state power made little, if any, progress since the year 1844. Certainly something very different is going to be required than an endless glossing and ornamentation of Marx's somewhat jejune reflections on the practices of the Commune of 1871. It is quite possible that the Marxist explanatory paradigm could be modified so that it both explained less dogmatically – and hence more accurately[47] – what does occur in men's political history and educated their practical anxieties over what is to be done without plunging them into inane euphoria or the fatalism of despair. But whether it *is* modified in this manner will depend on the courage, frankness, imagination and energy of those who try to understand politics in Marxist terms. It is certainly not a resource firmly inscribed in the body of Marxist theory, in the writings of Marx or Lenin or Mao or Gramsci or Althusser.

This is all very brusque and dogmatic. But I trust that at least it sets out clearly one particular judgement. Marxism as a discrete body of theory has no *privileged* role in the future of political philosophy, anywhere where political philosophy does *have* a future. But it has precisely the same opportunities as any other profound intellectual and cultural tradition to address the vertiginous problems of political and social organization which face the human race today and to consider the significance of different projects for resolving these, at particular times and places, in the light of the fundamental categories of human apprehension: reason, passion, truth.

In one major respect, of course, the socialist revolutions of the twentieth century have altered the subject matter of political phil-osophy very drastically indeed. But they have not done so, as Marxists might initially have hoped and expected, by counterposing to the intrinsic disfigurements of capitalist society the moral elegance of a set of plainly superior social orders. Instead, such comparisons of the domestic properties of capitalist and socialist societies are irretrievably messy and complicated – and thus far distressingly ambiguous. The most unequivocal impact of the socialist revolutions has fallen in fact on the relations between states. It has left the still wealthier states of advanced capitalism with an increasing sense of harrassment and beleaguerment, a sense which is naturally more than matched in the sentiments of their socialist antagonists whose own state powers were in most instances born in direct military confrontation with those of capitalist states. The incessant scrabbling for advantage, military, economic and ideological, and the consequent instability of this fren-zied competitive field is difficult to see at all clearly. But there is one simple and dramatic fact which figures prominently within it and which is awesome enough in its potential significance to demand recognition in any serious modern philosophy of politics. I refer, of course, to the fantastic increase in human powers of destruction signalled by the invention of nuclear weapons. Today for the first time since the Garden of Eden men have not merely the physical power to exterminate their own species but very possibly, in some circum-stances, the socially institutionalized will to use this power. Of course the presumption that they will actually in any circumstance coolly *choose* to use it still beggars belief. But that certainly is no guarantee that they *will* never in fact elect to do so deliberately, still less that they will avoid stumbling inadvertently into having done so.

The grounds for supposing this possibility to mark a decisive transformation in the subject matter of political philosophy are obvious enough. Up till the year of Hiroshima the outer limit of hazard in political agency has always remained the destruction or degradation of individual human lives in larger or smaller numbers. Ever since Hiroshima in prospect, and today already in actuality, the scale of hazard has become utterly different: no less than the extirpation for ever of human life itself (along, no doubt, with myriads of other forms of life). For a species to acquire the capacity to exterminate itself is something wholly new in the history of our world – a second Fall of Man, but unlike the first a wholly historical occurrence. Any naturalistic approach to political philosophy must be sharply altered by this change. If we consider the central roles played in the history of political philosophy by the relation between protection and allegiance, by the right to take human life or the duty to preserve it, it is clear enough how much must have changed when the primary political value becomes the preservation of the species itself and when the political agencies available for securing this value are as bizarrely unsuited to their task as those which we now possess. If much of the vapidity and vacuousness of modern political philosophy stems from its failure to confront political causality, then this particular range of causal potentiality, this possible unintended outcome of intended political practices, marks the most resonant of all its silences.

There are three outstanding weaknesses of modern political understanding in the face of this transformation. One is the absurd overemphasis in political philosophy, ever since the constitution of political economy and the formation in reaction to it of socialist theories, upon distributive justice. In any political society which permits the open discussion of political choices, justice in the distribution of material goods is an inevitable focus of dispute. But the degree to which modern political philosophers, whether Marxist or liberal, concentrate their imaginative energies upon this problem reflects a quite ludicrous level of misjudgement. Even within the sphere of the production of goods, it was a common presupposition of Adam Smith and Marx that efficacy in production was of greater human importance than the somewhat fugitive moral charm of distributive arrangements. Nothing which has happened since 1775 or 1843 or 1916 has done anything to lessen the cogency of this assessment of priorities. But one thing at least – the invention of nuclear weapons (to say nothing of others such as the First and Second World Wars or the Nazi seizure of power and its consequences for the Jewish people) has cruelly exposed the facile nineteenth-century eudaemonism of concentrating one's political imagination on the production and distribution of material goods and their alleged political requirements. It is not merely life chances but also death chances with which political theory must finally make its reckoning.

On the whole those who have grasped the scale of this change have found their political intelligences paralysed by this insight, descending into inane populist phrase-making and hoping blindly that the depth of the horror alone will at last enable men to dispense in safety with coherent political beliefs and to master the recalcitrant causality of politics without even *trying* to understand it. The prospects for these ventures are bleak indeed: to tame the prodigiously intricate menaces spawned by human history with the innocent politics of the Children's Crusade. But bathetic though they are in themselves, these responses do register one essential moment of consciousness, a quite indispensable and highly discomfiting revulsion from the sacralization of political power and authority. It is the compulsive self-righteousness of modern political authorities, capitalist as well as socialist, which makes it so easy for them to construe as a requirement of defensive prudence a relentless attempt to surpass the destructive capacities of their political enemies. The causal forces which have permitted the construction of modern state powers have not weakened; and there is no possibility, short of Armageddon, of their capacity to pursue such courses of action faltering through their own debility. The only countervailing force which might in time bring them under a measure of control is the politically articulated consciousness of sections of the populace at large, operating organizationally within much the same political repertoire as they have had at their disposal for the last century or more.[48] To be optimistic about the prospects of success, accordingly, would be to be a fool indeed; but to be indifferent to these prospects would be to be more than a cynic.

This homily has strayed some distance from political philosophy proper. But its bearing on the latter is direct enough. What it shows, I believe, is the indispensability of thinking about political value, political reason and political duty in the first instance in relation to existing political instruments (states, parties and so on) and the existing causal field of political power, but also the corresponding indispensability of treating these instruments with a high degree of evaluative detachment. Because of the priority of the economic in modern political reflection, modern state powers, both capitalist and socialist, are viewed predominantly in terms of an exculpatory or accusatory functionalism, as docile instruments for the reproduction of particular modes of production. Now that their courtship dances and ritual challenges may terminate in the extinction of human life itself, this is a blisteringly inadequate conception through which to view them. Even in terms of their productive prowess, let alone in terms of their existential contributions as a whole, none of the major power blocs in the world today has the least title to be seen as the standard-bearer of the interests of the human future. Each, after its fashion, is doing its best to cope with an unenviable legacy; but none is coping handsomely enough to deserve even a *trace* of veneration.

In a world of societies dynamically in motion, and increasingly interrelated with one another by economics, politics and military threat, individually incapable of ensuring their own good and collectively capable of exterminating mankind, the privileged focus on sovereign states is a conceptual anachronism in political philosophy. We certainly need in practice new political agencies, both broader and narrower than sovereign states, to pursue our collective interests more effectively and to express our rational solidarities more compellingly. but they must be agencies able to operate within the disorderly nexus of the world we inhabit, not rationalist fantasies of a new order miraculously capable of generating the power to impose itself upon history from the outside. (Before the Last Judgement, the Riddle of History *has* no solution.) Because politics is mired so deeply in consequences, causal recognition has always been just as important for political value as moral testimony. Political philosophy must come to terms with the shabbiness and intricacy as well as with the grandeur of political struggle. It must face political causality as this is and as it can be caused to become, not dream of a blither world.[49] Philosophers, of course, cannot *master* political causality and bend it to their whims. (We do not expect philosophers of natural science to be responsible for the safety of nuclear power stations.) But political philosophers must *face* political causality because the frame of human obligations and the modalities of men's rational cooperation are never simply given *a priori* but always produced through historical agency. Whether conceived through the narrowest egoism or the broadest altruism, the rationality of political action for any individual or class or nation depends inextricably on the properties of the causal field surrounding their potential actions. The resulting indeterminacies baffle our moral and political understanding;[50] perhaps increasingly also, they paralyse our capacity to act collectively. But they simply *constitute* the setting of our political lives. Political philosophers have always disagreed over the relations between rationality and moral strenuousness: the continuum from appropriation, through investment to pure self-sacrifice. And this disagreement is scarcely susceptible of intellectual resolution. But philosophers who have taken politics seriously, whatever the variations in their personal moral tastes, have all in some measure seen the centrality of judging the scope of rational cooperation between men. Even the theory of Hobbes, for example, is perhaps best represented as hinging more on the moral and practical benefits of rationally trustworthy cooperation than on the maximal satisfaction of intractably egoistic desires.[51]

In political philosophy, as in ethics, the correct view in the first instance is the view from here and now: from where and when one is.[52] This is true, and must be true, for nations and classes, as well as for individuals, even if to speak of the view of a nation or a class is to speak less clearly and more metaphorically than to speak of the view of an individual. This is not to dignify myopia or to commend unthinking greed. It is simply to recognize the ties between agency and responsibility and to acknowledge that agency is a causal category. There is no way of prescribing the rational limits on human imagination or emotional susceptibility.[53] But history prescribes the limits of our causal powers and we must assess them as skilfully as we can.

What a political philosophy for the turbulent world of today and tomorrow needs at its centre is a theory of prudence – a theory adequate to the historical world in which we *have* to live, if we are fortunate enough to be given the opportunity to continue to live at all. It cannot be said that political philosophers have made much effort to face this challenge in recent decades. Perhaps they will continue to ignore it – in which case the future of political philosophy in the West, like its recent past – and whatever its intellectual elegancies and ingenuities – is likely to be fairly trivial. In some ways this is a very old challenge. There has never been a time in politically organized societies when prudence was other than indispensable. But the cognitive requirements of prudence in our world are savagely more demanding and the scale of risk, to the species as a whole and to particular human collectivities within it, is breathtakingly more extreme. In its modern form, therefore, the challenge to understand what it is to be prudent – as individuals, as members of communities or classes, as citizens or political leaders – is necessarily an unnerving one.

But it is not a challenge from which we can, with honour, simply turn away.

Notes

Introduction

1 Charles Taylor, 'Political Theory and Practice', in Christopher Lloyd (ed), *Social Theory and Political Practice*, Clarendon Press, Oxford 1983, pp. 61–86; Alasdair MacIntyre, 'The Indispensability of Political Theory', in David Miller and Larry Siedentop (eds), *The Nature of Political Theory*, Clarendon Press, Oxford 1983, pp. 17–34.

2 See John Dunn, *Locke*, Oxford University Press 1984.

3 The younger Hume appears to have worried also that it might be subverted by the prevalence of superstitious or misconceived political ideologies – Jacobitism or even vulgar Whiggism. See Duncan Forbes, *Hume's Philosophical Politics*, Cambridge University Press, Cambridge 1975, esp. pp. 93–101, 204–6; F. J. McLynn, 'Jacobitism and David Hume: the Ideological Backlash Foiled', *Hume Studies*, IX, 2, November 1983, 171–99.

4 John Locke, *Essays on the Law of Nature*, ed. W. von Leyden, Clarendon Press, Oxford 1954, esp. pp. 204–14.

5 See also, John Dunn, *Political Obligation in its Historical Context*, Cambridge University Press, Cambridge 1980, ch. 9.

6 See John Dunn, *The Politics of Socialism*, Cambridge University Press, Cambridge 1984.

7 See also for an anthropological expression of this judgement Clifford Geertz, *Local Knowledge*, Basic Books, New York 1983. But cf. Ernest Gellner, *Legitimation of Belief*, Cambridge University Press, Cambridge 1974.

8 Dunn, *Political Obligation*, ch. 10.

9 Dunn, *Politics of Socialism*.

10 Paul Bracken, *The Command and Control of Nuclear Forces*, Yale University Press, New Haven 1983.

11 Bracken, *Command and Control of Nuclear Forces*. For an illuminating history of how this state of affairs came about see Lawrence Freedman, *The Evolution of Nuclear Strategy*, Macmillan, London 1981.

1 Individuality and clientage in the formation of Locke's social imagination

1 John Locke, *An Essay concerning Human Understanding*, ed P. H. Nidditch, Oxford, 1975, Bk II, xxvii, 9, ll 18–19.

2 *Essay*, II, xxvii, 27, ll 16–18.

3 See helpfully Henry E. Allison, 'Locke's Theory of Personal Identity: A

Re-examination', in I. C. Tipton (ed), *Locke on Human Understanding: Selected Essays*, Oxford, 1977, pp. 105–22.

4 See, for example, the essays by David Lewis, Derek Parfit, David Wiggins and Bernard Williams in Amélie O. Rorty (ed), *The Identities of Persons*, Berkeley, Calif. 1976 and cf. Bernard Williams, 'The Self and the Future', in his *Problems of the Self*, Cambridge 1973, pp. 46–63 and Derek Parfit, 'Personal Identity', *Philosophical Review*, LXXX, 1, Jan 1971, 3–27.

5 *Essay*, II, xxvii, 26, ll 26–28.

6 See Molyneux to Locke, 23 December 1693, *The Correspondence of John Locke*, ed E. S. de Beer, Vol IV, Oxford, 1979, p. 767 and for Locke's immediate responses, 19 January 1694, see pp. 784–6.

7 For an illuminating brief account of eighteenth century responses to Locke's position see Allison, *op cit*. For a more elaborate discussion of some aspects of what was at issue between Locke and Butler see David Wiggins, 'Locke, Butler and the Stream of Consciousness: And Men as a Natural Kind', in Rorty (ed), *Identities of Persons*, 139–73.

8 See particularly Nicholas Jolley, 'Leibniz on Locke and Socinianism', *Journal of the History of Ideas*, XXXIX, 2, April 1978, 233–50, esp 244.

9 Compare Bernard Williams, 'Persons, Character and Morality' in Rorty (ed), *Identities of Persons*, 197–216 with Derek Parfit, 'Later Selves and Moral Principles', in Alan Montefiore (ed), *Philosophy and Personal Relations*, London, 1973, 137–69; and for emphasis on the reflexiveness of human consciousness as the key condition for moral aspiration see Harry Frankfurt, 'Identification and Externality' and Charles Taylor, 'Responsibility for Self' in Rorty (ed), *Identities of Persons*, 239–51, 281–99.

10 See for example the ambivalence of his discussion in a letter to Edward Clarke, 19/29 April 1687 (one of the series subsequently incorporated in *Some Thoughts concerning Education: The Correspondence of John Locke*, ed E. S. de Beer, Vol III, Oxford, 1978, p. 182) of the possibility that youthful human beings might be by nature not merely proud, selfish and greedy but also quite specifically cruel ('the pleasure they take, to put any thing in pain that is capable of it'). This ill disposition Locke '*cannot yet believe* to come from nature' and blames accordingly on the corrupting influence of adult example; but when he considers the appropriate remedy the metaphor which he employs – 'to *plant* the contary, or more natural tempers of good nature, and Compassion in the roome of it' – displays decidedly less assurance. (italics added).

11 See particularly Von Leyden's Introduction to John Locke, *Essays on the Law of Nature*, Oxford 1954; Hans Aarsleff, 'The State of Nature and the Nature of Man in Locke' and Richard Ashcraft, 'Faith and Knowledge in Locke's Philosophy' in J. W. Yolton (ed), *John Locke: Problems and Perspectives*, Cambridge, 1969, 99–139, 194–223; John Dunn, *The Political Thought of John Locke*, Cambridge, 1969; James Tully, *A Discourse on Property: John Locke and his Adversaries*, (Cambridge 1980).

12 See eg Dunn, *Political Thought of Locke*, 32–40, 186–99, 234–35, esp 189–90.

13 A very interesting exploration of the possibilities of success in a venture of this kind (thought not focused in any way on the intellectual experience of Locke) can be found in David Wiggins, *Truth, Invention and the Meaning of Life*, Henriette Hertz Philosophical Lecture, British Academy, 1976.

14 See Williams, 'Persons, Character and Morality', Rorty (ed), *Identities of*

Persons; and for emphasis on its ethical significance see e.g. 'The Makropoulos Case', Williams, *Problems of the Self*, esp. p. 90 and Williams, 'A Critique of Utilitarianism' in J. J. C. Smart and Bernard Williams, *Utilitarianism For and Against*, Cambridge 1973, esp. p. 104.

15 See especially the work of Richard Aaron, Hans Aarsleff, Philip Abrams, Richard Ashcraft, M. R. Ayers, Peter Laslett, Raymond Polin, James Tully, C. A. Viano, W. von Leyden and John Yolton. It is only just to acknowledge that the largest single contribution to the enhancement of our understanding in this period has come from the work of Dr von Leyden.

16 Martin Hollis, *Models of Man*, Cambridge 1977.

17 Cf John Dunn, 'The Identity of the History of Ideas', *Philosophy*, XLIII, April 1968, 85–104; and Dunn, 'Practising History and Social Science on 'Realist Assumptions', in Christopher Hookway and Philip Pettit (eds), *Action and Interpretation: studies in the philosophy of the social sciences*, Cambridge, 1978, 145–75.

18 Cf Frank Manuel, *A Portrait of Isaac Newton*, Cambridge, Mass. 1968, esp pp. 83–5; C. B. Macpherson, *The Political Theory of Possessive Individualism*, Oxford 1962, pp. 194–271.

19 Anthony Kenny, *Will, Freedom and Power*, Oxford, 1975, 108.

20 See helpfully Bernard Williams, 'Deciding to Believe', *Problems of the Self*, 136–51.

21 'Sed ut verum fatear ego a rixosis hujusmodi disputatoribus non multum expecto qui in alienis convellendis, non suis astruendis quaerunt gloriam. Artificis et laudem merentis est aedificare.' Locke to Limborch 1/11 October, *Correspondence of John Locke*, vol III, p. 44.

22 Cf David Lewis, 'Radical Interpretation', *Synthèse*, XXVII, 1974, 331–44.

23 This conception has been elaborated with most care within the philosophy of natural science, particularly under the influence of Quine's treatment of referential opacity. It is employed here as a (deliberately) loose metaphor. For a brief presentation see W. V. Quine and J. S. Ullian, *The Web of Belief*, New York 1970.

24 Varieties of relativism centred upon a conception of belief as a web readily elevate credal habit to an epistemically implausible level of respectability. (Is being much in the habit of believing something really a *good reason* for believing it?) The fact that I cannot accept some of Locke's arguments might simply be an index of my (historical) inability to understand them: 'Two souls may be too widely met.' (Robert Frost, 'A Missive Missile', *Selected Poems*, Harmondsworth 1955, 215). The claim which is presumed here is that it is *because* I do understand them that I cannot accept them.

25 The will that can be weak in an instance of akrasia is 'the faculty for giving effect in one's life to long-term projects and stable purposes'. (Kenny, *Will, Freedom and Power*, p. 107). Locke's own grasp of this point falters on occasion cf, in context, his use as an excuse of the formula 'ita sunt fere res humanae ut nihil praeter voluntatem in nostra sit potestate', (Locke to Limborch 6/16 Feb 1689, *Correspondence of Locke*, Vol III, p. 558).

26 Kenny, *Will, Freedom and Power*, p. 129.

27 Kenny, *Will, Freedom and Power*, p. 130.

28 Compare the argument of Hilary Putnam, 'Philosophy and our Mental Life' in his *Mind, Language and Reality (Philosophical Papers*, Vol II), Cambridge, 1975, 295–8.

29 Frankfurt in Rorty (ed), *Identities of Persons*, 250–1. For the importance of distinguishing inconsistent desires from desires which are merely incompatible see Bernard Williams, *Problems of the Self*, chapters 11 and 12, esp. pp. 203–6 and Ronald de Sousa, 'Rational Homunculi', in Rorty (ed), *Identities of Persons*, esp. 231–6.

30 There are intimate links between the ways in which we conceive, apprehend, experience and feel the world and our place in it. The conceptual difficulty of distinguishing categorically between beliefs and sentiments is developed illuminatingly (from very different viewpoints) in Richard E. Grandy, 'Reference, Meaning and Belief', *Journal of Philosophy*, LXX, 14, 16 August 1973, 439–52 and Robert C. Solomon, 'Emotions and Anthropology: The Logic of Emotional World Views', *Inquiry*, XXI, 1978, 181–99.

31 A very schematic presentation of this kind can be found in Dunn, *Political Thought of Locke*. The degree of intricacy which a more adequate biographical account would require can be inferred from the biographical studies of Cranston (Maurice Cranston, *John Locke: A Biography*, London 1957) and Viano (Carlo Augusto Viano, *John Locke: Dal Razionalismo all' Illuminismo*, Turin 1960). Extremely valuable contextual presentations of individual works in print can be found in the editions of the *Essays on the Law of Nature* (ed. Von Leyden), the *Two Treatises of Government* (ed. Laslett), the *Treatises on the Civil Magistrate* (*Two Tracts on Government*, ed. Abrams) and the *Educational Writings* (ed. Axtell). A very fine analysis of the treatment of the central category of property is now available in James Tully, *A Discourse on Property: John Locke and his Adversaries*, Cambridge 1980 (see also his Cambridge University Ph. D. thesis 1977).

32 For the significance of this see Locke's letter to Edward Clarke, 29 Jan/8 Feb 1689 (*Correspondence of John Locke*, Vol III, 545–6) and John Dunn, 'Consent in the Political Theory of John Locke', *Historical Journal*, X, 2, June 1967, 153–82. Julian H. Franklin's excellent study *John Locke and the Theory of Sovereignty*, Cambridge 1978, is misleading on this point (See esp pp. 121–2).

33 The problems within the natural law tradition which this shift opened up can be seen clearly by contrasting the treatment of moral knowledge in the *Essay* with the preparedness of the great Spanish natural law theorists of the sixteenth century to place their confidence in a moral reason written in the hearts of all mankind. (Cf Quentin Skinner, *The Foundations of Modern Political Thought*, Cambridge 1979, Vol II, pp. 151, 157, 166, 169, 203). For the development in Locke's own thinking see von Leyden's Introduction to the *Essays on the Law of Nature* and Dunn, *Political Thought of Locke*, pp. 19–26, 187–99.

34 See, in general, Dunn, *Political Thought of Locke*; and esp pp. 27–40, 248–54, 257.

35 Pascal's position is perhaps best seen as a second-order fideism: See eg Ian Hacking, *The Emergence of Probability*, Cambridge 1975, chh. 7 and 8. The precise character of Bayle's literary intentions is still in very active dispute. But if, as seems likeliest, he was a believing Christian, his 'reasons' for so being were certainly fideist. For recent discussions see: Paul Dibon, 'Redécouverte de Bayle', in P. Dibon (ed), *Pierre Bayle le philosophe de Rotterdam*, Amsterdam 1959, vii–xvii (and see the review of this by Herbert Dieckmann, *Journal of the History of Ideas*, XXI, 1, January 1961, 131–6); Elisabeth Labrousse, *Pierre*

Bayle, 2 vols, The Hague, 1963–4; Walter Rex, *Essays on Pierre Bayle and Religious Controversy*, The Hague 1965; Karl C. Sandberg, *At the Crossroads of Faith and Reason*, Tucson, Arizona 1966; Craig B. Bush, *Montaigne and Bayle: variations on the theme of scepticism*, The Hague 1966; Gianfranco Cantelli, *Teologia e Ateismo: saggio sul pensiero filosofico e religioso di Pierre Bayle*, Florence 1969; J. P. Jossua, *Pierre Bayle ou l'obsession du mal*, Paris 1977. There is an extremely interesting study of the intellectual reactions to Bayle's greatest work of his contemporaries and eighteenth century successors in Pierre Rétat, *Le Dictionnaire de Bayle et la lutte philosophique au XVIIIe siècle*, Paris 1971. (*Bibliothèque de la Faculté des Lettres de Lyon*, XXVII).

36 The transition from *Two Tracts on Government* to the *Essays on the Law of Nature* might be seen in these terms. Abrams' Introduction gives an interesting discussion of the internal instability of the position adopted in the *Tracts*.

37 John Dunn, 'The Politics of Locke in England and America in the Eighteenth Century', in J. W. Yolton (ed), *John Locke: Problems and Perspectives*, Cambridge 1969, 45–80; Martyn P. Thompson, 'The Reception of Locke's *Two Treatises of Government* 1690–1715', *Political Studies*, XXIV, 2, June 1976, 184–91.

38 The profound intellectual importance of this issue for Hume is brought out admirably in Duncan Forbes, *Hume's Philosophical Politics*, Cambridge 1975. It made Hume, particularly in his essay on the original contract, a textually somewhat high-handed critic of Locke. (See Martyn P. Thompson, 'Hume's Critique of Locke and the Original Contract', *Il Pensiero Politico*, II, 2, 1977, 189–201).

39 *Conduct of the Understanding (The Works of John Locke*, 4 Vols, London 1768, IV, p. 166).

40 See the Journal entry printed by von Leyden in *Essays on the Law of Nature*, pp. 265–72. And see von Leyden's Introduction, 79–80). Cf also John W. Yolton, *Locke and the Compass of Human Understanding*, Cambridge 1970, pp. 145–9.

41 This view of the implications of Hobbes's writings does not depend upon a more or less contentious judgement as to the character of Hobbes's own religious conviction or agnosticism. It simply depends on the evident and unmistakably intended theoretical property of Hobbes's work, displayed with particular force in *Leviathan*, of depriving all theological categories of any intrinsic theoretical implications of their own. For a helpful discussion of Hobbes's arguments on the subject and of the inferences which they permit as to the content of his own religious beliefs see Ronald Hepburn, 'Hobbes on the Knowledge of God', in Maurice Cranston and Richard S. Peters (ed), *Hobbes and Rousseau*, Garden City, N. Y., 1972, 84–108.

42 *Bodleian MS Locke* c 28, 141. (Dunn, *Political Thought of Locke*, p. 1)

43 Cf 'He that has not a mastery over his inclinations, he that knows not how to resist the importunity of present pleasure, or pain, for the sake of what, reason tells him, is fit to be donne, wants the true principle of Vertue, and industry; and is in danger never to be good for anything.' (Letter to Edward Clarke 19/29 April 1687, *Correspondence*, III, p. 173. And see *Correspondence*, III, pp. 94, 108, 130, 179–82.)

44 *The Correspondence of John Locke*, ed E. S. de Beer, Oxford 1976. 7 vols published to date. 1 to follow.

45 *Two Treatises* (ed Laslett), II, 6, ll 10–14. For a fine demonstration of the

194

fundamental role played by this argument in the *Two Treatises*, see Tully, *A Discourse on Property*.

46 *Correspondence*, ii, p. 733.

47 See *Two Treatises*, ii, p. 54, ll 1–12.

48 Locke to his father, May 11th 1652, *Correspondence*, I, pp. 7–8 and see also an earlier letter to his father, 4 May 1652, *Correspondence*, I, pp. 6–7.

49 *Correspondence*, I, pp. 10–11 (date and recipient's name omitted. de Beer's translation).

50 *ibid* (cited in my own translation).

51 *Correspondence*, I, pp. 145–46 (undated).

52 *Correspondence*, I, pp. 60 (misdated).

53 *Correspondence*, I, pp. 162–3 (20 Dec? 1660).

54 *Correspondence*, I, pp. 122–4 (20 Oct 1659).

55 See Locke, *Paraphrase of the Epistles of St Paul to the Galatians*. Note to the Reader (*Works* iii, pp. 290): '... if there be nothing else worth notice in him, accept of his good intention'.

56 Dunn, *Political Thought of Locke*, chh. 3–19.

57 The differences between friendship, kinship and patronage as modes of social relationship have been very elaborately discussed by anthropologists over the last twenty-five years. No clear consensus has emerged on the appropriate manner in which to demarcate the scope of each. A helpful introductory discussion can be found in Eric R. Wolf, 'Kinship, Friendship and Patron–Client Relations in Complex Societies', M. Banton (ed), *The Social Anthropology of Complex Societies*, London 1966, 1–22. For my purposes the distinction can be seen as lying between the relations of kin (into which one enters by 'birth' in Locke's terminology) and the relations of clientage (which are generated by the bestowal of 'benefits' to all but the closest of kin, where the benefactor is interested in sustaining a social relationship with the beneficiary). Alliance between equals is, in my usage, a matter of friendship. However, all social relationships of any significance or durability tend to be moralized in terms of a vocabulary of friendship (patron–client ties are ties of 'lop-sided friendship') and the divisions between kinship and friendship do not appear to have been at all clearly demarcated in English vocabulary at this period. (See eg Randolph Trumbach, *The Rise of the Egalitarian Family*, London 1978, esp p. 65). The first 200 pages of volume I of the *Correspondence* is particularly illuminating on the conceptions of the character and significance of these modes of relationship among Locke's acquaintance as a young man and on Locke's own responses to them. Since the *Correspondence* is as yet unindexed it may be of some help to list summarily some of the more revealing contexts in the first four volumes:

I, p. 215 ('let him study but complyance, he neede want noe preferment'), pp. 225, 264 ('letting slip the minute they say everyone has once in his life to make himself'), pp. 266, 281–2, 287, 301, 303–5, 328 ('feel nothing at all of other's misfortunes and as little as you can of your owne'), pp. 367–8, 401, 420, 464, 466–7, 479, 513, 520, 575, 577, 599, 648, 649 ('Espetially this civilized world wherein you are obleiged to keepe your rank and station, and which if by mismanagement or neglect of your temporall affairs you fall from, you by your own fault put your self out of a condition of doeing that good and performing those offices requird from one in that station ...' 'We are borne members of common wealths, beset with relations, and in need of friends, and under a necessity of acquaintance '), pp. 672, 691, 700.

II, pp. 61, 76–7, 90, 103–4, 124, 160, 226, 269, 274, 353–54, 386, 403, 406, 453–4, 496, 498, 502, 519–20, 523, 549, 551–2, 556, 568–9, 591 ('There is a commerce of Friendship as well as merchandise...' etc.), pp. 595, 626, 662–3, 721 (and see 661–2, 671, 673, 742, 745–6), 756, 764–5. III, pp. 76, 79, 94, 108, 114, 116–17, 128–30, 131, 153, 175, 179–82, 229, 251–2, 255–6, 269,274, 306, 322–3, 343–7, 351–3, 387, 409–10, 429, 440, 446–7, 471–2, 543, 553, 556–58, 573*, 577, 603, 606, 634 (and 648, 674, 693), 645, 680, 715, 718, 725, 726, 730, 761, 787. IV, pp. 176, 288, 459–60, 643–4, 654–5.

58 For these (and several other illuminating) references see Forbes, *Hume's Philosophical Politics*, p. 125n. The poise displayed in this social attitude illuminated Hume's imaginative capacity in his philosophy of religion fully to entertain a conception of nature as 'blind' or 'indifferent'. See especially his *Dialogues concerning Natural Religion*, ed. Norman Kemp Smith, London 1947. There are helpful discussions of precisely where Hume himself should be seen as standing within the argument of the *Dialogues* in Kemp Smith's introduction, in Anders Jeffner, *Butler and Hume on Religion. A Comparative Analysis*, Stockholm 1966, esp pp. 192–209, and in two articles by Ernest C. Mossner, 'The Religion of David Hume', *Journal of the History of Ideas*, XXXIX, 4, October 1978, 653–63 and 'Hume and the Legacy of the Dialogues' in George Morice (ed), *David Hume: Bicentenary Papers*, Edinburgh 1977, 1–22.

59 See classically Adam Smith, *An Inquiry into the Nature and Causes of the Wealth of Nations*, ed R. Campbell, A. Skinner and W. Todd, Oxford, 1976, esp vol. I, pp. 412–22 and vol II, p. 712 (esp 'as he gives scarce any thing to any body but in exchange for an equivalent, there is scarce any body who considers himself as entirely dependent upon him'). This is a central theme for all the major Scots writers on social development, Hume, Smith, Adam Ferguson, John Millar, Sir James Steuart, Lord Kames, William Robertson etc.

60 There are good reasons for refusing to endorse this particular modern judgement. Cf David Gauthier, 'The Social Contract as Ideology', *Philosophy and Public Affairs*, VI, 2, Winter 1977, 130–64 and, more vulgarly, John Dunn, *Western Political Theory in the Face of the Future*, Cambridge 1979.

61 Lawrence Stone, *The Crisis of the Aristocracy 1558–1641*. Oxford 1965, 214.

2 Trust in the politics of John Locke

1 Cf G. A. Cohen, *Karl Marx's Theory of History*, Clarendon Press, Oxford 1978 and 'Reply to Elster on Marxism, Functionalism and Game Theory', *Theory and Society*, XI, 4, July 1982, 483–96 with Jon Elster, 'Marxism, Functionalism and Game Theory: the Case for Methodological Individualism', *Theory and Society*, XI, 4, July 1982, 453–82.

2 John Locke, *Essays on the Law of Nature*, ed. W. von Leyden, Clarendon Press, Oxford 1954, p. 212.

3 Barrington Moore, *Injustice: The Social Bases of Obedience and Revolt*, M. E. Sharpe, White Plains, N.Y. 1978. And cf John Dunn, 'Understanding Revolutions', ch. 4 below.

4 David Hume, *A Treatise of Human Nature*, 2 vols J. M. Dent & Sons, London 1911, Bk III, Pt II (esp section 8: Vol 2 pp. 242–3) and *Essays, Moral, Political and Literary*, Henry Frowde, Worlds Classics, London 1903, 'Of the Original Contract', esp pp. 466–7; and see Martyn P. Thompson, 'Hume's Critique of

Locke and the "Original Contract"', *Il Pensiero Politico*, x, 2, 1977, 189–201; and John Dunn, 'From Applied Theology to Social Analysis', chapter 3 below.

5 John Dunn, *Political Obligation in its Historical Context*, Cambridge University Press 1980, ch. 3.
6 Niklas Luhmann, *Trust and Power*, ed T. Burns and G. Poggi, John Wiley, Chichester and New York 1979, p. 30.
7 Luhmann, *op cit*, p. 87.
8 Luhmann, *op cit*, p. 15.
9 Luhmann, *op cit*, p. xiv.
10 Luhmann, *op cit*, p. 4.
11 Luhmann, *op cit*, pp. 50, 69.
12 Luhmann, *op cit*, p. 16.
13 Luhmann, *op cit*, p. xiv.
14 Luhmann, *op cit*, p. xiv.
15 Luhmann, *op cit*, p. 22.
16 Luhmann, *op cit*, p. 69.
17 Luhmann, *op cit*, pp. 87 etc.
18 See Dunn, *Political Obligation in its Historical Context*, ch. 10; and 'Social Theory, Social Understanding and Political Action', ch. 7 below.
19 Bernard Williams, *Moral Luck*, Cambridge University Press, Cambridge 1981.
20 Dunn, *Political Obligation*, chh. 8 and 10.
21 Dunn, *Political Obligation*, ch. 10.
22 For an illuminating study of Locke's moral thinking see John Colman, *John Locke's Moral Philosophy*, Edinburgh University Press, Edinburgh 1983.
23 *The Correspondence of John Locke*, ed. E. S. de Beer, Clarendon Press, Oxford, Vol 1, 1976, p. 122.
24 John Locke, *Two Tracts on Government*, ed Philip Abrams, Cambridge University Press, Cambridge 1967, pp. 231–2.
25 Locke, *Two Tracts*, pp. 78, 231.
26 Locke, *Two Tracts*, p. 146.
27 Locke, *Two Tracts*, p. 150.
28 John Locke, *An Essay concerning Human Understanding*, ed. Peter H. Nidditch, Clarendon Press, Oxford 1975. Contents summary of Bk I, ch. iv, 23 (p. 19).
29 Locke, *Essays on the Law of Nature*, pp. 128–9.
30 Locke, *Law of Nature*, pp. 166–7.
31 Locke, *Law of Nature*, p. 128.
32 Locke, *Law of Nature*, pp. 126–9.
33 Locke, *Law of Nature*, p. 128.
34 Locke, *Law of Nature*, p. 130 (and see p. 176).
35 Locke, *Law of Nature*, p. 126.
36 Locke, *Law of Nature*, pp. 212–14.
37 Locke, *Law of Nature*, p. 212.
38 See Bodleian MS Locke, c 28, ff 21–32, cited by J. W. Gough in John Locke, *Epistola de Tolerantia (A Letter on Toleration)*, ed. R. Klibansky and J. W. Gough, Clarendon Press, Oxford 1968, pp. 15–16.
39 Locke, *Epistola de Tolerantia*, p. 134.
40 Locke, *Tolerantia*, p. 134.

41 Pierre Bayle, *Pensées diverses sur la Comète*, ed A. Prat, E. Cornély, Paris, 2 vols, 1911–12; Vol. 1, pp. 301–20, 366–50; Vol. 2, pp. 5–21, 102–51.
42 Locke, *Essay concerning Human Understanding*, II, xxviii, 10–12 (pp. 353–7).
43 John Locke, *Two Treatises of Government*, ed Peter Laslett, Cambridge University Press, Cambridge 1960, II, 14, ll 17–19.
44 Locke, *Two Treatises*, II, 6, l. 6.
45 Locke, *Two Treatises*, II, 195, ll 4–7.
46 Locke, *Essay concerning Human Understanding*, II, xxi, 49 (p. 265).
47 Locke, *Human Understanding*, II, xxi, 47 (p. 264).
48 Bodleian MS Locke c 28, ff. 139–40. For an excellent discussion, see Colman, *John Locke's Moral Philosophy*, pp. 194–9.
49 William Wollaston, *The Religion of Nature Delineated*, 6th ed., London 1738, I, iii–vi, pp. 8–20.
50 Hume, *Treatise of Human Nature*, III, I, i (Vol. 2, pp. 170–71 n.).
51 For a helpful discussion of these two components of Locke's thinking see Colman, *Locke's Moral Philosophy*.
52 Leo Strauss, *Natural Right and History*, University of Chicago Press, Chicago 1954, pp. 202–51; Richard H. Cox, *Locke on War and Peace*, Clarendon Press, Oxford 1960.
53 Locke, *Two Treatises of Government*, II, 19 (pp. 298–9).
54 Locke, *Human Understanding*, IV, xiv (esp 2, ll 16–19: 'So in the greatest part of our Concernment, he has afforded us only the twilight, as I may so say, of *Probability*, suitable, I presume, to that state of Mediocrity and Probationership, he has been pleased to place us in here').
55 See John J. Jenkins, *Understanding Locke*, Edinburgh University Press, Edinburgh 1983, ch. 7, esp. pp. 150–52; Colman, *Locke's Moral Philosophy*, ch. 8, esp. p. 207.
56 Locke, *Human Understanding*, II, xxvii (esp. 26, pp. 346–7), II, xxi, 44; 47–53; 56 etc.
57 Locke, *Human Understanding*, II, xxi, 70 (and see also 44, 65).
58 Locke, *Human Understanding*, II, xxviii, 10–12 (pp. 353–57, esp. p. 357); *Some Thoughts Concerning Education* in *The Educational Writings of John Locke*, ed James Axtell, Cambridge University Press, Cambridge 1968.
59 As Colman rightly insists: *Locke's Moral Philosophy*, p. 171.
60 Locke, of course, does not himself employ the term 'socialization'. But he gives an exceedingly penetrating account in the *Essay* and in *Some Thoughts Concerning Education* of what we now mean by the term.
61 See John Dunn, *The Political Thought of John Locke*, Cambridge University Press, Cambridge 1969: Part III.
62 For a general formulation of the duty see his Journal entry for 15 July 1678 (Bodleian MS Locke f. 3, 202, cited in Dunn, *Political Thought of Locke*, p. 49 n; and see Dunn, *Political Obligation*, ch. 3).
63 Locke, *Two Treatises*, II, 77, ll 1–4; and see *Essays on the Law of Nature*, p. 156.
64 Locke, *Two Treatises*, II, 31, ll 5–7; II, 34, ll 1–3.
65 Locke, *Law of Nature*, pp. 204–15. This is why 'An Hobbist with his principle of self-preservation whereof him self is to be judge, will not easily admit a great many plain duties of morality' (Bodleian MS Locke, f 2, 128).
66 Locke, *Two Treatises*, II, 46 and 48.
67 Hume, *Treatise*, III, II, ii (Vol. 2, pp. 199–200).

68 Some continue to doubt how far it does serve to *explain* these: cf Elster, *Theory and Society*, XI, 4, July 1982, 453–82.
69 Locke, *Human Understanding*, II, xxi, 47–53 etc.
70 Locke, *Human Understanding*, IV, xx, 17 (p. 718).
71 Locke, *Human Understanding*, II, xxi, 55 (pp. 269–70).
72 Locke, *Human Understanding*, I, iii, 13 (p. 75).
73 Locke, *Human Understanding*, I, iii, 13 (p. 74).
74 See John Passmore, 'Locke and the Ethics of Belief', *Proceedings of the British Academy*, LXIV, 1978, pp. 185–208; and John Dunn, *Locke*, Oxford University Press, Oxford 1984, ch. 3.
75 Locke, *Two Treatises*, II, ch. 2.
76 Locke, *Human Understanding*, IV, xx, 17, ll 33–5.
77 Locke, *Two Treatises*, II, 124, ll 5–12; and cf. II, 90, 131 etc.
78 Locke, *Two Treatises*, II, 11, ll 16–27; 172, ll 9–19.
79 Locke, *Human Understanding*, II, xxi, 56 (pp. 270–1).
80 Bodleian MS Locke c. 28, f. 85ʳ (quoted in Dunn, *Political Thought of Locke*, p. 148 n. 1).
81 Locke, *Two Treatises*, II, 171, ll 1–5.
82 J. W. Gough, *John Locke's Political Philosophy* Clarendon Press, Oxford 1950, ch. vii.
83 Locke, *Two Treatises*, II, ch. 14.
84 Locke, *Two Treatises*, II, 166, ll 20–21.
85 *Correspondence of John Locke*, IV, p. 148.
86 Passmore, 'Locke and the Ethics of Belief'.
87 Locke, *Human Understanding*, IV, xiv, 2 (esp. ll. 16–29); II, xxi, 47–71.
88 *Correspondence of John Locke*, I p. 122. This places Locke in an intriguing relation to the trajectory sketched by Alasdair MacIntyre, *After Virtue*, Duckworth, London 1981.
89 Cf works cited in n. 18 above.
90 Cf Dunn, *Western Political Theory in the Face of the Future*, Cambridge University Press, Cambridge 1979; 'Totalitarian Democracy and the Legacy of Modern Revolutions' ch. 5 below.

3 *From applied theology to social analysis: the break between John Locke and the Scottish Enlightenment*

1 David Gauthier, 'Why Ought One Obey God? Reflections on Hobbes and Locke', *Canadian Journal of Philosophy*, 7 (1977), 425–46, especially p. 432.
2 John Dunn, *The Political Thought of John Locke: An Historical Account of the Argument of the 'Two Treatises of Government'*, Cambridge 1969; James Tully, *A Discourse of Property: John Locke and his Adversaries*, Cambridge 1980.
3 Gauthier, 'Why Ought One Obey God?', p. 435.
4 Ernest Campbell Mossner, *The Life of David Hume*, Edinburgh 1954, pp. 586–7. Even during this final illness Hume retained the capacity to tease Boswell with the greatest finesse. See the account of their last meeting in Boswell's journal, 3 March 1777, in *Boswell in Extremis, 1776–1778*, ed. Charles M. Weis and Frederick A. Pottle, London 1971, pp. 11–15, especially p. 11: 'He then said flatly that the Morality of every Religion was bad, and I really thought, was not jocular when he said that when he heard a man was

religious, he concluded he was a rascal, though he had known some instances of very good men being religious.'

5 The question of Smith's theological beliefs is an extremely intricate one. Jacob Viner, for example, *The Role of Providence in the Social Order*, Philadelphia 1972, ch. 3, especially pp. 79, 81–2 and also p. 60, lays considerable emphasis on the providentialist dimension of Smith's social thought. It is certainly easy enough to find such themes articulated by Smith in his earlier writings and in the early editions of the *Theory of Moral Sentiments*. In later life, however, Smith appears to have become considerably more sceptical (or considerably less discreet). Special attention must be paid to the so-called 'Passage of Atonement' in Appendix II, *Theory of Moral Sentiments*, edd. D. D. Raphael and A. L. Macfie, Oxford 1976, pp. 383–401. See also notes 67 and 68.

6 John Locke, *Epistola de Tolerantia*, ed. and trans. R. Klibansky and J. W. Gough, Oxford 1968, p. 135. (See also the Latin text of the whole of paragraph 4, p. 134.) It is not, however, clear that Locke's views on this matter were wholly consistent. Why, on this view, should promises and oaths 'tye the infinite Deity'? (*Two Treatises of Government*, ed. Peter Laslett, Cambridge, 1960, 1.2.6 line 6.) And see the, at first sight, slightly more naturalistic drift of: 'Truth and Keeping of Faith belongs to Men, as Men, and not as Members of Society'. (*Two Treatises*, 2.2.14 lines 17–19.)

7 See, for example, the introductions of Klibansky and Gough to Locke, *Epistola de Tolerantia*, esp. pp. xxxv, 40–1, etc. For a very helpful historical survey of attitudes towards disbelief in God in seventeenth-century England, see G. E. Aylmer, 'Unbelief in Seventeenth-Century England', in Donald Pennington and Keith Thomas (eds.), *Puritans and Revolutionaries: Essays in Seventeenth-Century History Presented to Christopher Hill*, Oxford 1978, pp. 22–46.

8 For Hume, see particularly David Gauthier, 'David Hume, Contractarian', *Philosophical Review*, 88 (1979), 3–38.

9 See e.g. Gauthier, 'Why Ought One Obey God?'; and the very clear analysis given by Bernard Williams, 'Internal and External Reasons', in Ross Harrison (ed.), *Rational Action*, Cambridge 1979, pp. 17–28.

10 See Philippa Foot, 'Morality as a System of Hypothetical Imperatives', *Philosophical Review*, 81, 1972, 305–16, and 'Reasons for Action and Desires', in Joseph Raz (ed.), *Practical Reasoning*, Oxford 1978, pp. 178–84; and John McDowell, 'Are Moral Requirements Hypothetical Imperatives?', *Proceedings of the Aristotelian Society*, supplementary vol. 62 (1978), 13–29.

11 See particularly Patrick Kelly, 'Locke on Money: An Edition of John Locke's Three Pamphlets on Money Published in the 1690s (unpublished Ph.D. thesis, University of Cambridge, 1973). Joyce Oldham Appleby, *Economic Thought and Ideology in Seventeenth-Century England*, Princeton, N.J., 1978, esp. pp. 221–54, 258, and 'Locke, Liberalism and the Natural Law of Money', *Past and Present*, no. 81 1976, 43–69, offers an illuminating discussion of the internal mechanisms of Locke's theory of the determinants of the value of coined gold and silver. But her efforts to relate his adoption of this theory to the trajectory of seventeenth-century English economic thought in general and more particularly to explain his abandonment of the more homogeneously causal theories of his predecessors and opponents is neither clear nor compelling. See also William Letwin, *The Origins of Scientific Economics: English Economic Thought 1660–1776*, London, 1963, ch. 6, esp. pp. 147–8.

12 For an important clarification of the implications of his doing so (which corrects many influential misunderstandings) see Tully, *A Discourse of Property*.

13 See John Locke, 'Venditio' (1695), printed in John Dunn, 'Justice and the Interpretation of Locke's Political Theory', *Political Studies*, 16, 1968, 84–7.

14 This preoccupation can be traced in his writings from the *Two Tracts on Government*, ed. Philip Abrams, Cambridge 1967, onwards. William G. Batz, 'This Historical Anthropology of John Locke', *Journal of the History of Ideas*, 34 1974, 663–70, gives some interesting information on one range of Locke's sources for these inquiries, though he shows little understanding of the relation which Locke himself claimed for his anthropological evidence to the theoretical structure of his argument.

15 Not reason, but 'passion and Superstition' 'share the bulk of mankinde and possesse them in their turnes'. (Bodleian Library, MS. Locke, fols. 5, 50.) Within Locke's moral psychology the predominance of this affective state necessarily implied that most men's moral beliefs were erroneous. Cf David Hume, *A Treatise of Human Nature*, ed. L. A. Selby Bigge, 2nd ed, Oxford 1979, 552–3.

16 See the interpretative and practical dilemma described by P. F. Strawson, in 'Freedom and Resentment' in Strawson (ed) *Studies in the Philosophy of Thought and Action*, London 1968, pp. 71–96.

17 Locke acknowledged frankly to his friend William Molyneux his incapacity to grasp how such moral freedom is in fact possible: letter to William Molyneux, 20 January 1693, *The Correspondence of John Locke*, ed. E. S. de Beer, iv Oxford 1979, pp. 625–6.

18 For the factors dictating this intricacy, see Dunn, *Political Thought of John Locke*, esp. chs. 4 and 14. And for an important correction of the context of these discussions, see Michael Ayers, 'Analytical Philosophy of History and the History of Philosophy', in Jonathan Rée *et al., Philosophy and its Past*, Hassocks, Sussex, 1979, pp. 46–7.

19 On the idea of an 'ethics of belief' generally, see E. M. Curley, 'Descartes, Spinoza and the Ethics of Belief', in Eugene Freeman and Maurice Mandelbaum (eds.), *Spinoza: Essays in Interpretation*, La Salle, Illinois 1975, pp. 159–89, and see Bernard Williams, 'Deciding to Believe', in *Problems of the Self*, Cambridge, 1973, ch. 9.

20 See particularly the correspondence with Philippus van Limborch, William Popple and Benjamin Furley in Locke, *Correspondence*, iii and iv.

21 Letter to Tom [Thomas Westrowe?], 20 October 1659. According to the editor of the Locke correspondence it is not likely that the letter was ever dispatched. (Locke, *Correspondence*, vol. 1, p. 123) see ch. 1 above, p. 30.

22 Locke, *Epistola de Tolerantia*, p. 122, lines 8–14.

23 Locke to William Molyneux, 26 December 1692: 'being fully persuaded there are very few things of pure speculation, wherein two thinking men who impartially seek truth can differ if they give themselves the leisure to examine their hypotheses and understand one another'. (Locke, *Correspondence*, vol. iv p. 609.)

24 See Richard H. Cox, *Locke on War and Peace*, Oxford 1960.

25 On Hobbes's theology, see Leopold Damrosch, Jr, 'Hobbes as Reformation Theologian', *Journal of the History of Ideas*, 40, 1979, 339–52: R. W. Hepburn, 'Hobbes on the Knowledge of God', in Maurice Cranston and

Richard S. Peters (eds.), *Hobbes and Rousseau*, Garden City, N.Y. 1972, pp. 85–108; Willis B. Glover, 'God and Thomas Hobbes', in K. C. Brown (ed.), *Hobbes Studies*, Oxford, 1965, pp. 141–68; J. G. A. Pocock, 'Time, History and Eschatology in the Thought of Thomas Hobbes', in his *Politics, Language and Time*, London, 1972, pp. 148–201; Gauthier, 'Why Ought One Obey God?' For the response to Hobbes as essentially a religious menace, see Samuel I. Mintz, *The Hunting of Leviathan*, Cambridge, 1962, and John Bowle, *Hobbes and his Critics*, London 1951. For more complex placing of Hobbes as philosopher and political theorist in the intellectual context of his time, see the work of Quentin Skinner, particularly 'The Context of Hobbes's Theory of Political Obligation', in Cranston and Peters, *Hobbes and Rousseau*, pp. 109–42, and 'Conquest and Consent: Thomas Hobbes and the Engagement Controversy', in G. E. Aylmer (ed.), *The Interregnum: The Quest for Settlement 1646–1600*, London 1972, pp. 79–98. See also Richard Tuck, *Natural Rights Theories: Their Origin and Development*, Cambridge, 1979, ch. 6.

26 See particularly the views of Locke's pupil the 3rd Earl of Shaftesbury, who decisively conflated the implications of his tutor's rejection of innate ideas with the fundamental tendency of Hobbes's thought. See his letter to Michael Ainsworth, 3 January 1709: 'It was Mr Locke that struck the home blow: for Mr Hobbes's character and base slavish principles in government took off the poison of his philosophy. 'Twas Mr Locke that struck at all fundamentals, threw all order and virtue out of the world, and made the very idea of these (which are the same as those of God) *unnatural* and without foundation in our minds ... Then comes Mr Locke with his Indian, barbarian stories of wild nations ...' (*The Life, Unpublished Letters, and Philosophical Regimen of Anthony, Earl of Shaftesbury, Author of the Characteristicks*, ed. Benjamin Rand, London, 1900, p. 403.) But also see his November 1709 letter to General Stanhope: 'Locke, whose *State of Nature* he supposes to be chimerical, and less serviceable to Mr Locke's own system than to Mr Hobbes's that is more of a piece as I believe.' (*Life, Unpublished Letters*, p. 415.) Shaftesbury's views on this question are not easy to disentangle and have been considerably misunderstood. See e.g. Jason Aronson, 'Shaftesbury on Locke', *American Political Science Review*, 53 (1959), 1101–4. The most illuminating brief formulation of his attitude is perhaps his *Second Characters or the Language of Forms*, ed. Benjamin Rand, Cambridge, 1914, pp. 106, 173–88 and esp p. 178. For the sense of the pervasiveness of Hobbism as an ideological menace and its extremely vague theoretical specification, see e.g. Margaret C. Jacob, *The Newtonians and the English Revolution 1689–1720*, Hassocks, Sussex 1976, pp. 24, 52, 65, 67, 198–9, 232, 238, and more broadly John Redwood, *Reason, Ridicule and Religion: The Age of Enlightenment in England 1660–1750*, London 1976.

27 See, more extendedly, 'Individuality and Clientage in the Formation of Locke's Social Imagination', chapter 1 above and John Dunn, *Locke*, Oxford 1984.

28 Locke to John Locke, sen., 6 April 1658, Locke, *Correspondence*, i, p. 60.

29 John Strachey to Locke, 13 November 1663, Locke, *Correspondence*, i, p. 215.

30 'when it was paid for with all that I had got in attending on him ten or a dozen of the best years of my life': Locke, *Correspondence*, iv, p. 411. For the context of this sense of injury see other letters in vol. iv, pp. 383, 398–9, 406–7, 412–13, 422–4, 452, 455–6, 698–9, 768, 773–4.

31 For a helpful account of this impact, see Paul Marshall, 'John Locke: Between God and Mammon', *Canadian Journal of Political Science*, 12, 1979, 73–98. For further treatment of the rejection of the substance of social relations as a foundation for value, see chapter 1 above.

32 See e.g. his claim to William Molyneux: 'The only riches I have valued or laboured to acquire has been the friendship of ingenious and worthy men', as cited in Patrick Kelly's interesting discussion, 'Locke and Molyneux: The Anatomy of a Friendship', *Hermathena*, no. 126, 1979, p. 43.

33 Bodleian Library, MS. Locke c.28, fol. 141, 'Ethica B', as quoted in Dunn, *Political Thought of John Locke*, p. 1; and also see there: 'Happiness is a continuation of content without any molestation. Very imperfect in this world. No body happy here certain.'

34 Adam Smith, *The Theory of Moral Sentiments*, VI, ii, 3.2. (p. 235).

35 Smith, *Theory of Moral Sentiments*, VII, ii. 1.20 (p. 276).

36 See particularly J. Dunn, 'Consent in the Political Theory of John Locke', in Dunn, *Political Obligation in its Historical Context*, Cambridge 1980, pp. 29–52, and more generally in Dunn, *Political Thought of John Locke*.

37 See the added footnote identifying Rapin, Locke, Sidney, Hoadley as the authors of 'Compositions the most despicable, both for style and matter' which Hume complained 'have been extolled, and propagated, and read; as if they had equalled the most celebrated remains of antiquity' (Hume, *History of England*, 8 vols., London 1778, viii, p. 323). Compare it with the earlier edition, Hume, *The History of Great Britain*, vol. II. *Containing the Commonwealth, and the Reigns of Charles II and James II*, London 1757, p. 445.

38 For a helpful treatment of Hume's misunderstanding, see Martyn P. Thompson, 'Hume's Critique of Locke and the "Original Contract"', *Il Pensiero Politico*, 10, 1977, 189–201.

39 See Adam Smith *An Inquiry into the Nature and Causes of the Wealth of Nations*, ed. R. H. Campbell, A. S. Skinner & W. B. Todd, 2 vols, Oxford 1976, V.i.f.31, vol 2, p. 772): 'a debased system of moral philosophy, which was considered as immediately connected with the doctrines of Pneumatology, with the immortality of the human soul, and with the rewards and punishments which, from the justice of the Deity, were to be expected in a life to come'. For Hume, see particularly his *Dialogues concerning Natural Religion* and Duncan Forbes, *Hume's Philosophical Politics*, Cambridge 1975, chs. 1 and 2, esp. pp. 45, 65, 80, and 'Hume's Science of Politics', in G. P. Morice (ed.), *David Hume: Bicentenary Papers*, Edinburgh 1977, pp. 39–50, esp. pp. 46–7; E. C. Mossner, 'The Religion of David Hume', *Journal of the History of Ideas*, 39, 1978, 653–63, and 'Hume and the Legacy of the *Dialogues*', in Morice, *David Hume: Bicentenary Papers*, pp. 1–22.

40 Hume, *Treatise*, p. 547. For the argument as a whole, see Bk. III, pt. II, sect. VIII, 'Of the source of allegiance'. For a placing of this argument, see Forbes, *Hume's Philosophical Politics*, pp. 91–101.

41 Hume, *Treatise*, pp. 542–3.

42 Hume, *Treatise*, p. 491.

43 Forbes, *Hume's Philosophical Politics*, esp. pp. 190, 192, 322.

44 Hume, *Treatise*, p. 552. 'The general opinion of mankind has some authority in all cases; but in this of morals it is perfectly infallible. Nor is it less infallible, because men cannot distinctly explain the principles on which it is founded.'

45 See his own anonymous puff for the work: David Hume, *An Abstract of a*

Treatise of Human Nature, ed. J. M. Keynes and P. Sraffa, Cambridge 1938, esp. p. 4; 'the Author seems to insinuate, that were his philosophy receiv'd, we must alter from the foundation the greater part of the sciences'.

46 But for direct evidence that he regarded Locke as a representative intellectual proponent of the error which he wished to correct, see his letter of 1743 to Francis Hutcheson on the latter's new *Philosophiae Moralis Institutio Compendiaria*: 'P.266.1.18 & quae seq: You imply a Condemnation of Locke's Opinion, which being the receiv'd one, I cou'd have wisht the Condemnation had been more express.' (*The Letters of David Hume*, ed. J. Y. T. Grieg, 2 vols, Oxford, 1932, i, p. 48.)

47 See 'Of the Original Contract', in Hume, *Philosophical Works*, iii, p. 460. Hume continued to alter this essay throughout his life adding one of its most important passages in the final edition published posthumously. The Locke references were included in the first publication of 1748. See also his letter of 8 January 1748 to Lord Elibank about this essay: 'I shall be very much mortify'd, if you do not approve, in some small degree, of the Reasonings with regard to the original Contract, which, I hope, are new and curious, & form a short, but compleat Refutation of the political Systems of Sydney, Locke, and the Whigs, which all the half Philosophers of the Nation have implicitely embrac'd for near a Century; tho' they are plainly, in my humble Opinion, repugnant to Reason & the Practice of all Nations.' ('New Hume Letters to Lord Elibank', ed. E. C. Mossner, *Texas Studies in Language and Literature*, 4 (1962), 437.)

48 For Smith's political theory in general, see especially the characteristically trenchant and illuminating article by Duncan Forbes, 'Sceptical Whiggism, Commerce and Liberty', in A. S. Skinner and T. B. Wilson (eds.), *Essays on Adam Smith*, Oxford 1975, pp. 179–201, and a more extended treatment by Donald Winch, *Adam Smith's Politics: An Essay in Historiographic Revision*, Cambridge 1978. For Smith's analysis of political obligation see Adam Smith, *Lectures on Jurisprudence*, ed. R. L. Meek, D. D. Raphael & P. G. Stein, Oxford 1978, 311–30, 401–4, 433–6.

49 Smith, *Lectures on Jurisprudence*, 311–15.

50 Smith, *Lectures on Jurisprudence*, 318–19.

51 Smith, *Lectures*, 318.

52 Smith, *Lectures*, 322–7.

53 Smith, *Lectures*, 318–19.

54 Smith, *Lectures*, 319–21.

55 Smith, *Lectures*, 320.

56 Smith, *Lectures*, 321–30.

57 See J. Dunn, 'Political Obligations and Political Possibilities', in Dunn, *Political Obligation in its Historical Context*, pp. 243–99. It is possible that, clearly understood, the position dictates a rigorous pragmatism, which begins from Smith's sardonic note; 'one who is to consider this matter must set out anew and upon his own bottom. All disputes of this sort have been decided by force and violence. If the sovereign got the better of the subjects, then they were condemned as traitors and rebels; and if the subjects have got the better of the sovereign, he is declared to be a tyrant and oppressor not to be endured.' Smith, *Lectures*, 311; but denies the legitimacy of his subsequent reservation in Smith, *Lectures*, 311: 'Sometimes the decision has been right and sometimes wrong.'

58 Smith, *Lectures*, 321.

59 Smith, *Lectures*, 315–16.

60 Smith, *Lectures*, 316, 402–3.
61 Smith, *Lectures*, 316–17.
62 Smith, *Lectures*, 316–18.
63 Cf. Michael Walzer, *Obligations: Essays on Disobedience, War and Citizenship*, Cambridge, Mass. 1970, esp. p. 207; Dunn, 'Political Obligations and Political Possibilities'; Carole Pateman, *The Problem of Political Obligation*, London 1978.
64 See notes 27 and 28 above.
65 This was not, of course, a simple failure in personal sensitivity or humanity – and least of all so in contrast with Locke. But it was a decisive shift in the angle of imaginative attention to the properties of society, in effect the disappearance of an entire dimension of assessment.
66 '... my own schemes of Study leave me very little leisure, which go forward too like the web of penelope so that I scarce see any Probability of their ending'. (Smith to Lord Hailes, 15 January 1769, Adam Smith, *Correspondence*, ed. E. C. Mossner & I. S. Ross, Oxford 1977, p. 140. It is a decidedly more illuminating fact about the tone and content of much of the *Theory of Moral Sentiments* than it is for example of those of the *Wealth of Nations* that each in a very extended sense began as a set of edifying university lectures.
67 See, *Theory of Moral Sentiments* I.iii.3.1–8 (pp. 61–66). For an account of the different editions of this work, see D. D. Raphael and A. L. Macfie, 'introduction', ibid., pp. 34–52.
68 See Smith, *Lectures*, 318. *Theory of Moral Sentiments* I.iii.2.1–4 (pp. 50–4). Smith's beliefs on this matter were in obvious tension with some other aspects of his thought, notably his sophisticated sociological conception of changes in relations of dependence which is set out most elaborately in the *Wealth of Nations*.
69 See F. A. Hayek, *New Studies in Philosophy, Politics, Economics and the History of Ideas*, London 1978; Keith Joseph and Jonathan Sumption, *Equality*, London, 1979.
70 David Gauthier, 'The Social Contract as Ideology', *Philosophy and Public Affairs*, 6, 1977, 130–64; Dunn, 'Political Obligations and Political Possibilities'.
71 Compare this with Gauthier, 'David Hume, Contractarian', esp. p. 38: 'Opinion is all; there is and can be no appeal against the present established practice of the age'.
72 See Hume's verdict on the political judgement of the ancients: 'These people were extremely fond of liberty; but seem not to have understood it very well.' ('Of the Populousness of Ancient Nations', *Philosophical Works*, iii, p. 403.)

4 Understanding revolutions

1 For a firm vindication of the virtue in this necessity see Elster 1978.
2 For an interesting discussion of how to distinguish legitimate from illegitimate entry see Tristram, *Sociology*, 1980 and cf. Hesse 1978. The issue is also at the centre of the very extensive recent discussion of 'essentially contested concepts'.
3 R. Aya, 'Theories of Revolution Reconsidered: Contrasting Models of Collective Violence', *Theory and Society*, VII, 1 July 1979, 39–99; A. S. Cohan, *Theories of Revolution: An Introduction*, Nelson, London 1975; M. Freeman, 'Theories of Revolution', *British Journal of Political Science*, II, 3, 339–59;

M. N. Hagopian, *The Phenomenon of Revolution*, Dodd, Mead, New York 1975; E. Hermassi, 'Towards a Comparative Study of Revolutions', *Comparative Studies in Society and History*, XVIII, 2, 211–35; E. J. Hobsbawm, 'Revolution', papers presented at XIVth International Congress of Historical Sciences, San Francisco, August 1975; I. Kramnick, 'Reflections on Revolution: Definition and Explanation in Recent Scholarship', *History and Theory*, XI, 1, 1972, 26–63; A. MacIntyre, 'Ideology, Social Science, and Revolution', *Comparative Politics*, V, 3, 321–42; J. M. Maravall, 'Subjective Conditions and Revolutionary Conflict: Some Remarks', *British Journal of Sociology*, XXVII, 1, 21–34; D. E. H. Russell, *Rebellion, Revolution and Armed Force*, Academic Press, New York 1974; B. Salert, *Revolutions and Revolutionaries*, Elsevier, New York 1976; C. Tilly, 'Does Modernization Breed Revolution?', *Comparative Politics*, V, 3, 1973, 425–47; P. Zagorin, 'Theories of Revolution in Contemporary Historiography', *Political Science Quarterly*, LXXXVIII, 1, 1973 23–52; P. Zagorin, 'Prolegomena to the Comparative History of Revolution in Early Modern Europe', *Comparative Studies in Society and History*, XVIII, 2, 1976 151–74.

4 E. Wolf, *Peasant Wars of the Twentieth Century*, Harper & Row, New York 1969; J. Dunn, *Modern Revolutions*, Cambridge University Press, Cambridge 1972; and, a more distinguished work less focused on the category of revolution, Barrington Moore, *Social Origins of Dictatorship and Democracy*, Beacon Press, Boston 1966.

5 Skocpol, *States and Social Revolutions*, pp. 4–6, 40, 163; and cf. Dunn (ed.), *West African States: Failure and Promise*, Cambridge University Press, Cambridge 1978, ch. 1.

6 Aya, 'Theories of Revolution Reconsidered', pp. 50–2.

7 C. Johnson, *Revolutionary Change*, Athlone Press, London 1968; but cf. C. Johnson, *Autopsy on People's War*, University of California Press, Berkeley 1973, p. 108.

8 T. Gurr, *Why Men Rebel*, Princeton University Press, Princeton 1970.

9 Aya, 'Theories of Revolution Reconsidered', etc.

10 C. Tilly, 'Does Modernization Breed Revolution?'; 'Revolutions and Collective Violence', in *Handbook of Political Science*, vol. 3, eds F. I. Greenstein and N. W. Polsby, Addison-Wesley, Reading, Mass. 1975; From *Mobilization to Revolution*, Addison-Wesley, Reading, Mass. 1978; and see Aya, 'Theories of Revolution Reconsidered'.

11 cf. P. Anderson, *Passages from Antiquity to Feudalism*, New Left Books, London 1974; *Lineages of the Absolutist State*, New Left Books, London 1974; J. Dunn, *Modern Revolutions*; J. Dunn, 'Revolutions as Class Struggle', *Government and Opposition*, XIV, 3, 398–403; E. Hermassi, 'Toward a Comparative Study of Revolutions', *Comparative Studies in Society and History*, XVIII, 2, 211–35; T. Skocpol, 'Wallerstein's World Capitalist System: A Theoretical and Historical Critique', *American Journal of Sociology*, LXXXII, 5, 1977, 1075–90; T. Skocpol and M. Fulbrook, review of P. Anderson, *Lineages of the Absolutist State* and *Passages from Antiquity to Feudalism*, in *Journal of Development Studies*, XIII, 3, 290–5; T. Skocpol and E. K. Trimberger, 'Revolutions and the World Historical Development of Capitalism', *Berkeley Journal of Sociology*, XXII, 101–13; E. K. Trimberger, *Revolution from Above*, Transaction Books, New Brunswick, N.J. 1978; and I. Wallerstein, *The Modern World-System: Capitalist Agriculture and the Origins of the*

European World-Economy in the Sixteenth Century, Academic Press, New York and London 1974.

12 Marx himself was certainly strongly committed to explaining historical change in terms of objective conditions. But after the experience of 1848–50, whether because of increased sagacity or simply because of diminished optimism, he was for the most part distinctly less forthcoming and programmatic in his observations on the relation between the mechanisms of historical change and the character and incidence of political revolution.

13 It is not clear that this is as searching a judgement in the case of China as it is in those of France and Russia.

14 J. Dunn, 'The Success and Failure of Modern Revolutions', in S. Bialer and S. Sluzar (eds), *Strategies and Impact of Contemporary Radicalism*, Westview Press, Boulder, Colo. 1977; A. MacIntyre, 'Ideology, Social Science and Revolution', *Comparative Politics*, v, 3, 321–42.

15 cf. Dunn, *Modern Revolutions*; 'The Success and Failure of Modern Revolutions'; *Political Obligation in its Historical Context*, Cambridge University Press, Cambridge 1980, pp. 91–4.

16 M. Hollis, *Models of Man*, Cambridge University Press, Cambridge, 1977.

17 K. Marx in, *Collected Works of Karl Marx and Frederick Engels*, Foreign Languages Publishing House, Moscow 1978, pp. 311, 314, 318.

18 E. J. Hobsbawm, 'Revolution', p. 12.

19 A. MacIntyre, 'Ideology, Social Science, and Revolution'; J. Dunn, *Political Obligation in its Historical Context*, ch. 5, esp. pp. 91–4.

20 Such a theory, it should be noted, is not merely unavailable and perhaps necessarily unavailable in practice (Putnam 1978, pp. 59–65); it also could not in principle, in any case, be included within the vantage point of human practical reason (Dunn 1980, cap. 10 esp. pp. 267–9, 283–5).

21 It is extremely hard, perhaps even simply impossible, to determine sociologically the limits of human inventiveness or folly. It is, for example, easy to detect the origins of the Leninist conception of the party in the special conditions of the Tsarist state. But it would be difficult to argue convincingly that such a conception was not *conceivable* at any point after Thermidor or (if the conception were to be defined more ambitiously) at least at any point after 1845 or 1850.

22 See, for example Levine in J. J. Linz and A. Stepan (eds), *The Breakdown of Democratic Regimes*, The Johns Hopkins University Press, Baltimore, Md. 1978, and the discussion of the impact of Castro on Latin American Politics throughout Part III of Linz and Stepan's book.

23 Dunn, 'The Success and Failure of Modern Revolutions'.

24 *Injustice: The Social Bases of Obedience and Revolt*, M. E. Sharpe, White Plains, N.Y. 1978.

25 Beacon Press, Boston, Mass. 1966.

26 J. V. Femia, 'Barrington Moore and the Preconditions for Democracy', *British Journal of Political Science*, ii, 1, 21–46; J. D. Y. Peel, 'Cultural Factors in the Contemporary Theory of Development', *Archives Européennes de Sociologie*, xiv, 2, 283–303; J. M. Weiner, 'The Barrington Moore Thesis and its Critics', *Theory and Society*, ii, 3, 301–30; 'Review of Reviews: *Social Origins of Dictatorship and Democracy*' in *History and Theory*, xv, 2, 146–75.

27 T. Skocpol, 'A Critical Review of Barrington Moore's *Social Origins of Dictatorship and Democracy*', in *Politics and Society*, IV, 1, 1–30.

28 H. Alavi, 'Peasants and Revolution', in R. Miliband and J. Saville (eds), *The Socialist Register*, The Merlin Press, London 1965; H. A. Landsberger, *Rural Protests: Peasant Movements and Social Change*, Macmillan, London 1974; 'The Sources of Rural Radicalism', in S. Bialer and S. Sluzar (eds), *Sources of Contemporary Radicalism*, pp. 247–91; J. W. Lewis (ed), *Peasant Rebellion and Communist Revolution in Asia*, Stanford University Press, Stanford, Calif. 1974; J. S. Migdal, *Peasants, Politics and Revolution*, Princeton University Press, Princeton, N.J. 1974; J. M. Paige, *Agrarian Revolution: Social Movements and Export Agriculture in the Underdeveloped World*, Free Press, New York 1975; J. C. Scott, *The Moral Economy of the Peasant*, Yale University Press, New Haven, Conn. 1976; 'Peasant Revolution: A Dismal Science', *Comparative Politics*, IX, 2, 231–48; E. Wolf, *Peasant Wars of the Twentieth Century*, Harper & Row, New York 1969.

29 Weiner, 'The Barrington Moore Thesis and its Critics', 309, 321–2.

30 Moore, *Social Origins of Dictatorship and Democracy*.

31 Cf. J. Gaventa, *Power and Powerlessness*, Clarendon Press, Oxford 1980.

32 Moore, *Injustice* p. 474. For the socially oppressed the good society typically is the society they know with its nastiest features mitigated (p. 370, etc.). This negative verdict on the contribution of proletarian understanding to the formation of revolutionary theory may require some revision in the light of Gareth Stedman Jones's studies of the formation of the views of Marx and Engels.

33 cf. Dunn, *Political Obligation in its Historical Context*, ch. 5.

34 Scott, *The Moral Economy of the Peasant*, p. 160. Compare the very active dispute at present amongst English Marxists over the role of human understanding and human agency in historical causation (E. P. Thompson, *The Poverty of Theory and Other Essays*, Merlin Press, London 1978, pp. 35–91, 193–406; P. Anderson, *Arguments Within English Marxism*, New Left Books, London 1980).

35 And see Hobsbawm, 'Revolution'.

36 K. Marx and F. Engels, *Marx and Engels on Britain*, Foreign Languages Publishing House, Moscow 1953, p. 499.

37 Aya, 'Theories of Revolution Reconsidered'; Tilly, 'Does Modernization Breed Revolution?'; 'Revolutions and Collective Violence'; *From Mobilization to Revolution*; etc.

38 J. Elster, *Logic and Society: Contradictions and Possible Worlds*, Wiley, London 1978; 'The Treatment of Counterfactuals: Reply to Brian Barry', *Political Studies*, XVIII, 1, 144–7; B. M. Barry, 'Superfox', *Political Studies* XXVIII, 1, 136–43.

39 cf. Dunn, 'The Success and Failure of Modern Revolutions', 107–14.

5 *Totalitarian democracy and the legacy of modern revolutions: explanation or indictment?*

1 See *L'Unità* (Milan), 16 December 1981, pp. 1, 24; 30 December 1981, pp. 1, 16; 12 January 1982, pp. 1, 8–9; 24 January 1982, pp. 1, 20.

2 *The Origins of Totalitarian Democracy* (1952), Mercury pb. ed., London 1961, esp pp. 3–8, 11, 249. There are a number of important differences of

emphasis between *The Origins* and the two later volumes (*Political Messianism* (1960) and *The Myth of the Nation and the Vision of Revolution* (1981)) but they do not affect this central judgement.

3 For the best outline of this tradition see J. G. A. Pocock, *The Machiavellian Moment*, Princeton University Press, Princeton 1975 and *Politics, Language and Time*, Methuen, London 1972, chh. 3 and 4.

4 Cf Stuart R. Schram, 'Introduction: The Cultural Revolution in historical perspective', in Stuart R. Schram (ed.), *Authority, Participation and Cultural Change in China*, Cambridge University Press, Cambridge 1973, pp. 1–108.

5 Zoltán Haraszti, *John Adams and the Prophets of Paris*, pp. ed. Grosset & Dunlap, New York 1964; Edward Handler, *American and Europe in the Political Thought of John Adams*, Harvard University Press, Cambridge, Mass. 1964; Jacob E. Cooke (ed.), *The Federalist*, Meridian Books pb ed, Cleveland, Ohio 1961.

6 John Lough, *The Philosophes and Post-Revolutionary France*, Clarendon Press, Oxford 1982.

7 George V. Taylor, 'Revolutionary and Non-revolutionary Content in the *Cahiers* of 1789', *French Historical Studies*, VII, 4, Fall 1972, pp. 479–502.

8 Cf. the somewhat unilluminating negative findings of Joan Macdonald, *Rousseau and the French Revolution*, Athlone Press, London 1965.

9 *The Origins*, p. 1.

10 *The Origins*, p. 8, 253.

11 See, for example, John Dunn, *Modern Revolutions; an Introduction to the Analysis of a Political Phenomenon*, Cambridge University Press, Cambridge 1972.

12 Compare Dunn, *Modern Revolutions*, chh. 1, 3 and 5 with ch. 8 and Jacques Rupnik, *Histoire du Parti Communiste Tchécoslovaque: des origines à la prise du pouvoir*, Presses de la Fondation Nationale des Sciences Politiques, Paris 1981.

13 For a well-informed and careful analysis of Lenin's political thought, insufficiently sensitive to its divergences from that of Marx, see Neil Harding, *Lenin's Political Thought*, 2 vols, Macmillan, London 1977–81.

14 See Dunn, *Modern Revolutions; Political Obligation in its Historical Context*, Cambridge University Press, Cambridge 1980, pp. 91–4, 217–39; 'Understanding revolutions', ch. 4 above.

15 Cf Karl Marx, *Economic and Philosophical Manuscripts* (1844), in Marx and Engels, *Collected Works*, Vol 3, Lawrence & Wishart, London 1975, pp. 296–7.

16 Cf Dunn, *Political Obligation*, ch. 9, esp pp. 227–33.

17 Francesco Guicciardini, *Maxims and Reflections of a Renaissance Statesman*, tr. Mario Domandi, Harper Torchbooks pb., New York 1965, p. 39.

18 See particularly, Theda Skocpol, *States and Social Revolutions*, Cambridge University Press, Cambridge 1979.

19 For a valuable treatment see Hélène Carrère d' Encausse and Stuart R. Schram, *Marxism and Asia; An Introduction with Readings*, Allen Lane, The Penguin Press, London 1969.

20 Karl Marx, *Contribution to the Critique of Hegel's Philosophy of Law: Introduction* (1844), Marx and Engels, *Collected Works*, vol. 3, 175–87.

21 There is no very satisfactory account of this phase of Marx's political thinking. For contrasting views see Alan Gilbert, *Marx's Politics: Communists and*

Citizens, Martin Robertson, London, 1981; R. N. Hunt, *The Political Ideas of Marx and Engels*, vol. 1, Macmillan, London 1975. See also Hal Draper, *Karl Marx's Theory of Revolution*, Part 1: *State and Bureaucracy*, 2 vols, Monthly Review Press, New York 1977.

22 Cf Pocock, *Politics, Language and Time*, ch. 4 and Caroline Robbins, *The Eighteenth Century Commonwealthman*, Harvard University Press, Cambridge, Mass, 1959.

23 F. Buonarroti, *Conspiration pour l'Égalité dite de Babeuf*, Éditions Sociales, Paris 1957, vol. 1, p. 25.

24 See especially Istvan Hont and Michael Ignatieff (eds), *Wealth and Virtue; the shaping of political economy in the Scottish Enlightenment*, Cambridge University Press, Cambridge 1983.

25 Buonarroti, *op cit*, vol. 1, p. 28.

26 Buonarroti, *op cit*, vol. 1, p. 26.

27 For helpful general points see Quentin Skinner, 'The Principles and Practice of Opposition: The Case of Bolingbroke versus Walpole', in Neil McKendrick (ed), *Historical Perspectives*, Europa Publications, London 1974, 93–128; 'Some Problems in the Analysis of Political Thought and Action', *Political Theory*, II, 3, August 1974, pp. 277–303.

28 For especially clear treatment of a delinquent example see Domenico Mario Nuti, 'The Polish Crisis: Economic Factors and Constraints', in Ralph Miliband and John Saville (eds), *The Socialist Register 1981*, The Merlin Press, London 1981, pp. 104–43; 'Open and Repressed Inflation in Poland, 1975–1981' (unpublished paper CREES, Birmingham, March 1982).

29 See János Kornai, *Economics of Shortage*, 2 vols, North Holland, Amsterdam 1980, esp conclusion, vol. 2, 569–71; Tamás Bauer, 'Investment Cycles in Planned Economies', *Acta Oeconomica*, XXI, 1978, 243–60; Wlodzimierz Brus, *Socialist Ownership and Political Systems*, tr R. A. Clarke, Routledge & Kegan Paul, London, 1975 and Brus, 'East European Economies Facing the Eighties': afterword to *The Economic History of Communist Eastern Europe*, Oxford University Press, Oxford 1984; Marc Rakovski (pseudonym), *Towards an East European Marxism*, Allison and Busby, London. For emphasis on the political relevance of the East European societies to the West see John Dunn, *The Politics of Socialism*, Cambridge University Press, Cambridge 1984.

30 Neal Ascherson, *The Polish August*, Penguin Books pb., Harmondsworth 1982 reprint.

31 Stefan Nowak, 'Values and Attitudes of the Polish People', *Scientific American*, CCXLV, 1, July 1981, 23–31.

6 *Unimagined community: the deceptions of socialist internationalism*

1 Particularly in the period 1843–50. For contrasting views see Michael Löwy, *La théorie de la révolution chez le jeune Marx*, Maspero, Paris 1970; *The Politics of Combined and Uneven Development*, Verso Editions, London 1981; Richard N. Hunt, *The Polticial Ideas of Marx and Engels*, vol. 1, Macmillan, London 1975; Alan Gilbert, *Marx's Politics: Communists and Citizens*, Martin Robertson, Oxford 1981.

2 Karl Marx and Frederick Engels, *Collected Works*, vol. 5, Lawrence & Wishart, London 1976, esp pp. 51–4.

3 Cf. G. A. Cohen, *Karl Marx's Theory of History: A Defence*, Clarendon Press, Oxford 1978 and 'Reply to Elster on "Marxism, Functionalism and Game Theory"', *Theory and Society*, XI, 4, July 1982, 483–96; Jon Elster, 'Marxism, Functionalism and Game Theory: The Case for Methodological Individualism', *Theory and Society*, XI, 4, July 1982, 453–82.

4 Cf John Dunn, 'The Identity of the History of Ideas', *Philosophy*, XLIII, April 1968, 85–104; Steven Lukes, *Emile Durkheim: His Life and Work. A Historical and Critical Study*, Allen Lane, The Penguin Press, London 1973, p. 1.

5 Karl Marx and Frederick Engels, *Manifesto of the Communist Party* (1848), *Collected Works*, vol. 6, Lawrence & Wishart, London 1976, p. 495.

6 Georges Haupt, *Socialism and the Great War: The Collapse of the Second International*, Clarendon Press, Oxford 1972.

7 Marx and Engels, *The German Ideology, Collected Works*, vol. 5, p. 54.

8 See particularly Karl Marx, *Contribution to the Critique of Hegel's Philosophy of Right: Introduction, Collected Works*, vol. 3, London 1975, pp. 175–87.

9 A. Walicki, *The Controversy over Capitalism*, Clarendon Press, Oxford 1969; Teodor Shanin, 'Marx and the Peasant Commune', *History Workshop*, 12, Autumn 1981, 108–28; Haruki Wada, 'Marx and Revolutionary Russia', *History Workshop*, 12, 129–50; Baruch Knei-Paz, *The Social and Political Thought of Leon Trotsky*, Clarendon Press, Oxford 1978, Appendix, pp. 585–98. For the relevant texts of Marx and Engels see most conveniently Marx and Engels, *The Russian Menace to Europe*, ed P. W. Blackstock and B. F. Hoselitz, George Allen & Unwin, London 1953, pp. 203–41; 273–84.

10 Leon Trotsky, *Results and Prospects* (1906) in Trotsky, *The Permanent Revolution and Results and Prospects*, Pathfinder Press, New York 1970; Löwy, *Combined and Uneven Development*, pp. 40–57.

11 Cf Löwy, *Combined and Uneven Development*.

12 Trotsky, *Results and Prospects*, p. 107.

13 Trotsky, *Results and Prospects*, p. 108.

14 Whatever else it may have indicated, twentieth-century experience of the consequences of combined and uneven development has certainly served also to confirm the disadvantages of backwardness.

15 Cf John Dunn, 'Understanding revolutions', ch. 4 above.

16 Cf Karl Marx, *Economic and Philosophical Manuscripts* (1844), Marx and Engels, *Collected Works*, vol. 3, London 1975, pp. 296–7.

17 For attempts to devise a more satisfactory structure of explanation see Theda Skocpol, *States and Social Revolutions*, Cambridge University Press, Cambridge 1979, and n. 15 above.

18 F. A. Hayek (ed.), *Collectivist Economic Planning: Critical Studies on the Possibilities of Socialism*, London 1935 (esp. Ludwig von Mises, 'Economic Calculation in the Socialist Commonwealth').

19 Cf particularly Alec Nove, *The Economics of Feasible Socialism*, George Allen & Unwin, London 1983, esp. p. 225.

20 A. C. Sutton, *Western Technology and Soviet Economic Development 1917 to 1930*, Hoover Institute Publications, Stanford, California 1968; *Western Technology and Soviet Economic Development 1930 to 1945*, Hoover Institute Publications, Stanford 1971; *Western Technology and Soviet Economic Development 1945 to 1965*, Hoover Institute Publications, Stanford 1973; but cf Michael Ellman, *Socialist Planning*, Cambridge University Press, Cambridge 1979, pp. 52–3.

21 Ellman (op cit, esp. p. 265) stresses the importance of the political order in any assessment of the comparative merits of an existing version of a socialist mode of production with those of its highly diverse capitalist rivals.

22 For a particularly fair and sympathetic account see Ellman, op cit, esp. pp. 37, 43, 65–79, 118, 126, 143, 176, 182, 185, 188, 209–10, 219 etc.

23 Marx, Contribution to the Critique of Hegel's Philosophy of Right, Collected Works, vol. 3, p. 186. (I have slightly emended the translation).

24 Behind modern international socialism there lies a misplaced providentialism which is an inadvertent descendant of the admiring self-understanding of earlier capitalist expansion. Cf. Jacob Viner, The Role of Providence in the Social Order: An Essay in Intellectual History, American Philosophical Society, Philadelphia 1972, esp ch. 3; and, residually, even Adam Smith, An Inquiry into the Nature and Causes of the Wealth of Nations, ed. R. H. Campbell, A. S. Skinner and W. B. Todd, 2 vols, Clarendon Press, Oxford 1976.

25 Cf Robert Nozick, Anarchy, State and Utopia, Basil Blackwell, Oxford 1974 and review by John Dunn, Ratio, XIX, 1, June 1977, 88–95; G. A. Cohen, 'Freedom, Justice and Capitalism', New Left Review, 126, March–April 1981, 3–16.

26 Ellman, op cit, pp. 222–44.

27 Cf Löwy, Combined and Uneven Development, p. 74.

28 The leading exponent of this point of view is the Egyptian economist Professor Samir Amin. But it appears to be accepted wholeheartedly by, for example, Löwy (Combined and Uneven Development).

29 On John Rawls (A Theory of Justice, Oxford University Press, Oxford 1972) see, for example, Michael J. Sandel, Liberalism and the Limits of Justice, Cambridge University Press, Cambridge 1982; but for an interesting attempt to indicate such a relevance see Salvatore Veca, La Società Giusta, Il Saggiatore, Milano 1982. Peter Singer, 'Famine, Altruism and Morality', in Peter Laslett and James Fishkin (eds) Philosophy, Politics and Society; Fifth Series, Basil Blackwell, Oxford 1979, 21–35; Julian Glover, Causing Death and Saving Lives, Penguin Books, pb., Harmondsworth 1977; John Harris, 'The Marxist Conception of Violence', Philosophy and Public Affairs, III, 2, Winter 1974, 192–220. But cf Susan James, 'The Duty to Relieve Suffering', Ethics, XCIII, 1, October 1982, 4–21.

30 Compare Edmund Burke, Reflections on the Revolution in France, Everyman ed., J. M. Dent & Son, London 1910: 'To be attached to the subdivision, to love the little platoon we belong to in society, is the first principle (the germ as it were) of public affections. It is the first link in the series by which we proceed towards a love to our country, and to mankind' (p. 44); Benedict Anderson, Imagined Communities: Reflections on the Origin and Spread of Nationalism, New Left Books, London 1983. And in a very different modality cf Brian Barry, 'Self-government Revisited', in David Miller and Larry Siedentop (eds), The Nature of Political Theory, Clarendon Press, Oxford 1983, 121–54.

31 Cf Norberto Bobbio, Quale Socialismo? discussione di un'alternativa, Giulio Einaudi, Torino 1976; and, a little less frankly and intrepidly, Ralph Miliband, Marxism and Politics, Oxford University Press, Oxford 1977.

32 The importance of this point is the central premiss of John Dunn, Political Obligation in its Historical Context, Cambridge University Press, Cambridge 1980, ch. 10 ('Political obligations and political possibilities').

33 Cf John Dunn, *Modern Revolutions; an Introduction to the analysis of a Political Phenomenon*, Cambridge University Press, Cambridge 1972.

34 For the importance of its variations in geographical scope see, for example, Dunn, *Political Obligation*, chh. 6 and 7; and cf John Dunn (ed), *West African States: Failure and Promise*, Cambridge University Press, Cambridge 1978, Introduction, esp. pp. 20–1.

35 Cf John Dunn, 'Social theory, social understanding and political action', ch. 7 below; *Political Obligation*, ch. 10; 'Country Risk: Social and Cultural Aspects', in Richard Herring (ed), *Managing International Risk*, Cambridge University Press, Cambridge 1983, 139–68.

36 Solomon F. Bloom, *The World of Nations*, Columbia University Press, New York 1941; Roman Rosdolsky, 'Worker and Fatherland: a Note on a Passage in the *Communist Manifesto*', *Science and Society*, XXIX, 3, Summer 1965, 330–37; Horace B. Davis, *Nationalism and Socialism: Marxist and Labor Theories of Nationalism to 1917*, Monthly Review Press, New York 1967; Horace B. Davis, *Toward a Marxist Theory of Nationalism*, Monthly Review Press, New York 1978.

37 Compare, for example, Anderson, *Imagined Communities*; Tom Nairn, *The Break-up of Britain*, 2nd ed., New Left Books, London 1981; J. M. Blaut, 'Nationalism as an autonomous force', *Science and Society*, XLVI, 1, Spring 1982, 1–23; Davis, *Toward a Marxist Theory of Nationalism*. But contrast Ernest Gellner, *Nations and Nationalism*, Basil Blackwell, Oxford 1983.

38 Cf R. N. Berki, 'On Marxian Thought and the Problem of International Relations', *World Politics*, XXIV, 1, October 1971, 80–105. I have tried to indicate some of the implications of this inadequacy in *Western Political Theory in the Face of the Future*, Cambridge University Press, Cambridge 1979 (Italian translation, Feltrinelli, Milano, October 1983), *Political Obligation in its Historical Context* (chh. 9 and 10) and in *The Politics of Socialism*, Cambridge University Press, Cambridge 1984.

7 Social theory, social understanding, and political action

1 David Hume, *An Enquiry concerning the Principles of Morals*, IX Pt 1, 219 (*Enquiries*, ed. L. A Selby-Bigge, Clarendon Press, Oxford, 2nd edn. 1902, p. 270). 'Celibacy, fasting, penance, mortification, self-denial, humility, silence, solitude, and the whole train of monkish virtues; for what reason are they everywhere rejected by men of sense, but because they serve to no manner of purpose; neither advance a man's fortune in the world, nor render him a more valuable member of society; neither qualify him for the entertainment of company, nor increase his power of self-enjoyment? We observe, on the contrary, that they cross all these desirable ends; stupify the understanding and harden the heart, obscure the fancy and sour the temper.... A gloomy, hare-brained enthusiast, after his death, may have a place in the calendar; but will scarcely ever be admitted, when alive, into intimacy and society, except by those who are as delirious and dismal as himself.'

2 Thomas Hobbes, *Leviathan*, ed. Michael Oakeshott, Basil Blackwell, Oxford, 1946, Pt I, Ch. II, pp. 9, 10. 'IMAGINATION therefore is nothing but *decaying sense*; and is found in men, and many other living creatures, as well sleeping, as waking ... This *decaying sense*, when we would express the thing itself, I mean *fancy* itself, we call *imagination*, as I said before: but when we

would express the decay, and signify that the sense is fading, old, and past, it is called *memory*. So that imagination and memory are but one thing, which for divers considerations hath divers names.'

3 But cf Blaise Pascal, *Pensées*, ed. L. Lafuma, Éditions du Seuil, Paris 1962, 103 (pp. 63–4): '+ Justice, force. Il est juste que ce qui est juste soit suivi; il est nécessaire que ce qui est le plus fort soit suivi. La justice sans la force est impuissante, la force sans la justice est tyrannique. La justice sans force est contredite, parce qu'ily y a toujours des méchants. La force sans la justice est accusée. Il faut donc mettre ensemble la justice et la force, et pour cela faire que ce qui est juste soit fort ou que ce qui est fort soit juste. La justice est sujette à dispute. La force est très reconnaissable et sans dispute. Aussi on n'a pu donner la force à la justice, parce que la force a contredit la justice et a dit qu'elle était injuste, et a dit que c'était elle qui était juste. Et ainsi ne pouvant faire que ce qui est juste fût fort on a fait que ce qui est fort fût juste.' And see *Pensées* 60 (pp. 51–2), 61 (p. 53), 81 (p. 57), and 85 (pp. 58–9).

4 See particularly Jürgen Habermas, *Toward a Rational Society*, translated J. J. Shapiro, Heinemann, London 1971; *Knowledge and Human Interests*, trans. J. J. Shapiro, Heinemann, London 1972; *Theory and Practice*, trans. J. Viertel, Heinemann, London 1974; *Legitimation Crisis*, trans. T. McCarthy, Heinemann, London 1976. For historical and analytical introductions to his work see David Held, *Introduction to Critical Theory: Horkheimer to Habermas*, Hutchinson, London 1980, and Thomas McCarthy, *The Critical Theory of Jürgen Habermas*, Hutchinson, London 1978.

5 Even amateur social theories are theories in the strong sense that they aim at explanation, prediction, or control. It is controversial whether there are ontological and moral constraints on the validity of social theories or whether the sole criterion of their validity is simply pragmatic. The view that human societies consist, *inter alia*, of all the human beings who constitute them, with all and only the beliefs and all and only the sentiments which these human beings happen to possess is not a social *theory*. It is simply a tautology. Because of the very evident pragmatic grounding of this tautology in the experience of all human beings, it is a constraint on any social theory that it preserve the full pragmatic force of this commonsense theory of social constitution (just as it is a constraint on any physical theory, however initially counterintuitive, that it preserve the full pragmatic force of the commonsense theory of material objects). The moral grounds for preserving this tautology, whether or not these are genuinely independent of the pragmatic grounds for doing so, are, as argued below, at least equally strong. (See John Dunn, *Political Obligation in its Historical Context*, Cambridge University Press, Cambridge 1980, ch. 5.)

6 For an interesting discussion of this question, particularly in relation to the work of Louis Althusser, see W. E. Connolly, *Appearance and Reality in Politics*, Cambridge University Press, Cambridge 1981, esp. pp. 48–62.

7 Bernard Williams, *Descartes: The Project of Pure Enquiry*, Penguin Books, Harmondsworth 1978, esp. pp. 65–7, 245–9, 301–3.

8 For an attempt to picture this transformation over the last century see J. Dunn and A. F. Robertson, *Dependence and Opportunity: Political Change in Ahafo*, Cambridge University Press, Cambridge 1973.

9 These social roles do not, of course, compel their occupants to adopt views of such arrogance. But they do foster an arrogant culture. Just as philosophers, in Richard Rorty's jibe, see themselves as 'knowing something about knowing

which nobody else knows so well' (Rorty, *Philosophy and the Mirror of Nature*, Basil Blackwell, Oxford 1980, p. 392), so social theorists and social scientists picture themselves as knowing something about knowing about society which no one else knows so well. Perhaps in many instances, indeed, they do; but like philosophers, they find it very hard to specify just what. The presumed possession of this happy epistemic knack is perhaps only an occupational disease. But it is apparent how hard it is to distinguish the occupational disease from the occupation.

10 Cf Dunn, *Political Obligation in its Historical Context*, ch. 10, esp pp. 284–5, 287–9; Rorty, *Philosophy and the Mirror of Nature*, pp. 376–7. And cf Williams, *Descartes*, pp. 162, 188, 195, 210, 268–9, etc.

11 See Dunn, *Political Obligation*, ch. 5.

12 See Connolly, *Appearance and Reality*.

13 This judgement, offered in March 1981, involves two presumptions: that the motive for workers to lower wage demands was to be the fear of becoming unemployed and that a lasting increase in unemployment levels would in itself be a cost rather than a gain for the national economy. The second presumption may appear to exaggerate the humanitarian concerns of the government. But the direct fiscal burden of unemployment relief and the indirect balance of trade impact of destroyed productive capacity are quite sufficient to establish its force (cf David Lipsey, 'Comment', *The Sunday Times*, 6 May 1984, p. 53).

14 Some more direct light is cast on Sir Keith Joseph's views in Sir Keith Joseph and Jonathan Sumption, *Equality*, John Murray, London 1979.

15 Cf Plato, *Gorgias*, 507e (trans. and ed. Terence Irwin, Clarendon Press, Oxford 1979, p. 86) and *passim*.

16 This is a central issue in Connolly, *Appearance and Reality*, esp. pp. 125, 127.

17 I have tried to bring out the fundamental significance of this point in political theory in *Political Obligation*, ch. 10.

18 *The Correspondence of John Locke*, ed. E. S. de Beer, Clarendon Press, Oxford, vol. I, 1976, p. 123.

8 Identity, modernity and the claim to know better

1 Richard Rorty, *Philosophy and the Mirror of Nature*, Basil Blackwell, Oxford 1980.

2 Richard Rorty, *Consequences of Pragmatism*, University of Minnesota Press, Minneapolis 1982, ch. 9.

3 J. C. Hurewitz, *Middle East Politics: the Military Dimension*, Frederick Praeger, New York, 1969, p. 44; John Dunn, *Modern Revolutions*, Cambridge University Press, Cambridge 1972, chh. 1, 3 and 7.

4 Cf John Dunn and A. F. Robertson, *Dependence and Opportunity: Political Change in Ahafo*, Cambridge University Press, Cambridge 1973.

5 Joseph R. Levenson, *Confucian China and its Modern Fate*, vol. 1, Routledge & Kegan Paul, London 1958; *Liang Ch'i-Ch'ao and the Mind of Modern China*, University of California Press, Berkeley 1967; Hao Chang, *Liang Ch'i-Ch'ao and Intellectual Transition in China*, Harvard University Press, Cambridge, Mass. 1971; Jerome B. Grieder, *Hu Shih and the Chinese Renaissance*, Harvard University Press, Cambridge, Mass. 1970; Philip C. Huang, *Liang Ch'i-Ch'ao and Modern Chinese Liberalism*, University of Washington Press, Seattle 1972; Benjamin Schwartz, *In Search of Wealth and Power: Yen*

Fu and the West, Harper Torchbooks, New York 1969; Maurice Meisner, *Li-Ta-Chao and the Origins of Chinese Marxism*, Harvard University Press, Cambridge, Mass. 1967, etc.

6 John K. Fairbank (ed), *The Chinese World Order: Traditional China's Foreign Relations*, Harvard University Press, Cambridge, Mass. 1968.

7 For comparable issues in the case of Egypt see Anouar Abdel-Malek, *Egypt: Military Society*, tr. Charles L. Markmann, Random House, New York 1968; *Idéologie et renaissance nationale: Égypte moderne*, Editions Anthropos, Paris 1969; and cf Nadav Safran, *Egypt in Search of Political Community*, Harvard University Press, Cambridge, Mass. 1961; Jacques Berque, *Egypt: Imperialism and Revolution*, tr. Jean Stewart, Faber & Faber, London 1972.

8 For a direct analogue on a more local scale see Dunn and Robertson, *Dependence and Opportunity*, pp. 121–37.

9 Raymond Vernon, *Storm over the Multinationals*, Macmillan, London 1977.

10 For a remarkably complacent statement of this point see David Apter, 'Introduction: Ideology and Discontent', in Apter (ed), *Ideology and Discontent*, Free Press, Glencoe, N.Y. 1964, pp. 15–46.

11 Rorty, *Philosophy*, p. 392.

12 Rorty, *Philosophy*.

13 John Dunn, *Western Political Theory in the Face of the Future*, Cambridge University Press, Cambridge 1979; *Political Obligation in its Historical Context*, Cambridge University Press, Cambridge 1980, etc.

14 Bernard Williams, *Descartes: The Project of Pure Enquiry*, Penguin Books pb., Harmondsworth 1978.

15 W. V. O. Quine, 'Two Dogmas of Empiricism', in Quine, *From a Logical Point of View*, Harper Torchbooks, New York 1963, pp. 20–46.

16 Hilary Putnam, *Meaning and the Moral Sciences*, Routledge & Kegan Paul, London 1978; Rorty, *Philosophy*; Mary Hesse, 'Theory and Value in the Social Sciences', in C. Hookway and P. Pettit (eds), *Action and Interpretation*, Cambridge University Press, Cambridge 1978, pp. 1–16; Christopher Hookway, 'Indeterminacy and Interpretation', in Hookway and Pettit (eds), *Action and Interpretation*, pp. 17–41, etc.

17 *The Correspondence of John Locke*, ed E. S. de Beer, Clarendon Press, Oxford, Vol. III, 1978, p. 182.

18 John Dunn, *The Political Thought of John Locke*, Cambridge University Press, Cambridge 1969.

19 John Locke, *An Essay concerning Human Understanding*, ed Peter H. Nidditch, Clarendon Press, Oxford 1975, p. 46.

20 Locke, *Essay*, pp. 328–48.

21 Locke, *Essay*, p. 335.

22 Locke, *Essay*, p. 346.

23 Henry E. Allison, 'Locke's Theory of Personal Identity: A Re-examination', in I. C. Tipton (ed.), *Locke on Human Understanding: Selected Essays*, Oxford University Press, Oxford 1977, pp. 105–22.

24 *Correspondence of John Locke*, Vol. 4, Oxford 1979, pp. 767, 784–6 etc.

25 Amélie Rorty (ed), *The Identities of Persons*, University of California Press, Berkeley, Calif. 1976.

26 Derek Parfit, 'Personal Identity', *Philosophical Review*, LXXX, 1, 1971, pp. 3–27; 'Later Selves and Moral Principles', in Alan Montefiore (ed), *Philosophy and Personal Relations*, Routledge & Kegan Paul, London 1973,

pp. 137–69. The interpretation of Parfit's ideas offered here is based upon these two articles alone. For the full development of his position see now Parfit, *Reasons and Persons*, Clarendon Press, Oxford 1984.

27 George Eliot, *The Mill on the Floss* (1860), Doubleday pb., Garden City, New York, n.d., p. 506.

28 Dunn, 'Social theory, social understanding and political action', ch. 7 above.

29 Dunn, *Western Political Theory*, ch. 1.

30 Karl Marx, *Critique of Hegel's Philosophy of Right*, ed J. O'Malley, Cambridge University Press, Cambridge 1970, p. 29.

31 Ch 7 above, Alasdair MacIntyre, *After Virtue: A Study in Moral Theory*, Duckworth, London 1981.

32 Roger Scruton, *The Meaning of Conservatism*, Penguin Books pb., Harmondsworth 1980.

33 Stuart Hampshire, 'Epilogue', in Leszek Kolakowski and Stuart Hampshire (eds), *The Socialist Idea: A Reappraisal*, Weidenfeld & Nicolson, London 1974, 247–9; Charles Taylor, *Hegel and Modern Society*, Cambridge University Press, Cambridge 1980; MacIntyre, *After Virtue*; Dunn, 'Social Theory', ch. 7 above; and cf the trajectory traced by Geoffrey Hawthorn, *Enlightenment and Despair: A History of Sociology*, Cambridge University Press, Cambridge 1976.

34 Isaiah Berlin, *Vico and Herder: Two Studies in the History of Ideas*, The Hogarth Press, London 1976; Friedrich Meinecke, *Historism: The Rise of a New Historical Outlook*, tr. J. E. Anderson, Routledge & Kegan Paul, London 1972; Peter H. Reill, *The German Enlightenment and the Rise of Historicism*, University of California Press, Berkeley 1975.

35 Dunn, *Political Obligation*, ch. 10.

36 Philippa Foot, 'Morality as a System of Hypothetical Imperatives', *Philosophical Review*, LXXXI, 3, 1972, 305–16; Gilbert Harman, 'Relativistic Ethics: Morality as Politics', *Midwest Studies in Philosophy*, III, 1978, 109–21; Bernard Williams, 'Internal and External Reasons', in Ross Harrison (ed), *Rational Action*, Cambridge University Press, Cambridge, 1979, 17–28.

37 Dunn, *Political Obligation*, ch. 5; and, much less confidently, Rorty, *Consequences of Pragmatism*, ch. 9.

The future of liberalism

1 Cf 'Individuality and Clientage in the Formation of Locke's Social Imagination', cap. 1 above.

2 See further, 'The future of political philosophy in the West', ch. 10 below.

3 Guido de Ruggiero, *The History of European Liberalism*, tr. R. G. Collingwood, pb. ed. Beacon Press, Boston 1959, pp. vii–viii.

4 de Ruggiero, *op cit*, p. viii.

5 J. Dunn, 'Country Risk: Social and Cultural Aspects', in Richard Herring (ed), *Managing International Risk*, Cambridge University Press, Cambridge 1983, pp. 138–67.

6 Stefan Collini, *Liberalism and Sociology: L. T. Hobhouse and Political Argument in England 1880–1914*, Cambridge University Press, Cambridge 1979.

7 H. L. A. Hart, *The Concept of Law*, Clarendon Press, Oxford 1961; *Punishment and Responsibility*, Clarendon Press, Oxford 1968. Ted Honderich, *Three Essays on Political Violence*, Basil Blackwell, Oxford 1976. Julian

Glover, *Causing Death and Saving Lives*, pb. Penguin Books, Harmondsworth 1977; Peter Singer, *Democracy and Disobedience*, Clarendon Press, Oxford 1973; *Practical Ethics*, Cambridge University Press, Cambridge 1980 etc.

8 For a sketch of these inadequacies see J. Dunn, *Western Political Theory in the Face of the Future*, Cambridge University Press, Cambridge 1979.

9 John Rawls, *A Theory of Justice*, Oxford University Press, Oxford 1971; 'Kantian Constructivism in Moral Theory', *Journal of Philosophy*, LXXVII, 1980, 515–72. Ronald Dworkin, *Taking Rights Seriously*, Duckworth, London 1977; 'Liberalism' in Stuart Hampshire (ed), *Public and Private Morality*, Cambridge University Press, Cambridge 1978, 113–43. Robert Nozick, *Anarchy, State and Utopia*, Basil Blackwell, Oxford 1974; *Philosophical Explanations*, Clarendon Press, Oxford 1981. Bruce Ackerman, *Social Justice in the Liberal State*, Yale University Press, New Haven 1980.

10 Not that Nozick has nothing to affirm about the nature of values (*Philosophical Explanations*, pp. 363–647). But it remains unclear, even on his own account (*Philosophical Explanations*, 498n–9n.) quite how what he does wish to affirm links up with what he has previously had to say about rights in *Anarchy, State and Utopia*.

11 Simon Blackburn, 'Reply: Rule-Following and Moral Realism', in Steven E. Holtzman and Christopher M. Leich (eds), *Wittgenstein: To Follow a Rule*, Routledge & Kegan Paul, London 1981, esp pp. 181–2.

12 John McDowell, 'Non-Cognitivism and Rule-Following', Holtzman and Leichs (eds), *op cit*, 141–63. And cf Jonathan Lear, 'Ethics, Mathematics and Relativism', *Mind*, XCII, January 1983, 38–60.

13 Cf James Griffin, 'Modern Utilitarianism', *Revue internationale de philosophie*, XXXVI, 3, 1982, 331–75; 'On Life's being valuable', *Dialectics and Humanism*, 2, 1981, 51–62.

14 This is shown very effectively and fairly by Michael J. Sandel, *Liberalism and the Limits of Justice*, Cambridge University Press, Cambridge 1982.

15 Cf J. Dunn, 'Political Obligations and Political Possibilities', in Dunn, *Political Obligation in its Historical Context*, Cambridge University Press, Cambridge 1980, ch. 10; 'Social theory, social understanding and political action', ch. 7 above. And cf Bernard Williams, 'Internal and External Reasons', in Ross Harrison (ed) *Rational Action*, Cambridge University Press, Cambridge 1979, 17–28.

16 Cf Patrick Riley, *Will and Political Legitimacy*, Harvard University Press, Cambridge, Mass. 1981.

17 See particularly Bernard Williams, *Moral Luck*, Cambridge University Press, Cambridge 1981; Bernard Williams and Amartya Sen (eds), *Utilitarianism and Beyond*, Cambridge University Press, Cambridge 1982. Thomas Nagel, *The Possibility of Altruism*, Clarendon Press, Oxford 1970; *Mortal Questions*, Cambridge University Press, Cambridge 1979; Stuart Hampshire, *Morality and Conflict*, Basil Blackwell, Oxford 1983.

18 See, inter alios, Stuart Hampshire (ed), *Public and Private Morality*, chh. 1 and 2; M. Cohen, T. Nagel and T. Scanlon (eds), *War and Moral Responsibility*, Princeton University Press, Princeton 1974; Michael Walzer, *Just and Unjust Wars*, Allen Lane, London 1978.

19 James Mill, *An Essay on Government*, Liberal Arts Press, New York 1955. For a sympathetic, if not wholly convincing, account of Bentham's mature

views see Frederick Rosen, *Jeremy Bentham and Representative Democracy*, Clarendon Press, Oxford 1983.
20 J. S. Mill, *On Liberty*, Introductory (J. S. Mill, *Utilitarianism, On Liberty and Representative Government*, J. M. Dent, London 1910, p. 73). For a powerful defence of Mill's view see John Gray, *Mill on Liberty: A Defence*, Routledge & Kegan Paul, London 1983.
21 Compare Mill, *Essay on Government*, p. 49, with pp. 90–91. And see the articles by William Thomas, *The Historical Journal*, June 1969 and December 1971 and *The Philosophic Radicals*, Clarendon Press, Oxford 1979, cap 3.
22 F. A. Hayek, *New Studies in Philosophy, Politics, Economics and the History of Ideas*, Routledge & Kegan Paul, London 1978, esp. chh. 8 and 10.
23 For this background see Larry Siedentop, 'Two Liberal Traditions', in Alan Ryan (ed), *The Idea of Freedom*, Oxford University Press, Oxford, 1979, 153–74; Nannerl O. Keohane, *Philosophy and the State in France*, Princeton University Press, Princeton 1980; Quentin Skinner, *The Foundations of Modern Political Thought*, Cambridge University Press, Cambridge 1978, Vol I, esp p. 45.
24 *The Miscellaneous Writings of Lord Macaulay*, London, Longman Green 1865, pp. 131–50.
25 Cf John Locke, *An Essay concerning Human Understanding*, ed Peter H. Nidditch, Clarendon Press, Oxford 1975 II, xxi, 55 (pp. 269–70). And see Dunn, *Locke*, Oxford University Press, Oxford 1984.
26 Dunn, *Political Obligation*, ch. 10.
27 Compare Williams, *Moral Luck* and Richard Rorty, *Consequences of Pragmatism*, University of Minnesota Press, Minneapolis 1982, esp. ch. 11.
28 Cf Dunn, *Western Political Theory*, ch. 18, 'Social theory, social understanding and political action', ch. 7 above.
29 For an exposition of Rawls's theory of justice which presents the latter as a politically relevant insistence on just this point see Salvatore Veca, *La Società Giusta: argomenti per il contrattualismo*, Il Saggiatore, Milan 1982.
30 J. Dunn, 'Trust in the political theory of John Locke', ch. 2 above.

10   *The future of political philosophy in the West*

1 See Jonathan Lear, 'Leaving the World Alone', *Journal of Philosophy*, LXXIX, 7, July 1982, 382–403.
2 See John W. Danford, *Wittgenstein and Political Philosophy*, Chicago University Press, Chicago 1978. Hanna F. Pitkin, *Wittgenstein and Justice*, University Press, Berkeley 1972.
3 See Peter Laslett (ed), *Philosophy, Politics and Society*, Basil Blackwell, Oxford 1956, pp. vii–xiv.
4 See Peter Laslett and W. G. Runciman (eds), *Philosophy, Politics and Society. Second Series*, Basil Blackwell, Oxford 1962, pp. vii–x.
5 Isaiah Berlin, 'Does Political Philosophy Still Exist?', in Laslett and Runciman (eds), *Philosophy, Politics and Society. Second Series*, pp. 1–33.
6 See Bernard Williams, 'Introduction' in Isaiah Berlin, *Concepts and Categories: Philosophical Essays*, ed Henry Hardy, The Hogarth Press, London 1978, pp. xi–xviii.
7 Cf T. D. Weldon, *The Vocabulary of Politics*, Penguin Books pb. ed., Harmondsworth 1953.

8 John Rawls, 'Two Concepts of Rules', *Philosophical Review*, LXIV, 1, January 1955, 3–32; 'Justice as Fairness', *Philosophical Review*, LXVII, 2, April 1958, 164–94.

9 H. L. A. Hart, *The Concept of Law*, Clarendon Press, Oxford 1961; *Law, Liberty and Morality*, Oxford University Press, London 1963; H. L. A. Hart and A. M. Honoré, *Causation in the Law*, Clarendon Press, Oxford 1959.

10 John Rawls, *A Theory of Justice*, Oxford University Press, Oxford 1972. Robert Nozick, *Anarchy, State and Utopia*, Basil Blackwell, Oxford 1974.

11 Bernard Williams, *Moral Luck*, Cambridge University Press, Cambridge 1981.

12 Thomas Nagel, *Mortal Questions*, Cambridge University Press, Cambridge 1979.

13 Richard Rorty, *Philosophy and the Mirror of Nature*, Basil Blackwell, Oxford 1980; *Consequences of Pragmatism*, University of Minnesota Press, Minneapolis 1982.

14 Alasdair MacIntyre, *After Virtue: a Study in Moral Theory*, Duckworth, London 1981; David Wiggins, *Truth, Invention and the Meaning of Life*, Henriette Hertz Lecture, British Academy 1976; Charles Taylor, *Hegel and Modern Society*, Cambridge University Press, Cambridge 1980; Hilary Putnam, *Meaning and the Moral Sciences*, Routledge & Kegan Paul, London 1978; *Reason, Truth and History*, Cambridge University Press, Cambridge 1981.

15 Rorty, *Philosophy and the Mirror of Nature*, 392.

16 Lear, 'Leaving the World Alone'.

17 Rorty, *Philosophy; Consequences of Pragmatism*, cap. 11.

18 Michael Oakeshott, *Rationalism in Politics*, Methuen & Co., London 1962.

19 Cf Taylor, *Hegel and Modern Society*.

20 Danford, *Wittgenstein*; Pitkin, *Wittgenstein*; Peter Winch, *The Idea of a Social Science and its Relation to Philosophy*, Routledge & Kegan Paul, London 1958; Peter Winch, 'Authority', in Anthony Quinton (ed), *Political Philosophy*, Oxford University Press, London 1967, pp. 97–111.

21 Ernest Gellner, 'Concepts and Society', in Bryan R. Wilson (ed), *Rationality*, Basil Blackwell, Oxford 1970, pp. 18–49; Gellner, *Legitimation of Belief*, Cambridge University Press, Cambridge 1974.

22 Winch, *The Idea of a Social Science*; A. R. Louch, *Explanation and Human Action*, Basil Blackwell, Oxford 1966; Alasdair MacIntyre, *Against the Self-images of the Age*, Duckworth, London 1971.

23 Alasdair MacIntyre, 'The Idea of a Social Science', in Wilson (ed), *Rationality*, ch. 6; John Dunn, *Political Obligation in its Historical Context*, Cambridge University Press, Cambridge 1980, ch. 5.

24 Pitkin, *Wittgenstein*; Danford, *Wittgenstein*; MacIntyre, *After Virtue*.

25 Michel Foucault, *Folie et déraison: histoire de la folie à l'âge classique*, Librairie Plon, Paris 1961; *Naissance de la clinique*, Presses Universitaires de France, Paris 1963; *Discipline and Punish: the Birth of the Prison*, Penguin Books pb., Harmondsworth 1979; *The History of Sexuality*. Vol 1, Penguin Books pb., Harmondsworth 1981.

26 MacIntyre, *After Virtue*; cf John Dunn, 'Grounds for Despair' (review of *After Virtue*) *London Review of Books*, 17 September 1981, p. 19.

27 Cf Derek Parfit, 'Later Selves and Moral Principles', in Alan Montefiore (ed.) *Philosophy and Personal Relations*, Routledge & Kegan Paul, London 1973, 137–69; 'Innumerate Ethics', *Philosophy and Public Affairs*, VII, 4, Summer

1978, 285–301; 'Prudence, Morality and the Prisoner's Dilemma', *Proceedings of the British Academy*, LXV, 1979, 539–64; 'Future Generations: Further Problems', *Philosophy and Public Affairs*, XI, 2, Spring 1982, 113–72. And see now in extenso Parfit, *Reasons and Persons*, Clarendon Press, Oxford 1984.

28 See Bernard Williams and Amartya Sen (eds), *Utilitarianism and Beyond*, Cambridge University Press, Cambridge 1982.

29 See e.g. Julian Glover, *Causing Deaths and Saving Lives*, Penguin Books pb. ed, Harmondsworth 1977; Ted Honderich, *Three Essays on Political Violence*, Basil Blackwell, Oxford 1976; Peter Singer, 'Famine, Affluence and Morality', in Peter Laslett and James Fishkin (eds), *Philosophy, Politics and Society: Fifth Series*, Basil Blackwell, Oxford 1979, pp. 21–35.

30 See John Rawls, 'Kantian Constructivism in Moral Theory', *Journal of Philosophy*, LXXVII, 9, September 1980, 515–72; and see Thomas Nagel, *The Possibility of Altruism*, Clarendon Press, Oxford 1970.

31 MacIntyre, *After Virtue*.

32 Taylor, *Hegel and Modern Society* etc.

33 Hilary Putnam, 'What is "Realism"?', *Proceedings of the Aristotelian Society*, New Series, LXXVI, 1975–6, 177–94.

34 Lear, 'Leaving the World Alone': Rorty, *Consequences of Pragmatism*; Williams, *Moral Luck*, ch. 12.

35 Cf Bernard Williams, *Descartes: The Project of Pure Enquiry*, Penguin Books pb., Harmondsworth 1978.

36 J. J. C. Smart and Bernard Williams, *Utilitarianism: For and Against*, Cambridge University Press, Cambridge 1973; Williams, *Moral Luck*; Williams and Sen (eds), *Utilitarianism and Beyond*.

37 Williams, *Moral Luck*; cf John Dunn, *Political Obligation in its Historical Context*, Cambridge University Press, Cambridge 1980, 244–50.

38 Dunn, *Political Obligation*, ch. 10.

39 Norman Daniels (ed.), *Reading Rawls*, Basil Blackwell, Oxford 1975; Brian Barry, *The Liberal Idea of Justice*, Clarendon Press, Oxford 1973; Williams, *Moral Luck*, ch. 7; John Dunn, 'Review of *Anarchy, State and Utopia*', *Ratio*, XIX, 1, June 1977, 88–95.

40 John Dunn, 'Rights', *London Review of Books*, 2, October 1980, 8–9.

41 Nagel, *Mortal Questions*, caps 5 and 6; Marshall Cohen, Thomas Nagel and Thomas Scanlon (eds), *War and Moral Responsibility*, Princeton University Press, Princeton, 1974.

42 Michael Walzer, *Just and Unjust Wars*, Allen Lane, London 1978.

43 Richard J. Bernstein, *The Restructuring of Social and Political Theory*, Basil Blackwell, Oxford 1976; Mary Hesse, 'Theory and Value in the Social Sciences', in Philip Pettit and Christopher Hookway (eds), *Action and Interpretation*, Cambridge University Press, Cambridge 1978, pp. 1–16.

44 Raymond Geuss, *The Idea of a Critical Theory*, Cambridge University Press, Cambridge 1981.

45 See e.g. Perry Anderson, *Passages from Antiquity to Feudalism*, New Left Books, London 1974; *Lineages of the Absolutist State*, New Left Books, London 1974; *Considerations on Western Marxism*, New Left Books, London 1976; *Arguments Within English Marxism*, New Left Books, London 1980. G. A. Cohen, *Karl Marx's Theory of History: A Defence*, Clarendon Press, Oxford 1978; G. A. Cohen, 'Reply to Elster on "Marxism, Functionalism and Game Theory"', *Theory and Society*, XI, 4, July 1982, 483–96; Jon Elster,

'Marxism, Functionalism and Game Theory: The Case for Methodological Individualism', *Theory and Society*, XI, 4, July 1982, 453–82.

46 Norberto Bobbio, *Quale Socialismo? discussione di un'alternativa*, Giulio Einaudi, Torino 1976.

47 Dunn, 'Understanding revolutions', ch. 4 above.

48 Charles Tilly, 'Britain Creates the Social Movement', working paper, Centre for Research on Social Organization, University of Michigan, March 1981.

49 John Dunn, *Western Political Theory in the Face of the Future*, Cambridge University Press, Cambridge 1979; *Political Obligation*.

50 Dunn, *Political Obligation*, ch. 10.

51 Wolfgang von Leyden, *Hobbes and Locke: The Politics of Freedom and Obligation*, Macmillan, London 1982.

52 Nagel, *Mortal Questions*, ch. 14; Williams, *Moral Luck*; Dunn, *Political Obligation*, ch. 10.

53 Williams, *Moral Luck*, ch. 8.

Index

223

Index

Index

Index

Index

Index

ALSO IN THE
CAMBRIDGE PAPERBACK LIBRARY

A Liberal Descent
Victorian Historians and the English Past

J. W. BURROW

An intriguing examination of the ideas of Macaulay, Stubbs, Freeman and Froude and of the cultural and historiographical context.

'... a subtle, witty and graceful analysis of the attitude of various nineteenth-century historians to key policies in English history.'

J. P. Kenyon, *The Observer*

This book was joint winner of the Wolfson Literary Award, 1981

Liberalism and Sociology

L. T. Hobhouse and Political Argument in England 1880–1914

STEFAN COLLINI

Providing the first full historical study of the thought of L. T. Hobhouse, this book examines the moral and intellectual inspiration of the New Liberalism which came to dominate Edwardian politics.

'... a scholarly, rich and illuminating piece of historiography.'

New Society

The Beginning of Ideology

Consciousness and Society in the French Revolution

D. R. KELLEY'

A new interpretation of a seminal phase in early modern European history. Professor Kelley examines the generation of sentiments, values, ideas, justifications and actions which underlie one spectacular case of profound intellectual and social change.

'a complex, stimulating and provocative work that is bound to alter historians' perceptions of the significance of the French Reformation.'

America

ALSO IN THE
CAMBRIDGE PAPERBACK LIBRARY

A Treatise on Social Theory
Volume 1: The Methodology of Social Theory
W. G. RUNCIMAN

In the first volume of a projected trilogy, W. G. Runciman argues that a methodology adequate to resolve the longstanding debate over the status of the social as against the natural sciences can be constructed in terms of a fourfold distinction between the reportage, explanation, description and evaluation of human behaviour.

'a masterly introduction to the topic.' *The Times*

The Development of the Family and Marriage in Europe
JACK GOODY

In this highly original and far-reaching study Professor Goody argues that from the fourth century the Church in Europe provoked a radical change in prevailing kinship patterns. He suggests that the Church regulated the rules of marriage so that wealth could be channelled away from the family and into the Church, thereby dramatically changing the structure of domestic life.

'We must admire the shrewdness with which the author of this billiant essay has done his research. He teaches professional historians a splendid lesson in rigour.'
The Times Literary Supplement

Karl Marx Collective
Economy, Society and Religion in a Siberian Collective Farm
CAROLINE HUMPHREY

The first ethnography based on fieldwork in a Soviet community by a Western anthropologist, this book describes the contemporary life of the Buryats, a Mongolian-speaking people in Siberia. Dr Humphrey presents a detailed, sympathetic and absorbing account of the actual functioning of a planned economy at local level.

'... a most important book, not only because it deals with such interesting subject-matter with great skill ...'
Maurice Bloch, *London Review of Books*